200 Crochet blocks

200 Crochet blocks

for blankets, throws, and afghans

JAN EATON

INTERWEAVE PRESS
www.interweave.com

A QUARTO BOOK

Copyright © 2004 by Quarto Inc.

Published in North America by
Interweave Press

201 East Fourth Street
Loveland, CO 80537-5655
www.interweave.com
All rights reserved.

QUAR.ABL
Conceived, designed, and produced by
Quarto Publishing plc
The Old Brewery
6 Blundell Street
London N7 9BH

Project Editor Jo Fisher
U.S. Edition Editor Jean Lampe
Senior Art Editor Sally Bond
Designer Jo Long
Copy Editor Hazel Williams
Photographer Colin Bowling
Illustrator Coral Mula
Proofreader Jan Eaton, Sally Maceachern
Indexer Pamela Ellis
Art Director Moira Clinch
Publisher Piers Spence

Library of Congress Cataloging-in-Publication
Data
Eaton, Jan.
  200 crochet blocks for blankets, throws and
afghans : crochet squares to mix and match /
Jan Eaton.
    p. cm.
  Includes index.
  ISBN-13: 978-1-931499-68-2
  ISBN-10: 1-931499-68-3
  1. Crocheting--Patterns. 2. Afghans
(Coverlets) I. Title: Two hundred crochet blocks
for blankets, throws and afghans. II. Title.
  TT825.E27967 2004
  746.43'40437--dc22
        2004003174

Manufactured by Universal Graphics,
Singapore
Printed by SNP Leefung Printers Limited, China

10 9 8 7

Contents

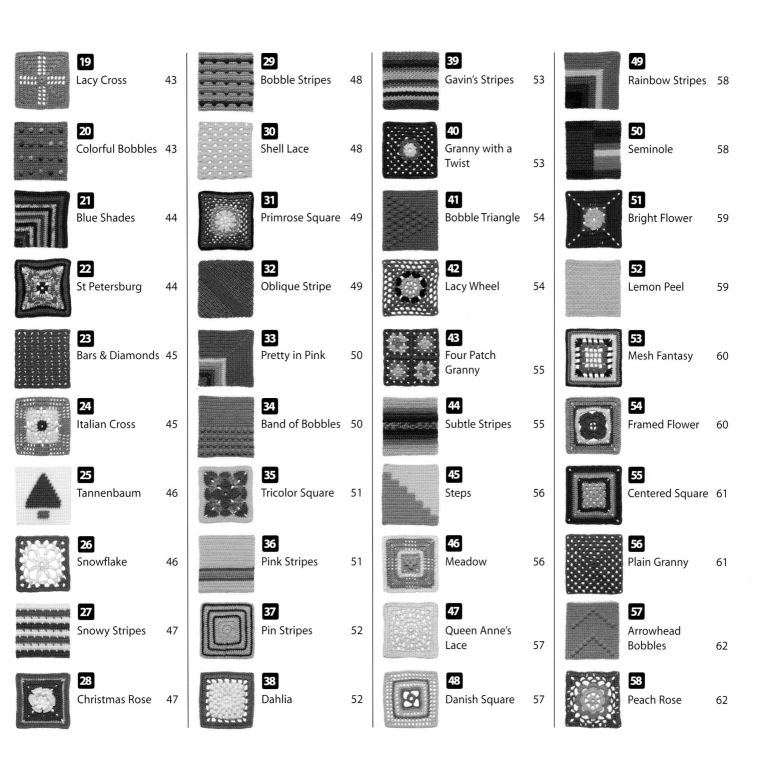

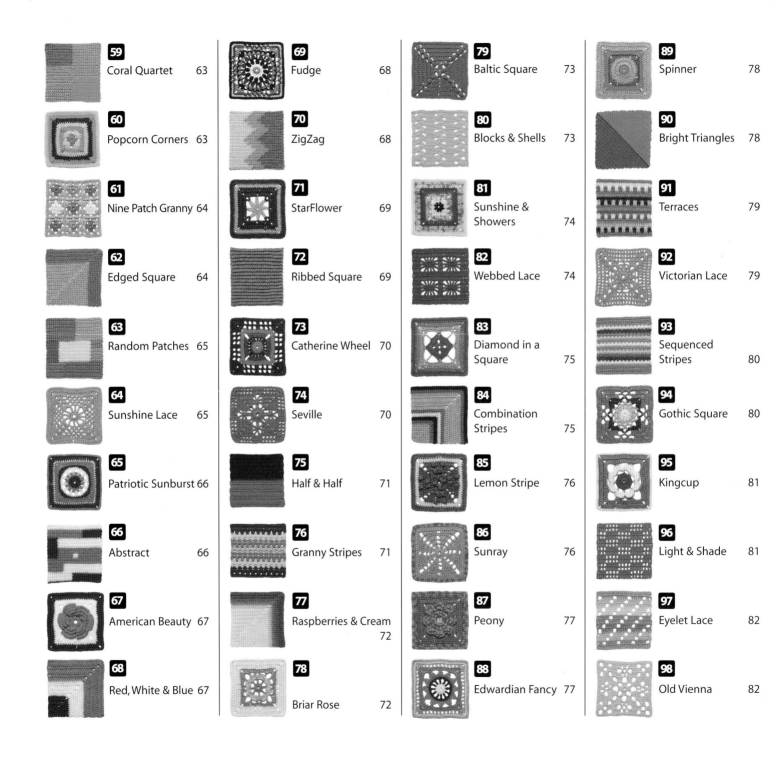

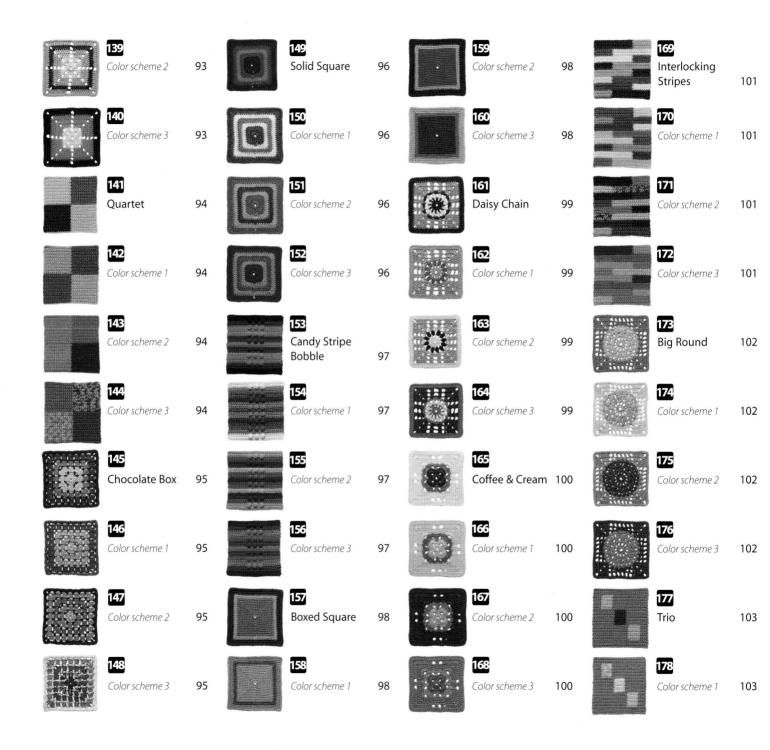

CHAPTER 3

Techniques 112

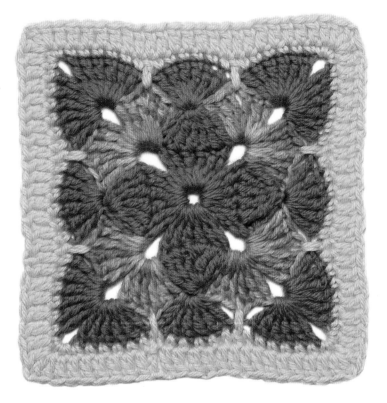

Tricolor Square, block 35

Lacy Cross, block 19

Introduction

Crochet is one of the oldest and most fascinating ways of creating a fabric with yarn. By using a hook to work loops with a continuous length of yarn, it's easy to produce a fabric with endless variations of texture, pattern, and color. Making small blocks out of crochet and joining them together to make a larger piece of fabric has long been a favorite way of working and incorporating odds and ends of yarn. Breaking a large piece of crochet down in small, easily transportable units means you can crochet blocks on a bus, train, or plane journey, as well as while watching television or listening to music or audio books. The author has been crocheting since she was a small child and finds picking up a ball of yarn and a hook and settling down to crochet the perfect way to unwind after a long stressful day. She is an avid collector of old crochet patterns and magazines and has reworked many traditional designs to make some of the blocks in the book, as well as creating many of the block patterns herself. After working more than 200 different blocks over the last few months, she is still as intrigued by the craft as ever.

Colors and yarns

The colors and yarns used to work each block are the author's own personal choice. It can't be stressed strongly enough that the patterns can be worked using any colors and combinations of colors that you prefer. Some useful guidelines about choosing and using color (page 20) are included and it is hoped that

Bobble Stripes, block 29

Alhambra, block 14

these will help you enjoy exploring the whole spectrum of colored yarns that are available. The author prefers working with a smooth, pure wool yarn. She has chosen to use double knitting (DK weight) yarn for all the blocks for several reasons—it is a good thickness to work with and shows up the different stitches well. It was also necessary to ensure that the blocks would be the same size when finished, so they can be mixed and joined without difficulty. Double knitting (DK weight) yarn also has the advantage of being available in a wonderful range of colors.

Wisteria, block 113

However, you should feel free to use whatever yarn suits you, whether it's made from wool, cotton, a synthetic fiber, such as acrylic, or a wool/synthetic blend. Always keep to the same weight of yarn throughout a project.

Combining blocks

As well as patterns for making over 200 blocks, a selection of block combinations is included to give you inspiration when arranging blocks to make throws, afghans, and pillow covers. The designs will provide you with a useful jumping-off point and encourage you to begin combining blocks in new and unusual ways. The author's aim is to inspire both new and experienced crafters to take on the challenge of designing and making their own personal, unique piece of crochet and transform the humble afghan into a wonderful and desirable item for the traditional or modern home.

Floral Fantasy, page 29

How to use this book

At the beginning of this book you'll find an illustrated contents list showing you photographs of all the main blocks—these are cross-referenced, according to the techniques used and the degree of difficulty of the pattern, from beginner to advanced. Look through and find one you like that matches your skill level.

Mix and Match

The Mix and Match section, pages 14-31, takes you through the process of creating your own afghan design, giving you advice on combining blocks, mixing techniques, and exploring the world of color. There are also plans for making 12 afghans, throws, and pillow covers using a selection of blocks from the book. They include large designs, as well as small, quick-to-make designs.

SIZE
All the blocks are the same size, 6" (15cm) square, and have been worked using the same weight of yarn and size of hook, so any block can be mixed and matched with others at will.

READING THE PLANS
Each afghan plan is accompanied by details of the finished size of the item, the type of yarn, colors, and hook size, as well as the names and reference numbers of the component blocks and how many to make of each one. This section also tells you how to finish off your blocks and join them together, and suggests a suitable edging to finish off your project.

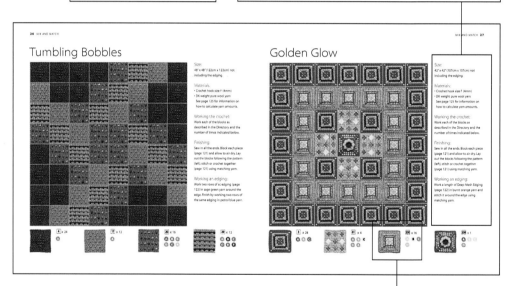

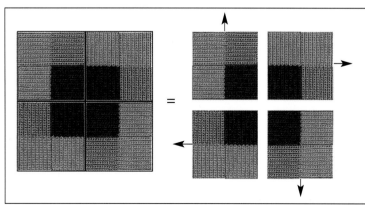

TURNING THE BLOCKS
Some of the blocks used in the plans need to be turned clockwise or counterclockwise by 90° or 180° to make up the design. When assembling your blocks, check the plan carefully and make sure the color and pattern within each block matches the plan.

QUANTITY & COLORS
Each block used for the design is shown below the plan, accompanied by its pattern reference number, yarn colors, and how many of that block you need to make.

The Block Directory

The afghan Block Directory contains a wide variety of block patterns, from well-loved traditional patterns to brand-new designs. Each block is accompanied by a photograph, pattern instructions, yarn colors, and helpful symbols. The Block Directory is divided into two sections. Section one (pages 34 to 83) contains patterns for 100 blocks, while section two (pages 84 to 111), includes more than 100 blocks and explores alternative color combinations.

Techniques

The final section of this book contains detailed information on the abbreviations and how to work the stitches and techniques used. Different methods of joining blocks are demonstrated, as well as patterns for a selection of edgings to finish off your projects beautifully. At the end of the section, there are tips on choosing yarns and a list of the actual yarns used in this book.

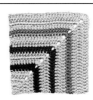

The second section of the book shows different color combinations for each block. Each yarn color is clearly referenced as used in the accompanying pattern.

PAGES 34–83

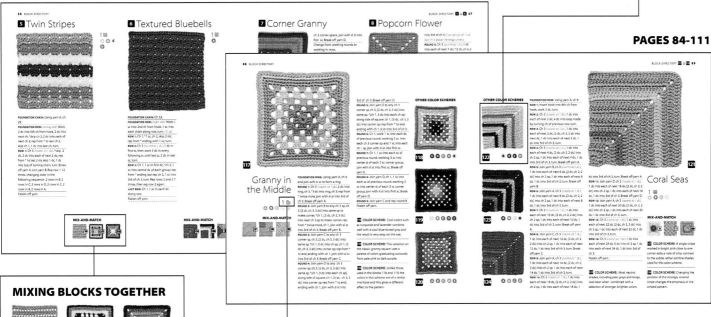

PAGES 84–111

MIXING BLOCKS TOGETHER

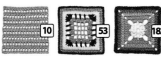

You can use your own imagination to mix blocks or experiment with the recommendations here.

UNDERSTANDING THE SYMBOLS

Each block pattern is accompanied by one or more symbols indicating how each pattern is worked, and a symbol indicating the pattern's degree of difficulty:

WORKED IN ROWS
This symbol shows that the block has been worked backward and forward in rows.

WORKED IN ROUNDS
This symbol is used for blocks worked in the round from the center outward. You will find some blocks, for example block 53 Mesh Fantasy, are accompanied by both symbols as they have part of the pattern worked in rows and part in rounds.

LEVEL OF DIFFICULTY

1 Beginner blocks

11 Some experience required

111 Challenging

Mix and Match

This chapter shows you how to choose and combine blocks from the directory and includes a selection of colorful design ideas for making items in various sizes from a large throw to a pillow cover plus tips on how to plan your own design. A further section explores selecting and using your own choice of color.

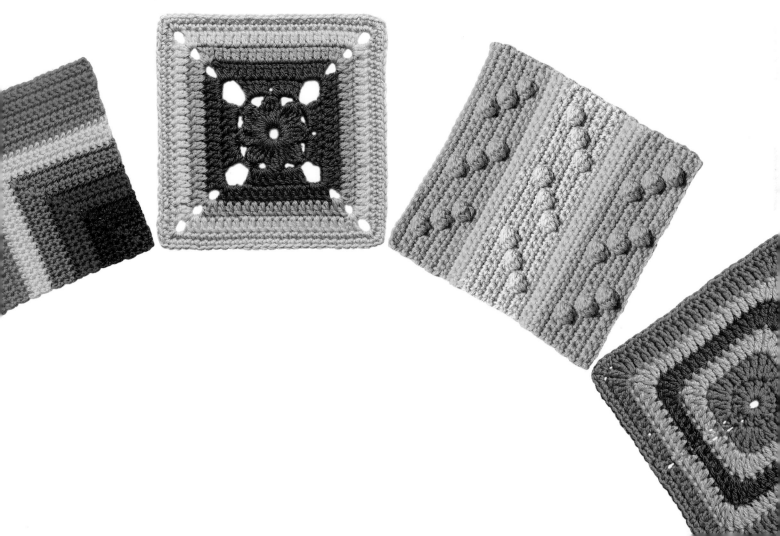

Mixing and matching blocks

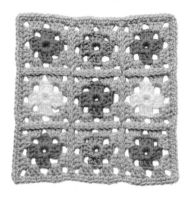

Choosing blocks

All the 212 blocks in the block directory are the same size, 6" (15cm), so there are thousands of possible combinations you could put together when designing your own afghan, throw, or pillow cover. The size of your finished project depends on its use—a throw to cover a double bed will need to be much larger than an everyday afghan for you to snuggle into when reading or watching television. You can work to whatever size feels comfortable for you; for example, a 42" (107cm) or 48" (122cm) square afghan is a good, all-purpose size for throwing over a sofa or chair. If you find the idea of working to this size too daunting or time consuming, you can put together the blocks to make an 18" (45cm) square pillow cover in a few evenings.

On pages 22 to 31, in the Mix and Match section, you'll find 12 colorful designs, in various sizes, including a large throw called Eastern Promise (page 25), which measures 72" by 84" (180cm by 210cm) and a 36" (91cm) square baby blanket called Pastel Rainbow (page 31). As well as working the designs as they are shown, you can change the yarn colors to suit your own tastes—for more information, refer to Using Colors, pages 20 and 21. You can also use the block arrangements to inspire you to begin mixing blocks and creating your very own original afghan. Begin by looking through the Block Directory (pages 32 to 111) and choose several blocks that appeal to you and are suitable for your current skill level. The degree of difficulty symbols, which accompany each block, are explained on page 13. Don't forget that you don't have to choose the same yarn colors used by the author when working the blocks.

Planning your design

When designing a piece made out of crochet blocks, it's a good idea to make a visual plan, so you can be sure you'll be happy with the look and size of your finished item. You can make a plan very simply by marking out the outline of the required number of blocks on graph paper to make a grid of squares. Make each block about 1" (2.5cm) square on the graph paper. Color the squares with pencils, or felt-tipped pens, in the colors and patterns of the blocks you have chosen.

Another way is to crochet one of each type of block you intend to use, then take the blocks to your local photocopy shop and get several copies of each one reduced to a smaller size, say about 1 ½" (4cm) square. You can do this yourself at home if you have access to a computer, printer, and scanner.

Cut out the copies and arrange them on a large sheet of plain paper. Move the blocks around until you're happy with the arrangement, then either tape them down or stick them in place using a glue stick. At the side of your plan, attach a copy of each block and write down the number you need to make and details of the colors you have chosen. There's information on page 125 telling you how to calculate the amounts of yarn you will need to buy.

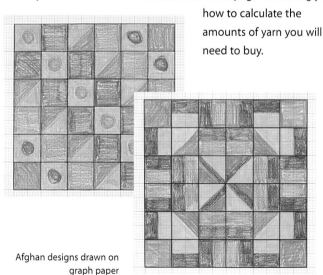

Afghan designs drawn on graph paper

Combining blocks

Crochet fabric can be smooth, lacy, or textured, depending on which technique you are using. Blocks can be worked in rows or in rounds and each way of working has its own visual appeal—for example, compare block 29 Bobble Stripes with block 55 Centered Square. Each block is worked in a similar color scheme, but the two look completely different. You can combine blocks at random just because you like their appearance or use a more measured approach. Look at the Floral Fantasy design on page 29 as an example of combining blocks worked in rounds together. Here, a strong checkerboard pattern, made with block 189 Willow, provides the perfect framework to show off paler blocks worked in shades of pink. Similarly, the Golden Glow design (page 27) combines blocks worked in the round, but this design builds outward from one central square.

LACE BLOCKS

Lace blocks work well when they are combined with each other, but they can also be used to add a touch of lightness to other block combinations. Lace blocks make perfect baby afghans, as the crochet

Worked in rows · Worked in rounds

Smooth · Lacy · Textured

Think about the different textures and methods of working blocks when deciding which to combine

Golden Glow, page 27— combines various blocks worked in rounds

fabric is soft and tends to drape well, whether used as a crib or bassinette cover or a shawl for wrapping baby. The author likes combining lace blocks with heavier, more closely worked ones but when doing this, you should bear in mind that not only the weight and density of individual blocks will be different but the amount of stretch and drape will vary too.

TEXTURED BLOCKS

Textured blocks combine well with each other, whether they are plain or patterned. Textures add surface interest to bold, modern designs, such as Deco Delight (page 23), where patterns of bobbles break up the large areas of plain color. The design on page 26, Tumbling Bobbles, shows how effective textured blocks in solid colors can be when combined with a small number of multicolored blocks.

Creating patterns

Different patterns start to appear when you arrange identical blocks into groups of four or more and start turning some of the blocks in different directions. For example, take a simple block made from two identical triangles *(block 90 Bright Triangles)* and see how many combinations you can make using four or more blocks.

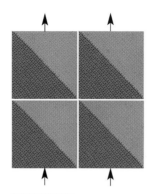

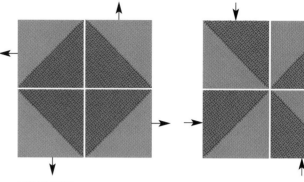

SAWTOOTH

Four blocks placed as shown above make a sawtooth pattern. This could be repeated across a whole afghan using colors that shade gradually into each other—think dark and light blues rippling into shades of mauve and pink.

DIAMOND

Create a simple, yet visually effective diamond shape by starting with the top right block the correct way up, then turning the other blocks 90° away from each other in turn.

WINDMILL

Form a windmill pattern by starting with the bottom right block the correct way up, then turning the other blocks 90° away from each other in turn.

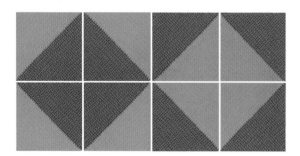

DIAMOND COMBINATIONS

Next to the first diamond, place a second made by turning individual blocks so that the diamond is now made from the background color *(left)*. Add two more four-block groups below the first two and you've got the beginning of an interesting repeat pattern *(right)*. This way of working with geometric shapes is very similar to making patchwork blocks out of fabric and you'll find lots of inspiration in books of traditional quilt block patterns.

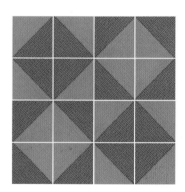

STRIPES

Striped blocks also offer a range of design possibilities. Using the simplest striped block in the book, block 75 Half & Half, arrange several with the top edges facing the same way, to make narrow horizontal or vertical stripes *(right)*, then turn one row to create a wider stripe *(far right)*.

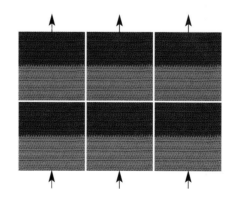

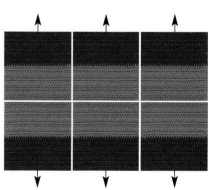

BROKEN STRIPES

Broken stripe patterns are made by alternating the top and bottom of each block *(right)* or by turning some blocks vertically *(below)*.

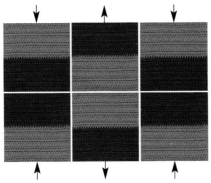

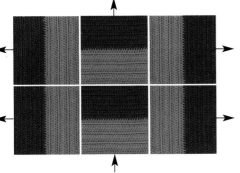

STEPPED ZIGZAG

One of the nicest patterns made with striped blocks is a stepped zigzag, made by turning alternate blocks vertically and horizontally *(right)*. The patterns you can make will also vary depending on the width and complexity of the stripes on the actual block you choose.

CREATING FRAMES

Striped blocks combined with corner blocks in matching or coordinating colors are useful as a way of making a "frame" around an afghan *(blocks 187 and 194 shown left)*.

Edgings

A compatible edging finishes off any piece of crochet made from blocks. Plain or striped rows of single crochet edging (page 122) look nice if you like a simple, straight edge, but for something more ornate choose one of the edging patterns on pages 122 to 123. The edgings shown on these pages are all worked in narrow rows across the width so it's easy to make the exact length of edging you need. Don't forget that you'll need to make the edging a little longer to stretch around the corners neatly—you can gather, pleat, or fold the edging strip into the corners, so that the strip lies flat without pulling. As a rule, apply an edging neatly by stitching it in place with yarn that matches the edging in color.

Looking after afghans

Afghans look wonderful used as bed, chair, or sofa throws and they add warmth, as well as decoration, to any room. Spruce up a plain, neutral décor with an afghan in bright, lively colors, or coordinate your throw with the existing color scheme. Baby afghans are popular items to make and give as presents.

Always clean your afghan regularly, according to the care instructions on the ball band of the yarns you have used. You may prefer to have very large throws and afghans professionally dry-cleaned. To store afghans not in use, never enclose them in a plastic bag, as the fibers will not be able to breathe and the static cling created by polythene will attract dust and dirt. Instead, wrap in a clean cotton pillowcase or sheet, depending on size. Store in a dry, cool, dust-free place, adding a bag of dried lavender to keep the crochet smelling sweet and to deter moths.

Using colors

There are no hard and fast rules governing the use of color in a crochet design—all colors combine and interact in different ways, some of which may appear more, or less pleasing to the eye. The most important thing to remember is that color is a very personal thing, so you could start exploring color by experimenting with colors that you find initially appealing. The range of colors you choose for your clothes and home decorations will give you a clear indication of your own color preferences. For example, you may like subtle shades of blue, but think red and orange are bright and garish, or love dark colors, such as black and brown, but dislike pale neutral shades.

Color palettes

A good way to begin exploring the wonderful world of color is to make your own personal color palette. Cut a strip of thin white card about 3″ x 12″ (8cm x 30cm) and punch a row of holes along one long edge. Collect a selection of yarns in colors that you know you like and loop a short length of each one through alternate holes. Now it's time to add some spice to your palette with different colors of yarn, adding new lengths gradually, one color at a time, to see what effect they create. For example, if you prefer pastel shades, see what happens when you combine deeper, brighter versions of your well-loved colors—try adding cobalt or royal blue to your favorite powder blue; fuchsia

or bright raspberry pink to pale baby pinks and creams; emerald and strong lime green to eau-de-nile.

You may have an instinctive feeling for warm colors (for example, yellow, mustard, orange, red, tan) or cool ones (lavender, blue, green, turquoise, blue gray) or you may prefer light-toned, pastel shades to strong, bright, or dark ones. Some colors (pink, for example) can be either warm or cool, depending on the particular shade you choose— peachy pinks are warm, as they contain some yellow, which is a warm color, while fuchsia pinks tend to be cool, as they contain blue, a cool color.

Color theory

A few basic color theory guidelines are useful to consider at this stage. Investigate the standard wheel arrangement of colors, where the three primary colors, red, yellow, and blue, are divided by the three secondary colors (orange, green, and purple), which are made by mixing two primary colors together. Generally, colors opposite each other on the color wheel (these are called complementary colors, for example, red and green) may clash with each other when used at full strength. Neighboring colors on the wheel, such as blue and purple, are usually harmonious, as they each contain some of the same color.

In general, warm colors tend to advance while cool colors tend to recede. The same is true with dark and light tones of the same color— dark tones tend to advance and light tones to recede. This effect can totally alter the appearance of a block pattern—see pages 84-111 for examples of how a block pattern varies when it is worked in four different color schemes. Individual colors also change according to how they are placed in a block. An area of scarlet surrounded by black or navy blue will look bold and striking, while the same scarlet area surrounded by white, pale gray, or cream will have less impact. By introducing more brightly colored areas into the block, the initial impact of the scarlet area will be diminished. Similarly, stripes and small

Color palettes: the one on the left shows cool pastel and bright colors, while the right one shows neutrals and warm shades

areas of black or dark brown can enhance a design, defining and accentuating the pattern. This works in the same way as the black leaded lines in a stained glass window that surround brilliantly colored glass shapes and create a glowing jewel-like effect.

Warm colors

Cool colors

Different color combinations of the same design (see pages 84-111)

Blocks with different designs but using similar or complementary colors

Creative color

When using your own color choice to work a crochet block, you may need to crochet more than one sample, as the colors may create a different effect from the one you anticipate when they are combined. It's interesting to see how different yarn colors in skeins or balls may look good when placed together, but the colors often change and react with each other when the yarns are combined in a piece of crochet.

Inspiration for color

For more inspiration and help with color, start by looking at the wide range of color-mixing books for water colorists and oil painters. They often include color suggestions for painting landscapes and interiors, when the painter wants to create a particular season or time of day.

Look around you at flowers, plants, parks, and gardens and the beautiful colors of birds, animals, and insects. View paintings and other works of art in museums and galleries and look at how different colors have been put together and what effect they create. For example, Tiffany glass and works by the Art Nouveau movement utilize different color palettes from the vibrant colors favored by America's Jazz Age and Art Deco Style. Hot African colors are very different from the restrained palette used in Japanese woodcuts by Hokusai and Hiroshige. Other beautifully colored museum objects to look at include Oriental textiles, particularly Japanese kimonos, brightly colored folk textiles from the Golden Triangle, and jewelry made from gems and semi-precious stones. Keep a scrapbook and paste into it anything that appeals to you colorwise—postcards, magazine cuttings, paint clips, swatches of fabric, and thread are all useful as reference.

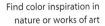

Find color inspiration in nature or works of art

Mix and match designs
Blue Horizons

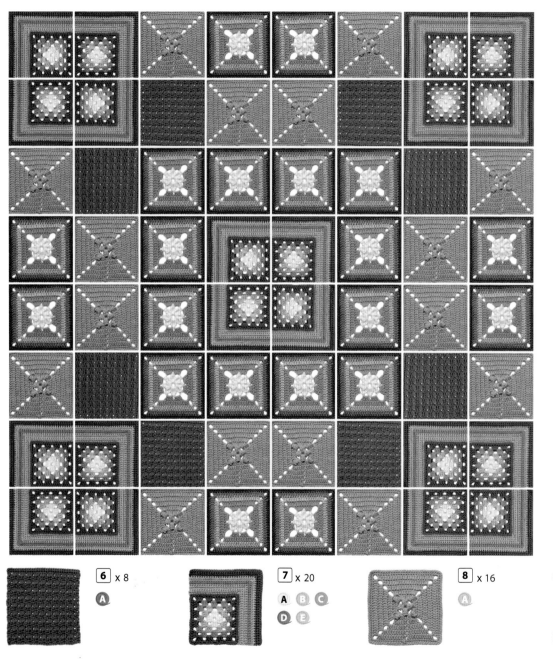

Size:
48" x 48" (122cm x 122cm) not including the edging.

Materials:
- Crochet hook size F (4mm)
- DK weight pure wool yarn
  See page 125 for information on how to calculate yarn amounts.

Working the crochet:
Work each of the blocks as described in the Directory and the number of times indicated below.

Finishing:
Sew in all the ends. Block each piece (page 121) and allow to dry. Lay out the blocks following the pattern (left), stitch or crochet together (page 121) using matching yarn.

Working an edging:
Work a length of Shamrock Edging (page 122) in cornflower blue yarn and stitch it around the edge using matching yarn.

6 x 8

A

7 x 20

A B C
D E

8 x 16

A

182 x 20

A B C
D E

Deco Delight

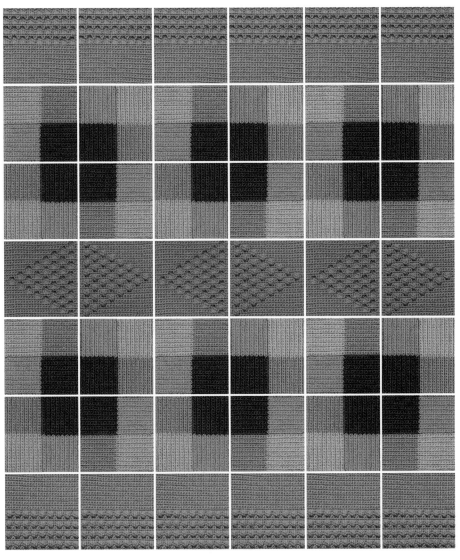

Size:
36″ x 42″ (91cm x 106cm) not including the edging.

Materials:
- Crochet hook size F (4mm)
- DK weight pure wool yarn
  See page 125 for information on how to calculate yarn amounts.

Working the crochet:
Work each of the blocks as described in the Directory and the number of times indicated below.

Finishing:
Sew in all the ends. Block each piece (page 121) and allow to dry. Lay out the blocks following the pattern (left), stitch or crochet together (page 121) using matching yarn.

Working an edging:
Work two rows of sc edging (page 122) in fuchsia yarn around the edge.

   x 12
A

   x 6
A

   x 24
A B C
D

Waterlily Pond

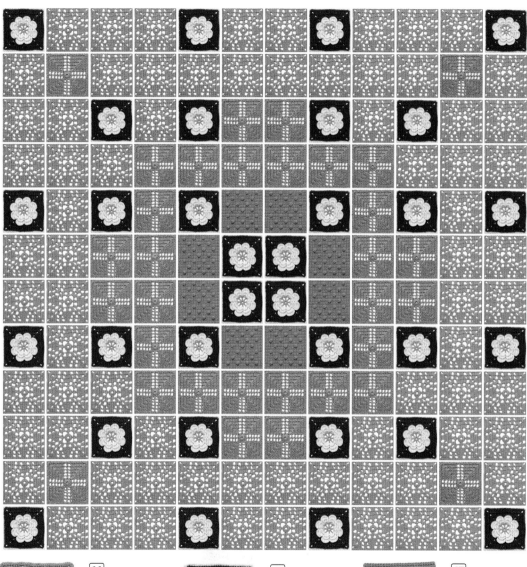

Size:
72″ x 72″ (180cm x 180cm) not including the edging.

Materials:
- Crochet hook size F (4mm)
- DK weight pure wool yarn
  See page 125 for information on how to calculate yarn amounts.

Working the crochet:
Work each of the blocks as described in the Directory and the number of times indicated below.

Finishing:
Sew in all the ends. Block each piece (page 121) and allow to air dry. Lay out the blocks following the pattern (left), stitch or crochet together (page 121) using matching yarn.

Working an edging:
To make a simple, narrow edging, work two rows of sc edging (page 122) in cream yarn around the edge. Alternatively, work a length of Shell and Lace Edging (page 123) in clover pink or cream yarn and stitch it around the edge using matching yarn.

 14 x 72

 A

 16 x 32

 A B C

 17 x 8

 A

19 x 32

A

Eastern Promise

Size:
72" x 84" (180cm x 210cm) not including the edging.

Materials:
- Crochet hook size F (4mm)
- DK weight pure wool yarn
  See page 125 for information on how to calculate yarn amounts

Working the crochet:
Work each of the blocks as described in the Directory and the number of times indicated below.

Finishing:
Sew in all the ends. Block each piece (page 121) and allow to air dry. Lay out the blocks following the pattern (left), stitch or crochet together (page 121) using matching yarn.

Working an edging:
Work two sc edging rows (page 122) in amethyst yarn and then another two sc edging rows in raspberry yarn.

 13 x 44
Ⓐ Ⓑ Ⓒ
Ⓓ Ⓔ

 15 x 124
Ⓐ Ⓑ Ⓒ
Ⓓ Ⓔ Ⓕ

Tumbling Bobbles

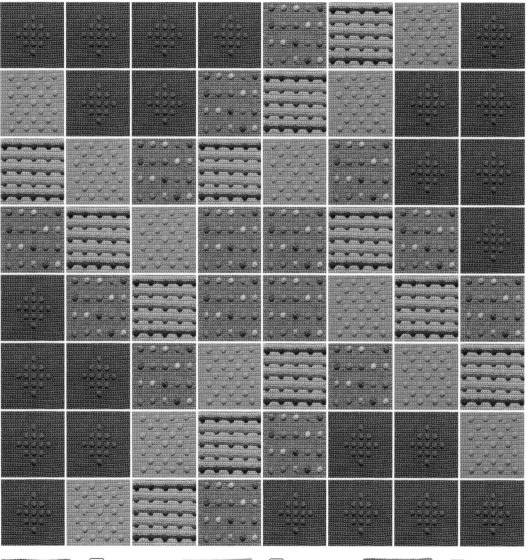

Size:
48" x 48" (122cm x 122cm) not including the edging.

Materials:
- Crochet hook size F (4mm)
- DK weight pure wool yarn
  See page 125 for information on how to calculate yarn amounts.

Working the crochet:
Work each of the blocks as described in the Directory and the number of times indicated below.

Finishing:
Sew in all the ends. Block each piece (page 121) and allow to air dry. Lay out the blocks following the pattern (left), stitch or crochet together (page 121) using matching yarn.

Working an edging:
Work two rows of sc edging (page 122) in sage green yarn around the edge. Finish by working two rows of the same edging in petrol blue yarn.

  4 x 24
A

 17 x 12
A

 20 x 16
A B C
D E F

     29 x 12
A B C
D E F

Golden Glow

Size:
42" x 42" (107cm x 107cm) not including the edging.

Materials:
- Crochet hook size F (4mm)
- DK weight pure wool yarn
  See page 125 for information on how to calculate yarn amounts.

Working the crochet:
Work each of the blocks as described in the Directory and the number of times indicated below.

Finishing:
Sew in all the ends. Block each piece (page 121) and allow to air dry. Lay out the blocks following the pattern (left), stitch or crochet together (page 121) using matching yarn.

Working an edging:
Work a length of Deep Mesh Edging (page 122) in burnt orange yarn and stitch it around the edge using matching yarn.

 3 x 28
 A B C

 61 x 4
 A B C
D E

 200 x 16
 A B C
D

 209 x 1
 A B C
D

Stripes & Squares

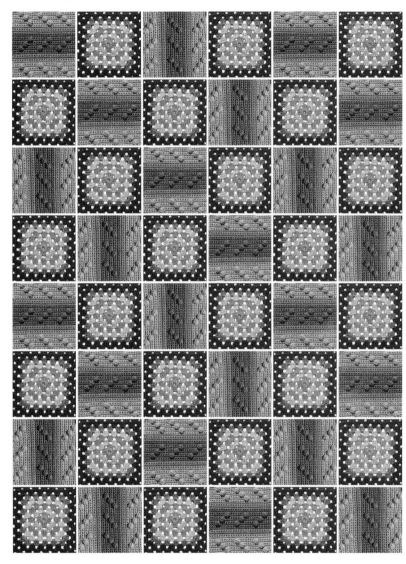

Size:
36" x 48" (91cm x 122cm) not including the edging.

Materials:
- Crochet hook size F (4mm)
- DK weight pure wool yarn
  See page 125 for information on how to calculate yarn amounts.

Working the crochet:
Work each of the blocks as described in the Directory and the number of times indicated below.

Finishing:
Sew in all the ends. Block each piece (page 121) and allow to air dry. Lay out the blocks following the pattern (left), stitch or crochet together (page 121) using matching yarn.

Working an edging:
Work two rows of sc edging (page 122) in bronze green yarn around the edge. Alternatively, work a length of Shamrock Edging (page 122) in sage green yarn and stitch it around the edge using matching yarn.

  18 x 24

A B C
D E F

  203 x 24

A B C

Floral Fantasy

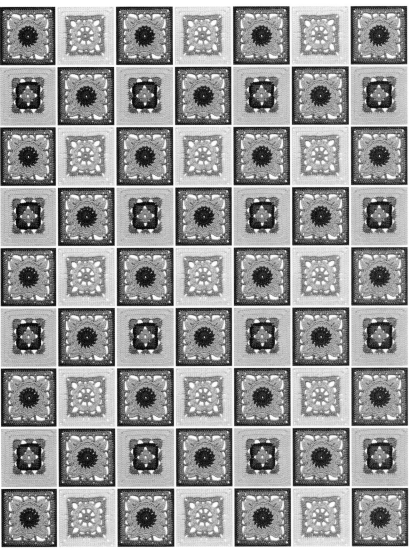

Size:
42" x 54" (107cm x 137cm) not including the edging.

Materials:
- Crochet hook size F (4mm)
- DK weight pure wool yarn
  See page 125 for information on how to calculate yarn amounts.

Working the crochet:
Work each of the blocks as described in the Directory and the number of times indicated below.

Finishing:
Sew in all the ends. Block each piece (page 121) and allow to air dry. Lay out the blocks following the pattern (left), stitch or crochet together (page 121) using matching yarn.

Working an edging:
Work a length of Scallop Edging (page 123) in bronze green and stitch it around the edge using matching yarn. Alternatively, work a length of Shell and Lace Edging (page 123) in pale pink and attach in the same way.

 78 x 15

 A B C
D

 129 x 16

 A B C
D

 189 x 32

 A B C

Happy Holidays

Size:

To fit pillow form 18″ x 18″ (45cm x 45cm)

Materials:

- Crochet hook size F (4mm)
- DK weight pure wool yarn
  See page 125 for information on how to calculate yarn amounts.

Working the crochet:

Work each of the blocks as described in the Directory and the number of times indicated below.

Finishing:

Sew in all the ends. Block each piece (page 121) and allow to air dry. Lay out the blocks following the pattern (left) to make two identical pieces for front and back of the pillow. Stitch the blocks together (page 121) using matching yarn. Place the front and back pieces together with right sides facing and stitch together around three sides. Turn to the right side, insert the pillow form and stitch the opening closed.

 25 x 2 Ⓐ Ⓑ Ⓒ

 27 x 8 Ⓐ B Ⓒ

 28 x 8 Ⓐ Ⓑ Ⓒ

Fourth of July

Size:

To fit pillow form 18″ x 18″ (45cm x 45cm)

Materials:

- Crochet hook size F (4mm)
- DK weight pure wool yarn
  See page 125 for information on how to calculate yarn amounts.

Working the crochet:

Work each of the blocks as described in the Directory and the number of times indicated below.

Finishing:

Sew in all the ends. Block each piece (page 121) and allow to air dry. Lay out the blocks following the pattern (left) to make two identical pieces for front and back of the pillow. Stitch the blocks together (page 121) using matching yarn. Place the front and back pieces together with right sides facing and stitch together around three sides. Turn to the right side, insert the pillow form and stitch the opening closed.

 65 x 8 Ⓐ Ⓑ C

 67 x 2 Ⓐ B Ⓒ

 68 x 8 Ⓐ B Ⓒ

Baby Stripes

Size:
36" x 42" (91cm x 107cm), without edging.

Materials:
- Crochet hook size F (4mm)
- DK weight pure wool yarn
  See page 125 for information on how to
  calculate yarn amounts.

Working the crochet:
Work each of the blocks as described in the
Directory and the number of times indicated
below.

Finishing:
Sew in all the ends. Block each piece (page
121) and allow to air dry. Lay out the blocks
following the pattern (right), stitch or crochet
together (page 121) using matching yarn.

Working an edging:
Work two rows of sc edging (page 122) in
cream yarn around the edge. Finish by
working two rows of the same edging in
mauve yarn.

 **108** x 42

   D

Pastel Rainbow

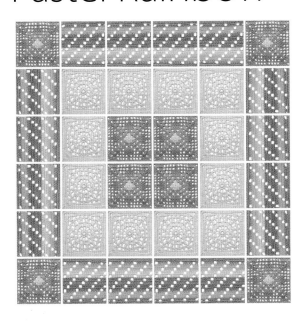

Size:
36" x 36" (91cm x 91cm), without edging.

Materials:
- Crochet hook size F (4mm)
- DK weight pure wool yarn
  See page 125 for information on how to
  calculate yarn amounts.

Working the crochet:
Work each of the blocks as described in the
Directory and the number of times indicated
below.

Finishing:
Sew in all the ends. Block each piece (page
121) and allow to air dry. Lay out the blocks
following the pattern (left), stitch or crochet
together (page 121) using matching yarn.

Working an edging:
To make a simple, narrow edging, work two
rows of sc edging (page 122) in sky blue yarn
around the edge. Alternatively, work a length
of Shamrock Edging (page 122) in sky blue
yarn and stitch it around the edge using
matching yarn.

 47 x 12

A

 97 x 16

 100 x 8

Block Directory

The Block Directory contains photographs and patterns for over 200 crochet blocks. Each block is graded by degree of difficulty so you can choose the ones which suit your own skill level. In the last section, each main pattern is shown in the original color with three different colorways to illustrate the variety of effects you can achieve.

1 Triangle Stripes

11 ≣
Ⓐ Ⓑ Ⓒ

2 Tiny Textures

1 ≣
Ⓐ

Special abbreviation

sc3tog = decrease 2 sts by working the next 3 sc together

FOUNDATION CHAIN: Using yarn A, ch 2.

FOUNDATION ROW: *(wrong side)* Work 3 sc into 2nd ch from hook, turn. *(3 sc)*

ROW 1: Ch 1, 2 sc into first sc, 1 sc into next sc, 2 sc into last sc, turn. *(5 sc)* Begin increase pattern.

ROWS 2 to 4: Ch 1, 2 sc into first sc, 1 sc into each sc along row to last st, 2 sc into last sc, turn.

ROW 5: Ch 1, 1 sc into each sc along row, turn. Rep rows 2 to 5 five times. *(41 sc)* Break off yarn A. Join yarn B and begin decrease pattern.

NEXT ROW: Ch 1, 1 sc into each sc along row, turn.

NEXT 3 ROWS: Ch 1, skip first sc, 1 sc into each sc along row to last 2 sts, skip 1 sc, 1 sc into last sc, turn. Break off yarn B. Rep 4-row decrease pattern five times using four-row stripes of color in the following sequence: C, A, B, C, A. *(5 sc)*

NEXT ROW: Continuing with A, ch 1, skip first sc, 1 sc into each of next 2 sc, skip next sc, 1 sc into next sc, turn. *(3 sc)*

NEXT ROW: Ch 1, work sc3tog. Fasten off yarn.

FOUNDATION CHAIN: Ch 32.

FOUNDATION ROW: *(right side)* Work 1 sc into 2nd ch from hook, 1 sc into each chain to end, turn. *(31 sc)*

ROW 1: Ch 1, 1 sc in first sc, *ch 1, skip 1 sc, 1 sc into next sc; rep from * to end, turn.

ROW 2: Ch 1, 1 sc in first sc, *1 dc in next ch 1 sp, 1 sc into next sc; rep from * to end, turn.

ROW 3: Ch 1, 1 sc in first sc, *ch 1, skip 1 sc, 1 sc into next sc; rep from * to end, turn. Rep rows 2 and 3 11 times, ending with a 3rd row.

NEXT ROW: Work 1 sc in each st along row.

Fasten off yarn.

MIX-AND-MATCH

MIX-AND-MATCH

3 Square Target

1 📷
Ⓐ Ⓑ Ⓒ

4 Bobble Diamond

11 ☰
Ⓐ

FOUNDATION RING: Using yarn A, ch 4 and join with sl st to form a ring.

ROUND 1: Ch 5 (counts as 1 dc, ch 2), [3 dc into ring, ch 2] 3 times, 2 dc into ring, join with sl st into 3rd of ch 5. (Four groups of 3 dc, four ch 2 spaces forming corners)

ROUND 2: Sl st into ch 2 sp, ch 7 (counts as 1 dc, ch 4), *2 dc into same ch 2 sp, 1 dc into each dc across side of square, **2 dc into next ch 2 sp, ch 4; rep from * twice and from * to ** again, 1 dc into last ch 2 sp, join with sl st to 3rd of ch 7. (Four groups of 7 dc, four 4ch spaces forming corners) Break off yarn A.

ROUND 3: Join yarn B to ch 4 sp, ch 7 (counts as 1 dc, ch 4), *2 dc into same ch 4 sp, 1 dc into each dc across side of square, **2 dc into next ch 4 sp, ch 4; rep from * twice and from * to ** again, 1 dc into last ch 4 sp, join with sl st to 3rd of ch 7. (Four groups of 11 dc, four ch 4 spaces forming corners) Break off yarn B.

ROUND 4: Join yarn C to ch 4 sp, rep round 3. (Four groups of 15 dc, four ch 4 spaces forming corners) Break off yarn C.

ROUND 5: Join yarn B to ch 4 sp, rep round 3. (Four groups of 19 dc, four ch 4 spaces forming corners) Break off yarn B.

ROUND 6: Join yarn A to ch 4 sp, rep round 3. (Four groups of 23 dc, four ch 4 spaces forming corners)

ROUND 7: Ch 1, 1 sc into each dc in previous round, working [2 sc, ch 1, 2 sc] into each ch 4 corner sp, join with sl st into first sc.

ROUND 8: Ch 1, 1 sc into each sc in previous round, working ch 2 at each corner, join with sl st into first sc.

Fasten off yarn.

Special abbreviation
MB = make bobble (work 4 open dc in same st leaving 5 loops on hook, draw yarn through all 5 loops at once)

FOUNDATION CHAIN: Ch 28.

FOUNDATION ROW: (wrong side) Work 1 sc into 2nd ch from hook, 1 sc into each ch to end, turn. (27 sc)

ROW 1: Ch 1, 1 sc into each sc, turn. (27 sc)

ROWS 2 to 7: Rep row 1.

ROW 8: Ch 1, 1 sc into each of next 13 sc, MB, 1 sc into each of next 13 sc, turn.

ROWS 9 to 11: Rep row 1.

ROW 12: Ch 1, 1 sc into each of next 10 sc, [MB, 1 sc into each of next 2 sc] twice, MB, 1 sc into each of next 10 sc, turn.

ROWS 13 to 15: Rep row 1.

ROW 16: Ch 1, 1 sc into each of next 7 sc, [MB, 1 sc into each of next 2 sc] 4 times, MB, 1 sc into each of next 7 sc, turn.

ROWS 17 to 19: Rep row 1.
ROW 20: Rep row 12.
ROWS 21 to 23: Rep row 1.
ROW 24: Rep row 8.
ROWS 25 to 32: Rep row 1.
Fasten off yarn.

MIX-AND-MATCH

 95 204 209

MIX-AND-MATCH

 157 193 203

5 Twin Stripes

1 ≣
Ⓐ Ⓑ Ⓒ
Ⓓ

FOUNDATION CHAIN: Using yarn A, ch 32.

FOUNDATION ROW: *(wrong side)* Work 2 dc into 5th ch from hook, 2 dc into next ch, *skip ch 2, 2 dc into each of next ch 2; rep from * to last ch 2, skip ch 1, 1 dc into last ch, turn.

ROW 1: Ch 3 *(counts as 1 dc)*, *skip 2 dc, 2 dc into each of next 2 dc; rep from * to last 2 sts, skip 1 dc, 1 dc into top of turning chain, turn. Break off yarn A. Join yarn B. Rep row 1 12 times, changing color in the following sequence: 2 rows in B, 2 rows in C, 2 rows in D, 2 rows in C, 2 rows in B, 2 rows in A.

Fasten off yarn.

6 Textured Bluebells

1 ≣
Ⓐ

FOUNDATION CHAIN: Ch 32.

FOUNDATION ROW: *(right side)* Work 1 sc into 2nd ch from hook, 1 sc into each chain along row, turn. *(31 sc)*

ROW 1: Ch 1, *1 sc, ch 2, skip 2 sts; rep from * ending with 1 sc, turn.

ROW 2: Ch 3 *(counts as 1 dc)*, 1 dc in first sc, then work 3 dc in every following sc until last sc, 2 dc in last sc, turn.

ROW 3: Ch 1, 1 sc in first dc, *ch 2, 1 sc into central dc of each group; rep from * ending last rep ch 2, 1 sc into 3rd of ch 3, turn. Rep rows 2 and 3 7 times, then rep row 2 again.

LAST ROW: Ch 1, 1 sc in each dc along row.

Fasten off yarn.

MIX-AND-MATCH

 10 53 182

MIX-AND-MATCH

 124 186 206

7 Corner Granny

   A **B** **C** **D** **E**

FOUNDATION RING: Using yarn A, ch 6 and join with sl st to form a ring.

ROUND 1: Ch 3 *(counts as 1 dc)*, 2 dc into ring, ch 3, *3 dc into ring, ch 3; rep from * twice, join with sl st into 3rd of ch 3. Break off yarn A.

ROUND 2: Join yarn B to any ch 3 sp, ch 3 *(counts as 1 dc)*, [2 dc, ch 3, 3 dc] into same sp to make corner, *ch 1, [3 dc, ch 3, 3 dc] into next ch 3 sp to make corner; rep from * twice, ch 1, join with sl st into 3rd of ch 3. Break off yarn B.

ROUND 3: Join yarn C to any ch 3 corner sp, ch 3, [2 dc, ch 3, 3 dc] into same sp, *ch 1, 3 dc into next ch 1 sp, ch 1, [3 dc, ch 3, 3 dc] into next ch 3 corner sp; rep from * to end, ending with ch 1, join with sl st into 3rd of ch 3. Break off yarn C.

ROUND 4: Join yarn D to any ch 3 corner sp, ch 3, [2 dc, ch 3, 3 dc] into same sp, *[ch 1, 3 dc into each ch 1 sp] along side of square, ch 1, [3 dc, ch 3, 3 dc] into next ch 3 corner sp; rep from * to end, ch 1, join with sl st into 3rd of ch 3.

ROUND 5: Ch 1, 1 sc into every dc and ch 1 sp of previous round, working [2 sc, ch 1, 2 sc] into each ch 3 corner space, join with sl st into first sc. Break off yarn D.
Change from working rounds to working in rows.

ROW 1: Join yarn E to any ch 1 corner sp. With RS of square facing and working through back loops of each st on this row only, ch 1, 1 sc into each sc along first side of square, 3 sc into next ch 1 corner sp, 1 sc into each sc along next side of square working last sc into corner ch 1 sp, turn.

ROW 2: Working through both loops of each st, ch 1, 1 sc into each sc of previous row, working 3 sc into center st of 3 sc corner group, turn. Rep row 2 9 times, changing yarn color in the following sequence: 2 more rows in E, two rows in C, two rows in B, 3 rows in D.
Fasten off yarn.

MIX-AND-MATCH

8 Popcorn Flower

 A

Special abbreviations

beg pc = beginning popcorn made from ch 3 and 4 dc sts, **pc** = popcorn made from 5 dc sts

FOUNDATION RING: Using yarn A, ch 8 and join with sl st to form a ring.

ROUND 1: Beg pc into ring, [ch 5, pc into ring] 3 times, ch 5, join with sl st into top of beg pc.

ROUND 2: Ch 3 *(counts as 1 dc)*, *[2 dc, ch 2, pc, ch 2, 2 dc] into next ch 5 sp, **1 dc into next pc; rep from * twice and from * to ** again, join with sl st into 3rd of ch 3.

ROUND 3: Ch 3 *(counts as 1 dc)*, 1 dc into each of next 2 sts, *3 dc into next ch 2 sp, ch 4, 3 dc into next ch 2 sp, **1 dc into each dc across side of square; rep from * twice and from * to ** again, 1 dc into each of last 2 sts, join with sl st into 3rd of ch 3. *(Four groups of 11 dc, four ch 4 spaces forming corners)*

ROUND 4: Ch 3 *(counts as 1 dc)*, 1 dc into each of next 5 sts, *[2 dc, ch 4, 2 dc] into corner sp, **1 dc into each dc across side of square; rep from * twice and from * to ** again, 1 dc into each of last 5 sts, join with sl st into 3rd of ch 3. *(Four groups of 15 dc, four ch 4 spaces forming corners)*

ROUND 5: Ch 3 *(counts as 1 dc)*, 1 dc into each of next 7 sts, *[2 dc, ch 4, 2 dc] into corner sp, **1 dc into each dc across side of square; rep from * twice and from * to ** again, 1 dc into each of last 7 sts, join with sl st into 3rd of ch 3. *(Four groups of 19 dc, four ch 4 spaces forming corners)*

ROUND 6: Ch 3 *(counts as 1 dc)*, 1 dc into each of next 9 sts, *[2 dc, ch 4, 2 dc] into corner sp, **1 dc into each dc across side of square; rep from * twice and from * to ** again, 1 dc into each of last 9 sts, join with sl st into 3rd of ch 3. *(Four groups of 23 dc, four ch 4 spaces forming corners)*

ROUND 7: Ch 1, 1 sc into each dc in previous round, working [2 sc, ch 1, 2 sc] into each ch 4 corner sp, join with sl st into first sc.

ROUND 8: Ch 1, 1 sc into each sc in previous round, working ch 2 at each corner, join with sl st into first sc.
Fasten off yarn.

MIX-AND-MATCH

9 Arcadia

FOUNDATION RING: Using yarn A, ch 6 and join with sl st to form a ring.

ROUND 1: Ch 3 *(counts as 1 dc)*, 15 dc into ring, join with sl st into 3rd of ch 3. *(16 dc)* Break off yarn A.

ROUND 2: Join yarn B, ch 5 *(counts as 1 dc, ch 2)*, [1 dc into next dc, ch 2] 15 times, join with sl st into 3rd of ch 5. *(16 spaced dc)* Break off yarn B.

ROUND 3: Join yarn C to any ch 2 sp, ch 3 *(counts as 1 dc)*, [1 dc, ch 3, 2 dc] into same sp, *[ch 2, 1 sc into next ch 2 sp] 3 times, ch 2, **[2 dc, ch 3, 2 dc] into next ch 2 sp; rep from * twice and from * to ** once again, join with sl st into 3rd of ch 3.

ROUND 4: Join yarn D to any ch 3 corner sp, ch 3 *(counts as 1 dc)*, [1 dc, ch 3, 2 dc] into same sp, *[ch 2, 1 sc into next ch 2 sp] 4 times, ch 2, **[2 dc, ch 3, 2 dc] into next ch 3 corner sp; rep from * twice and from * to ** once again, join with sl st into 3rd of ch 3.

ROUND 5: Sl st in next dc and into next ch 3 sp, ch 3 *(counts as 1 dc)*, [2 dc, ch 2, 3 dc] into same sp, *[ch 2, 1 dc into next ch 2 sp] 5 times, ch 2, **[3 dc, ch 2, 3 dc] into next ch 3 corner sp; rep from * twice and from

* to ** once again, join with sl st into 3rd of ch 3.

ROUND 6: Join yarn E to any ch 2 corner sp, ch 3 *(counts as 1 dc)*, [2 dc, ch 2, 3 dc] into same sp, *[ch 2, 1 dc into next ch 2 sp] 6 times, ch 2, **[3 dc, ch 2, 3 dc] into next ch 2 corner sp; rep from * twice and from * to ** once again, join with sl st into 3rd of ch 3.

ROUND 7: Sl st in next 2 dc and into next ch 2 sp, ch 3 *(counts as 1 dc)*, [1 dc, ch 2, 2 dc] into same sp, *1 dc into each dc and 2 dc into each ch 2 sp along side of square, **[2 dc, ch 2, 2 dc] into next ch 2 corner sp; rep from * twice and from * to ** once again, join with sl st into 3rd of ch 3. Fasten off yarn.

10 Openwork Square

FOUNDATION CHAIN: Ch 34.

FOUNDATION ROW: *(right side)* 1 sc into 2nd ch from hook, 1 sc into each ch, turn. *(33 sc)*

ROW 1: Ch 4 *(counts as 1 dc, ch 1)*, skip 1 sc, 1 dc into next sc, *ch 1, skip 1 sc, 1 dc into next sc; rep from * to end, turn.

ROW 2: Ch 1, 1 sc into first dc, 2 sc into each ch 1 sp along row, ending with 2 sc into ch 1 sp formed by turning ch, turn. *(33 sc)*

ROW 3: Ch 1, 1 sc into each sc, turn. Rep rows 1 to 3 7 times. Fasten off yarn.

MIX-AND-MATCH

MIX-AND-MATCH

11 Baby Blocks

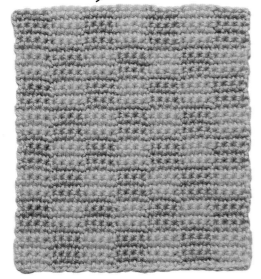

11 ☰
Ⓐ Ⓑ

12 Fine Lines

1 ☰
Ⓐ Ⓑ Ⓒ
Ⓓ Ⓔ Ⓕ

FOUNDATION CHAIN: Using yarn A, ch 29.

WORKING THE PATTERN: When following the chart, read odd-numbered rows (right side rows) from right to left and even-numbered rows (wrong side rows) from left to right.

Starting at the bottom right-hand corner of the chart, work the 34 row pattern from the chart in sc. On the first row, work first sc into 2nd ch from hook, 1 sc into each ch along row. *(28 sc)*

Fasten off yarn.

■ YARN A

■ YARN B

FOUNDATION CHAIN: Using yarn A, ch 29.

FOUNDATION ROW: *(right side)* 1 sc into 2nd ch from hook, 1 sc into each ch, turn. *(28 sc)*

ROW 1: Ch 1, 1 sc into each sc, turn. *(28 sc)*

Rep row 1, working the following color sequence: 4 more rows in A, 1 row in B, 3 rows in A, 1 row in C, 1 row in A, 1 row in D, 5 rows in A, 1 row in E, 3 rows in A, 1 row in F, 1 row in A, 1 row in C, 3 rows in A, 1 row in B, 6 rows in A.

Fasten off yarn.

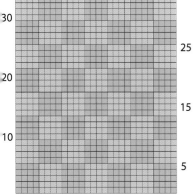

30
25
20
15
10
5

MIX-AND-MATCH

 117 121 141

MIX-AND-MATCH

 57 59 207

13 Circle in a Square

11 📷

(A) (B) (C)
(D) (E)

FOUNDATION RING: Using yarn A, ch 8 and join with sl st to form a ring.

ROUND 1: Ch 3 *(counts as 1 dc)*, 15 dc into ring, join with sl st into 3rd of ch 3. *(16 dc)* Break off yarn A.

ROUND 2: Join yarn B, ch 5 *(counts as 1 dc, ch 2)*, [1 dc into next dc, ch 2] 15 times, join with sl st into 3rd of ch 5. *(16 spaced dc)* Break off yarn B.

ROUND 3: Join yarn C to any ch 2 sp, ch 3 *(counts as 1 dc)*, 2 dc into same sp, ch1, *[3 dc, ch 1] into next ch 2 sp; rep from * to end, join with sl st into 3rd of ch 3. Break off yarn C.

ROUND 4: Join yarn D to any ch 1 sp, *[ch 3, 1 sc into next ch 1 sp] 3 times, ch 6 to make corner sp, 1 sc into next ch 1 sp; rep from * to end. Join with sl st into first of ch 3.

ROUND 5: Ch 3 *(counts as 1 dc)*, 2 dc into first ch 3 sp, 3 dc into each of next two ch 3 sps, *[5 dc, ch 2, 5 dc] into ch 6 corner sp, 3 dc into each ch 3 sp; rep from * to end. Join with sl st into 3rd of ch 3. Break off yarn D.

ROUND 6: Join yarn E to any dc along side of square, ch 3, work 1 dc into each dc of previous round, working [1 dc, 1tr, 1 dc] into each ch 2 corner sp, join with sl st into 3rd of ch 3. Break off yarn E.

ROUND 7: Join yarn A to any dc along side of square, ch 1, 1 sc into every dc of previous round, working [1 sc, ch 1, 1 sc] into each tr at corner, join with sl st into first sc. Break off yarn A.

ROUND 8: Join yarn B, ch 1, 1 sc into every sc of previous round, working 3 sc into each ch 1 corner sp, join with sl st into first sc.

Fasten off yarn.

MIX-AND-MATCH

15   33   153

14 Alhambra

11 📷 (A)

Special abbreviation

dc2tog = work 2 double crochet stitches together to make cluster

FOUNDATION RING: Ch 8 and join with sl st to form a ring.

ROUND 1: Ch 1, 16 sc into ring, join with sl st into first sc. *(16 sc)*

ROUND 2: Ch 1, 1 sc into same place, [ch 7, skip 3 sc, 1 sc into next sc] 3 times, ch 7, skip 3 sc, join with ss into first sc.

ROUND 3: Sl st into 3rd ch of next ch 7 sp, ch 3 *(counts as 1 dc)*, 1 dc into same place, *ch 3, 2 dc into same sp, ch 3, dc2tog inserting hook into same sp for first leg and into next ch 7 sp for second leg, ch 3, 2 dc into same sp; rep from * 3 times omitting 2 dc at end of last rep, join with sl st into 3rd of ch 3.

ROUND 4: Sl st in next dc and into next ch 3 corner sp, ch 3 *(counts as 1 dc)*, 1 dc into same place, *ch 3, 2 dc into same ch 3 sp, ch 3, skip 2 dc, 3 dc into next ch 3 sp, 1 dc into top of next cluster, 3 dc into next ch 3 sp, ch 3, skip 2 dc, 2 dc into next ch 3 sp; rep from * 3 times, omitting 2 dc at end of last rep, join with sl st into

3rd of ch 3.

ROUND 5: Sl st in next dc and into next ch 3 sp, ch 3 *(counts as 1 dc)*, 2 dc into same place, *ch 3, 3 dc into same ch 3 sp, ch 2, 2 dc into next ch 3 sp, ch 2, skip 1 dc, 1 dc into each of next 5 dc, ch 2, 2 dc into next ch 3 sp, ch 2, 3 dc into next ch 3 sp; rep from * 3 times, omitting 3 dc at of last rep, join with sl st into 3rd of ch 3.

ROUND 6: Ch 3, 1 dc into each of next 2 dc, *[3 dc, ch 3, 3 dc] into next ch 3 sp, 1 dc into each of next 3 dc, ch 2, 2 dc into next 2 dc, ch 2, skip 1 dc, 1 dc into each of next 3 dc, ch 2, 1 dc into each of next 2 dc, ch 2, 1 dc into each of next 3 dc; rep from * 3 times, omitting 3 dc at end of last rep, join with sl st into 3rd of ch 3.

ROUND 7: Ch 1, 1 sc into every dc of previous round, working 2 sc into every ch 2 sp and 5 sc into each ch 3 corner sp, join with sl st into first sc.

Fasten off yarn.

MIX-AND-MATCH

36   77   86

15 Corner Square

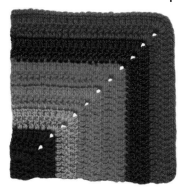

1 ☰ **A** **B** **C** **D** **E** **F**

FOUNDATION CHAIN: Using yarn A, ch 6.

ROW 1: *(right side)* Insert hook into 4th ch from hook, work 3 dc, turn.

ROW 2: Ch 3 *(counts as 1 dc)*, 1 dc into each of next 2 dc, 4 dc into loop made by turning ch of previous row, turn.

ROW 3: Ch 3 *(counts as 1 dc)*, 1 dc into each of next 2 dc, [2 dc, ch 2, 2 dc] into next dc, 1 dc into each of next 2 dc, 1 dc into 3rd of 3 ch, turn.

ROW 4: Ch 3 *(counts as 1 dc)*, 1 dc into each of next 4 dc, [2 dc, ch 2, 2 dc] into ch 2 sp, 1 dc into each of next 4 dc, 1 dc into 3rd of ch 3, turn. Break off yarn A.

ROW 5: Join yarn B, ch 3 *(counts as 1 dc)*, 1 dc into each of next 6 dc, [2 dc, ch 2, 2 dc] into ch 2 sp, 1 dc into each of next 6 dc, 1 dc into 3rd of ch 3, turn.

ROW 6: Ch 3 *(counts as 1 dc)*, 1 dc into each of next 8 dc, [2 dc, ch 2, 2 dc] into ch 2 sp, 1 dc into each of next 8 dc, 1 dc into 3rd of ch 3, turn. Break off yarn B.

ROW 7: Join yarn C, ch 3 *(counts as 1 dc)*, 1 dc into each of next 10 dc, [2 dc, ch 2, 2 dc] into ch 2 sp, 1 dc into each of next 10 dc, 1 dc into 3rd of ch 3, turn.

ROW 8: Ch 3 *(counts as 1 dc)*, 1 dc into each of next 12 dc, [2 dc, ch 2, 2 dc] into ch 2 sp, 1 dc into each of next 12 dc, 1 dc into 3rd of ch 3, turn. Break off yarn C.

ROW 9: Join yarn D, ch 3 *(counts as 1 dc)*, 1 dc into each of next 14 dc, [2 dc, ch 2, 2 dc] into ch 2 sp, 1 dc into each of next 14 dc, 1 dc into 3rd of ch 3, turn.

ROW 10: Ch 3 *(counts as 1 dc)*, 1 dc into each of next 16 dc, [2 dc, ch 2, 2 dc] into ch 2 sp, 1 dc into each of next 16 dc, 1 dc into 3rd of ch 3, turn. Break off yarn D.

ROW 11: Join yarn E, ch 3 *(counts as 1 dc)*, 1 dc into each of next 18 dc, [2 dc, ch 2, 2 dc] into ch 2 sp, 1 dc into each of next 18 dc, 1 dc into 3rd of ch 3, turn.

ROW 12: Ch 3 *(counts as 1 dc)*, 1 dc into each of next 20 dc, [2 dc, ch 2, 2 dc] into ch 2 sp, 1 dc into each of next 20 dc, 1 dc into 3rd of ch 3, turn. Break off yarn E.

ROW 13: Join yarn F, ch 3 *(counts as 1 dc)*, 1 dc into each of next 22 dc, [2 dc, ch 2, 2 dc] into ch 2 sp, 1 dc into each of next 22 dc, 1 dc into 3rd of ch 3, turn.

ROW 14: Ch 3 *(counts as 1 dc)*, 1 dc into each of next 24 dc, 5 dc into ch 2 sp, 1 dc into each of next 24 dc, 1 dc into 3rd of ch 3.

Fasten off yarn.

MIX-AND-MATCH

 34
 75
 197

16 Waterlily

111 📷 **A** **B** **C**

FOUNDATION RING: Using yarn A, ch 8 and join with sl st to form a ring.

ROUND 1: Ch 6 *(counts as 1 dc, ch 3)*, [1 dc into ring, ch 3] 7 times, join with sl st into 3rd of ch 3. *(8 spaced dc)* Break off yarn A.

ROUND 2: Join yarn B to any ch 3 sp, [1 sc, ch 2, 3 dc, ch 2, 1 sc] into same sp, *[1 sc, ch 2, 3 dc, ch 2, 1 sc] into next ch 3 sp; rep from * 7 times, do not join. *(8 petals)*

ROUND 3: *Ch 5, working behind petals, skip 1 petal, 1 sc into top of next dc of round 1; rep from * to end, do not join. *(8 ch 5 loops)*

ROUND 4: *[1 sc, ch 2, 5 dc, ch 2, 1 sc] into next ch 5 loop; rep from * to end, do not join. *(8 petals)*

ROUND 5: *Ch 7, working behind petals, skip 1 petal, 1 sc into next sc of round 3; rep from * to end, do not join. *(8 ch 7 loops)*

ROUND 6: *[1 sc, ch 2, 7 dc, ch 2, 1 sc] into next ch 7 loop; rep from * to end, join with sl st into first sc. *(8 petals)* Break off yarn B.

ROUND 7: Working behind petals, join yarn C to any sc on round 5, ch 3, *(counts as 1 dc)*, 2 dc into same sc, ch 3, *[3 dc, ch 3, 3 dc] into next sc of round 5 to make corner, ch 3, **3 dc into next sc, ch 3; rep from * twice and from * to ** once again, join with sl st into 3rd of ch 3.

ROUND 8: Ch 3 *(counts as 1 dc)*, 1 dc into every dc and 3 dc into each ch 3 sp of previous round, working [2 dc, ch 3, 2 dc] into each ch 3 corner sp, join with sl st into 3rd of ch 3.

ROUND 9: Ch 3 *(counts as 1 dc)*, 1 dc into each dc of previous round, working [2 dc, ch 3, 2 dc] into each ch 3 corner sp, join with sl st into 3rd of ch 3.

ROUND 10: Ch 1, 1 sc into each dc of previous round, working [2 sc, ch 1, 2 sc] into each ch 3 corner sp, join with sl st into first sc. Break off yarn C.

ROUND 11: Join yarn B, ch 1, 1 sc into each sc of previous round, working 3 sc into each ch 1 corner sp, join with sl st into first sc.

Fasten off yarn.

MIX-AND-MATCH

 43
 44
 167

17 Alternate Bobbles

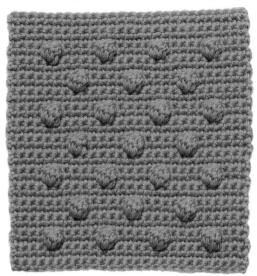

11

 A

Special abbreviation

MB = make bobble (work 4 open dc in same st leaving 5 loops on hook, draw yarn through all 5 loops at once)

FOUNDATION CHAIN: Ch 28.

FOUNDATION ROW: *(wrong side)* Working first sc into 2nd ch from hook, work 1 sc into each ch, turn. *(27 sc)*

ROW 1: Ch 1, 1 sc into each sc, turn. *(27 sc)*

ROWS 2 & 3: Rep row 1.

ROW 4: *(wrong side)* Ch 1, 1 sc into each of next 4 sc, [MB, 1 sc into each of next 5 sc] 3 times, MB, 1 sc into each of next 4 sc, turn.

ROWS 5 to 7: Rep row 1.

ROW 8: Ch 1, 1 sc into each of next 7 sc, [MB, 1 sc into each of next 5 sc] twice, MB, 1 sc into each of next 7 sc, turn.

Rep rows 1 to 8 twice, and then rep rows 1 to 7 once again.

NEXT ROW: Rep row 1.
Fasten off yarn.

MIX-AND-MATCH

 104   118   177

18 Traditional Granny

1 A B C D E F

FOUNDATION RING: Using yarn A, ch 6 and join with sl st to form a ring.

ROUND 1: Ch 3 *(counts as 1 dc)*, 2 dc into ring, ch 3, *3 dc into ring, ch 3; rep from * twice more, join with sl st into 3rd of ch 3. Break off yarn A.

ROUND 2: Join yarn B to any ch 3 sp, ch 3 *(counts as 1 dc)*, [2 dc, ch 3, 3 dc] into same sp *(corner made)*, *ch 1, [3 dc, ch 3, 3 dc] into next ch 3 sp; rep from * twice more, ch 1, join with sl st into 3rd of ch 3. Break off yarn B.

ROUND 3: Join yarn C to any ch 3 corner sp, ch 3 *(counts as 1 dc)*, [2 dc, ch 3, 3 dc] into same sp, *ch 1, 3 dc into ch 1 sp, ch 1, **[3 dc, ch 3, 3 dc] into next ch 3 corner sp; rep from * twice and from * to ** once again, join with sl st into 3rd of ch 3. Break off yarn C.

ROUND 4: Join yarn D to any ch 3 corner sp, ch 3 *(counts as 1 dc)*, [2 dc, ch 3, 3 dc] into same sp, *[ch 1, 3 dc] into each ch 1 sp along side of square, ch 1, **[3 dc, ch 3, 3 dc] into next ch 3 corner sp; rep from * twice and from * to ** once again, join with sl st into 3rd of ch 3. Break off yarn D.

ROUND 5: Join yarn E to any ch 3 corner sp, ch 3 *(counts as 1 dc)*, [2 dc, ch 3, 3 dc] into same sp, *[ch 1, 3 dc] into each ch 1 sp along side of square, ch 1, **[3 dc, ch 3, 3 dc] into next ch 3 corner sp; rep from * twice and from * to ** once again, join with sl st into 3rd of ch 3. Break off yarn E.

ROUND 6: Join yarn F to any ch 3 corner sp, ch 3 *(counts as 1 dc)*, [2 dc, ch 3, 3 dc] into same sp, *[ch 1, 3 dc] into each ch 1 sp along side of square, ch 1, **[3 dc, ch 3, 3 dc] into next ch 3 corner sp; rep from * twice and from * to ** once again, join with sl st into 3rd of ch 3.

ROUND 7: Sl st in next 2 dc and into next ch 3 corner sp, ch 3 *(counts as 1 dc)*, [2 dc, ch 3, 3 dc] into same sp, *[ch 1, 3 dc] into each ch 1 sp along side of square, ch 1, **[3 dc, ch 3, 3 dc] into next ch 3 corner sp; rep from * twice and from * to ** once again, join with sl st into 3rd of ch 3. Fasten off yarn.

MIX-AND-MATCH

 20   29   63

19 Lacy Cross

1 🖕 Ⓐ

FOUNDATION RING: Using yarn A, ch 6 and join with sl st to form a ring.

ROUND 1: Ch 3 *(counts as 1 dc)*, 15 dc into ring, join with sl st into 3rd of ch 3.

ROUND 2: Ch 3 *(counts as 1 dc)*, 2 dc into same place, ch 2, skip 1 dc, 1 dc into next dc, ch 2, skip 1 dc, *3 dc into next dc, ch 2, skip 1 dc, 1 dc into next dc, ch 2, skip 1 dc; rep from * twice, join with sl st into 3rd of ch 3.

ROUND 3: Ch 3 *(counts as 1 dc)*, 5 dc into next dc, *1 dc into next dc, [ch 2, 1 dc into next dc] twice, 5 dc into next dc; rep from * twice, [1 dc into next dc, ch 2] twice, join with sl st into 3rd of ch 3.

ROUND 4: Ch 3 *(counts as 1 dc)*, 1 dc into each of next 2 dc, 5 dc into next dc, *1 dc into each of next 3 dc, ch 2, 1 dc into next dc, ch 2, 1 dc into each of next 3 dc, 5 dc into next dc; rep from * twice, 1 dc into each of next 3 dc, ch 2, 1 dc into next dc, ch 2, join with sl st into 3rd of ch 3.

ROUND 5: Ch 3 *(counts as 1 dc)*, 1 dc into each of next 4 dc, 5 dc into next dc, *1 dc into each of next 5 dc, ch 2, 1 dc into next dc, ch 2, 1 dc into each of next 5 dc, 5 dc into next dc; rep from * twice, 1 dc into each of next 5 dc, ch 2, 1 dc into next dc, ch 2, join with sl st into 3rd of ch 3.

ROUND 6: Ch 3 *(counts as 1 dc)*, 1 dc into each of next 6 dc, 5 dc into next dc, *1 dc into each of next 7 dc, ch 2, 1 dc into next dc, ch 2, 1 dc into each of next 7 dc, 5 dc into next dc; rep from * twice, 1 dc into each of next 7 dc, ch 2, 1 dc into next dc, ch 2, join with sl st into 3rd of ch 3.

ROUND 7: Ch 3 *(counts as 1 dc)*, work 1 dc into each dc and 2 dc into each ch 2 sp of previous round, working [2 dc, ch 1, 2 dc] into center st of each 5 dc corner group, join with sl st into 3rd of ch 3.

Fasten off yarn.

MIX-AND-MATCH

 137 158 162

20 Colorful Bobbles

111 ≋ Ⓐ Ⓑ Ⓒ Ⓓ Ⓔ Ⓕ

Special abbreviation

MB = make bobble (work 4 open dc in same st leaving 5 loops on hook, draw yarn through all 5 loops at once)

FOUNDATION CHAIN: Using yarn A, ch 28.

FOUNDATION ROW: *(wrong side)* Working first sc into 2nd ch from hook, work 1 sc into each ch, turn. *(27 sc)*

ROW 1: Ch 1, 1 sc into each sc, turn.

ROWS 2 & 3: Rep row 1.

ROW 4: *(wrong side)* Ch 1, 1 sc into each of next 3 sc, MB in B, 1 sc into each of next 4 sc, MB in C, 1 sc into each of next 4 sc, MB in D, 1 sc into each of next 4 sc, MB in E, 1 sc into each of next 4 sc, MB in F, 1 sc into each of next 3 sc, turn.

ROWS 5 to 11: Rep row 1.

ROW 12: Ch 1, 1 sc into each of next 3 sc, MB in D, 1 sc into each of next 4 sc, MB in F, 1 sc into each of next 4 sc, MB in E, 1 sc into each of next 4 sc, MB in B, 1 sc into each of next 4 sc, MB in C, 1 sc into each of next 3 sc, turn.

ROWS 13 to 19: Rep row 1.

ROW 20: Ch 1, 1 sc into each of next 3 sc, MB in E, 1 sc into each of next 4 sc, MB in B, 1 sc into each of next 4 sc, MB in C, 1 sc into each of next 4 sc, MB in F, 1 sc into each of next 4 sc, MB in D, 1 sc into each of next 3 sc, turn.

ROWS 21 to 27: Rep row 1.

ROW 28: Ch 1, 1 sc into each of next 3 sc, MB in C, 1 sc into each of next 4 sc, MB in D, 1 sc into each of next 4 sc, MB in F, 1 sc into each of next 4 sc, MB in B, 1 sc into each of next 4 sc, MB in E, 1 sc into each of next 3 sc, turn.

ROWS 29 to 32: Rep row 1.

Fasten off yarn.

MIX-AND-MATCH

 127 131 175

21 Blue Shades

Special abbreviation

sc3tog = decrease 2 sts by working the next 3 sc together

FOUNDATION CHAIN: Using yarn A, ch 58.

FOUNDATION ROW: *(wrong side)* 1 sc into 2nd ch from hook, 1 sc into each ch, turn. *(57 sc)*

ROW 1: Ch 1, 1 sc into each of next 27 sc, sc3tog, 1 sc into each of rem 27 sc, turn. *(55 sc)*

ROW 2: Ch 1, 1 sc into each of next 26 sc, sc3tog, 1 sc into each of rem 26 sc, turn. *(53 sc)* Break off yarn A.

ROW 3: Join yarn B, ch 1, 1 sc into each of next 25 sc, sc3tog, 1 sc into each of rem 25 sc, turn. *(51 sc)*

ROW 4: Ch 1, 1 sc into each of next 24 sc, sc3tog, 1 sc into each of rem 24 sc, turn. *(49 sc)* Break off yarn B. Join yarn C. Cont in pattern as set, working sc3tog over 3 center sts on every row. At the same time, change yarn colors in the following color sequence: Work 2 rows in yarn C,

2 rows in yarn D, 2 rows in yarn E, 2 rows in yarn F, 2 rows in yarn G, 2 rows in yarn F, 2 rows in yarn E, 2 rows in yarn D, 2 rows in yarn C, 2 rows in yarn B. Join yarn A and cont in pattern until 3 sc rem.

NEXT ROW: Work sc3tog.

Fasten off yarn.

MIX-AND-MATCH

22 St Petersburg

Special abbreviations

fpdc = front post double crochet
bpdc = back post double crochet

FOUNDATION RING: Using yarn A, ch 8 and join with sl st to form a ring.

ROUND 1: Ch 6 *(counts as 1 dc, ch 3)*, [3 dc into ring, ch 3] 3 times, 2 dc into ring, join with sl st into 3rd of ch 6. Break off yarn A.

ROUND 2: Join yarn B to any ch 3 corner sp, ch 3 *(counts as 1 dc)*, 2 dc into same sp, *1 fpdc round each of next 3 dc, **[3 dc, ch 3, 3 dc] into next ch 3 corner sp; rep from * twice and from * to ** once again, [3 dc, ch 3] into next ch 3 corner sp, join with sl st into 3rd of ch 3. Break off yarn B.

ROUND 3: Join yarn C to any ch 3 corner sp, ch 6 *(counts as 1 dc, ch 3)*, 3 dc into same sp, *1 bpdc round each of next 3 sts, 1 fpdc round each of next 3 sts, 1 bpdc round each of next 3 sts, **[3 dc, ch 3, 3 dc] into next ch 3 corner sp; rep from * twice and from * to ** once again, 2 dc into next ch 3 corner sp, join with sl st into 3rd of ch 6. Break off yarn C.

ROUND 4: Join yarn B to any ch 3

corner sp, ch 3 *(counts as 1 dc)*, 2 dc into same sp, *[1 fpdc round each of next 3 sts, 1 bpdc round each of next 3 sts] twice, 1 fpdc round each of next 3 sts, **[3 dc, ch 3, 3 dc] into next ch 3 corner sp; rep from * twice and from * to ** once again, [3 dc, ch 3] into next ch 3 corner sp, join with sl st into 3rd of ch 3. Break off yarn B.

ROUND 5: Join yarn A to any ch 3 corner sp, ch 1, [2 sc, ch 1, 2 sc] into same sp, *1 sc into each of next 3 dc, 1 hdc into each of next 15 dc, 1 sc into each of next 3 dc, **[2 sc, ch 1, 2 sc] into next ch 3 corner sp; rep from * twice and from * to ** once again, join with sl st into first sc. Break off yarn A.

ROUND 6: Join yarn C to any ch 1 corner sp, ch 2 *(counts as 1 hdc)*, 2 hdc into same sp, *1 hdc into each of next 5 sc, 1 dc into each of next 15 hdc, 1 hdc into each of next 5 sc, **3 hdc into next ch 1 corner sp; rep from * twice and from * to ** once again, join with sl st into 2nd of ch 2. Break off yarn C.

ROUND 7: Join yarn A to any dc, ch 1, 1 sc into each hdc and dc of previous round, working 3 sc into center st of 3 hdc corner group, join with sl st into first sc.

Fasten off yarn.

MIX-AND-MATCH

23 Bars & Diamonds

11 ≣
Ⓐ

FOUNDATION CHAIN: Ch 34.

FOUNDATION ROW: (wrong side) 1 sc into 2nd ch from hook, 1 sc into each ch, turn. (33 sc)

ROW 1: Ch 3 (counts as 1 dc), 1 dc into next sc, *skip 2 sc, 1 dc into next sc, ch 3, work block of 3 evenly spaced dc into side of dc just made, skip 2 sc, 1 dc into each of next 3 sc; rep from * ending last rep with 2 dc, turn.

ROW 2: Ch 3 (counts as 1 dc), 1 dc into next dc, *ch 2, 1 sc into 3rd of ch 3 at top corner of next block, ch 2, 1 dc into each of next 3 dc; rep from * ending last rep with 2 dc, turn.

ROW 3: Ch 3 (counts as 1 dc), 1 dc into next dc, *1 dc into next sc, ch 3, work block of 3 evenly spaced dc into side of dc just made, 1 dc into each of next 3 dc; rep from * ending last rep with 2 dc, turn. Rep rows 2 and 3 5 times, then rep row 2 once again.

NEXT ROW: Ch 1, 1 sc into each of next 2 dc, *2 sc into next ch 2 sp, 1 sc into next sc, 2 sc into next ch 2 sp, 1 sc into each of next 3 dc; rep from * ending last rep with 2 sc. Fasten off yarn.

MIX-AND-MATCH

 56 82 105

24 Italian Cross

11 📷 Ⓐ Ⓑ Ⓒ

Special abbreviations

beg pf = beginning puff st of hdc3tog, pf = puff stitch of hdc4tog

FOUNDATION RING: Using yarn A, ch 4 and join with sl st to form a ring.

ROUND 1: Ch 3 (counts as 1 dc), 11 dc into ring, join with sl st into 3rd of ch 3. (12 dc) Break off yarn A.

ROUND 2: Join yarn B, ch 2 (counts as 1 hdc), beg pf in same place, *[ch 1, pf into next st] twice, ch 5, **pf into next st; rep from * twice and from * to ** once again, join with sl st into top of beg pf.

ROUND 3: Sl st into next ch 1 sp, ch 2 (counts as 1 hdc), beg pf into same sp, * ch 1, pf into next sp, ch 2, 5 dc into next ch 5 sp, ch 2, **pf into next ch 1 sp; rep from * twice and from * to ** once again, join with sl st into top of beg pf.

ROUND 4: Sl st into next ch 1 sp, ch 2 (counts as 1 hdc), beg pf into same sp, *ch 3, skip ch 2, [1 dc into next dc, ch 1] twice, [1 dc, ch 1, 1 dc, ch 1, 1 dc] into next dc, [ch 1, 1 dc into next dc] twice, ch 3, skip ch 2, **pf into next ch 1 sp; rep from * twice and from * to ** once again, join

with sl st into top of beg pf. Break off yarn B.

ROUND 5: Join yarn C to first dc of any 7 dc corner group, ch 4 (counts as 1 dc, ch 1), *[1 dc into next dc, ch 1] twice, [1 dc, ch 1, 1 dc, ch 1, 1 dc] into next dc, [ch 1, 1 dc into next dc] 3 times, 3 dc into next ch 3 sp, ch 1, 3 dc into next ch 3 sp, **1 dc into next dc, ch 1; rep from * twice and from * to ** once again, join with sl st into 3rd of ch 4.

ROUND 6: Ch 4 (counts as 1 dc, ch 1), * [1 dc into next dc, ch 1] 3 times, [1 dc, ch 1, 1 dc, ch 1, 1 dc] into next dc, [ch 1, 1 dc into next dc] 4 times, 1 dc into each of next 3 dc, 1 dc into ch 1 sp, 1 dc into each of next 3 dc, **1 dc into next dc, ch 1; rep from * twice and from * to ** once again, join with sl st into 3rd of ch 4.

ROUND 7: Ch 4 (counts as 1 dc, ch 1), *[1 dc into next dc, ch 1] 4 times, [1 dc, ch 1, 1 dc, ch 1, 1 dc] into next dc, [ch 1, 1 dc into next dc] 5 times, **1 dc into each of next 8 dc, ch 1; rep from * twice and from * to ** once again, 1 dc into each of next 7 dc, join with sl st into 3rd of ch 4. Fasten off yarn.

MIX-AND-MATCH

 47 81 84

25 Tannenbaum

11 ☰
Ⓐ Ⓑ Ⓒ

FOUNDATION CHAIN: Using yarn A, ch 29.

WORKING THE PATTERN: When following the chart, read odd-numbered rows (right side rows) from right to left and even-numbered rows (wrong side rows) from left to right.

Starting at the bottom right-hand corner of the chart, work the 34 row pattern from the chart in sc. On the first row, work first sc into 2nd ch from hook, 1 sc into each ch along row. *(28 sc)*

Fasten off yarn.

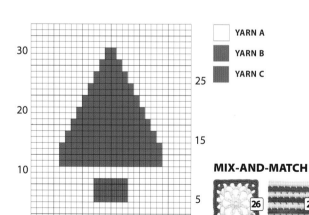

YARN A
YARN B
YARN C

MIX-AND-MATCH

 26   27   28

26 Snowflake

11 ⟳ Ⓐ Ⓑ

Special abbreviations

beg cl = beginning cluster made from 3 dc stitches, **cl** = cluster made from 4 dc stitches

FOUNDATION RING: Using yarn A, ch 8 and join with sl st to form a ring.

ROUND 1: Ch 3 *(counts as 1 dc)*, 2 dc into ring, ch 7, [3 dc, ch 7] 7 times into ring, join with sl st into 3rd of ch 3.

ROUND 2: Sl st across next 2 dc and ch 2, ch 3 *(counts as 1 dc)*, beg cl into first ch 7 sp, *ch 9, cl into next ch 7 sp; rep from *6 times, ch 9, join with sl st into top of beg cl.

ROUND 3: Ch 1, *[2 sc, ch 5, 2 sc] into next ch 9 sp, ch 7, [cl, ch 5, cl] into next ch 9 sp, ch 7; rep from * 3 times, join with sl st into first sc. Break off yarn A.

ROUND 4: Join yarn B to ch 5 sp between 2 groups of 2 sc, 2 sc into same sp, *ch 5, 2 sc into next ch 7 sp, ch 5, [cl, ch 5, cl] into next ch 5 sp, ch 5, 2 sc into ch 7 sp, ch 5, **2 sc into next ch 5 sp; rep from * twice and from * to ** once again, join with sl st into first sc.

ROUND 5: Ch 2 *(counts as 1 hdc)*, 1 hdc into next sc, 3 sc into next ch 5 sp, 1 hdc into each of next 2 sc, 3 sc into next ch 5 sp, *1 sc into top of next cl, [1 sc, 1 hdc, 1 dc, 1 hdc, 1 sc] into next ch 5 corner sp, 1 sc into next cl, **[3 sc into next ch 5 sp, 1 hdc into each of next 2 sc] 3 times, 3 sc into next ch 5 sp; rep from * twice and from * to ** once again, 3 sc into next ch 5 sp, 1 hdc into each of next 2 sc, 3 sc into next ch 5 sp, join with sl st into 2nd of ch 2.

ROUND 6: Ch 1, 1 sc into each sc and hdc of previous round, working 5 sc into center st of each corner group. Fasten off yarn.

MIX-AND-MATCH

25   27   28

27 Snowy Stripes

11 ≣
A B C

Special abbreviation

sp = spike (insert hook 1 row below next st, pull up loop of yarn, insert hook into top of next st, yo, draw loop through, yo, draw through all 3 loops on hook)

FOUNDATION CHAIN: Using yarn A, ch 30.

FOUNDATION ROW: *(right side)* 1 sc into 2nd ch from hook, 1 sc into each ch to end, turn. *(29 sc)*

ROW 1: Ch 1, 1 sc into each st of previous row, turn. *(29 sc)*

ROWS 2 & 3: Rep row 1. Break off yarn A.

ROW 4: Join yarn B, ch 1, 1 sc into each of next 2 sc, *sp into next st, 1 sc into each of next 3 sc; rep from * to last 2 sts, 1 sc into each of next 2 sc, turn.

ROWS 5 to 7: Rep row 1. Break off yarn B.

ROW 8: Join yarn C, ch 1, 1 sc into each of next 4 sc, *sp into next st, 1 sc into each of next 3 sc; rep from *

to last 4 sts, 1 sc into each of next 4 sc, turn.

ROWS 9 to 11: Rep row 1. Break off yarn C.

ROW 12: Join yarn B, rep row 4.

ROWS 13 to 15: Rep row 1. Break off yarn B.

ROW 16: Join yarn A, rep row 8. Rep rows 1 to 15 once again. Fasten off yarn.

MIX-AND-MATCH

 25 26 28

28 Christmas Rose

11 ⟳ A B C

FOUNDATION RING: Using yarn A, ch 12 and join with sl st to form a ring.

ROUND 1: Ch 1, 18 sc into ring, join with sl st into first sc.

ROUND 2: Ch 1, 1 sc into same place, [ch 3, skip 2 sc, 1 sc into next sc] 5 times, ch 3, skip 2 sc, join with sl st into first sc. *(6 ch 3 loops)*

ROUND 3: Ch 1, [1 sc, ch 3, 5 dc, ch 3, 1 sc] into each of next 6 ch 3 loops, join with sl st into first sc. *(6 petals)*

ROUND 4: Ch 1, 1 sc into same place, [ch 5 behind petal of previous round, 1 sc between 2 sc] 5 times, ch 5 behind petal of previous round, join with sl st into first sc. *(6 ch 5 loops)*

ROUND 5: Ch 1, [1 sc, ch 3, 7 dc, ch 3, 1 sc] into each of next 6 ch 5 loops, join with sl st into first sc. *(6 petals)* Break off yarn A.

ROUND 6: Join yarn B between any 2 sc, ch 1, [1 sc between 2 sc, ch 6 behind petal of previous round] 6 times, join with sl st into first sc. *(6 ch 6 loops)*

ROUND 7: Sl st into next ch 6 loop, ch 3 *(counts as 1 dc)*, [4 dc, ch 2, 1 dc] into same loop, *6 dc into next ch 6 loop, [2 dc, ch 2, 4 dc] into next ch 6

loop, **[5 dc, ch 2, 1 dc] into next ch 6 loop; rep from * to ** once, join with sl st into 3rd of ch 3. *(9 dc along each side of square)*

ROUND 8: Ch 3 *(counts as 1 dc)*, 1 dc into each dc of previous round, working [3 dc, ch 2, 3 dc] into each ch 2 corner sp, join with sl st into 3rd of ch 3.

ROUND 9: Ch 3 *(counts as 1 dc)*, 1 dc into each dc of previous round, working [2 dc, 1 tr, ch 2, 1 tr, 2 dc] into each ch 2 corner sp, join with sl st into 3rd of ch 3. Break off yarn B.

ROUND 10: Join yarn A to any dc of previous round, ch 1, 1 sc into each dc and tr of previous round, working [2 sc, ch 2, 2 sc] into each ch 2 corner sp, join with sl st into first sc. Break off yarn A.

ROUND 11: Join yarn C, ch 1, 1 sc into each sc of previous round, working 3 sc into each ch 2 corner sp, join with sl st into first sc.

ROUNDS 12 & 13: Ch 1, 1 sc into each sc of previous round, working 3 sc into center st of each 3 sc corner group, join with sl st into first sc. Fasten off yarn.

MIX-AND-MATCH

 25 26 27

29 Bobble Stripes

11

A B C
D E F

Special abbreviation

MB = make bobble (work 4 open dc in same st leaving 5 loops on hook, draw yarn through all 5 loops at once)

FOUNDATION CHAIN: Using yarn A, ch 28.

FOUNDATION ROW: (wrong side) Working first sc into 2nd ch from hook, work 1 sc into each ch, turn. (27 sc)

ROW 1: Ch 1, 1 sc into each sc, turn.

ROWS 2 & 3: Rep row 1. Break off yarn A.

ROW 4: Join yarn B, ch 1, 1 sc into next sc, *MB, 1 sc into each of next 5 sc; rep from * three times, MB, 1 sc into next sc, turn. Break off yarn B.

ROW 5: Join yarn A and rep row 1.

ROWS 6 to 9: Rep row 1. Break off yarn A.

ROW 10: Join yarn C, ch 1, 1 sc into next sc, *MB, 1 sc into each of next 5 sc; rep from * three times, MB, 1 sc into next sc, turn. Break off yarn C.

ROW 11: Join yarn A and rep row 1.

ROWS 12 to 15: Rep row 1. Break off yarn A.

ROW 16: Join yarn D, ch 1, 1 sc into next sc, *MB, 1 sc into each of next 5 sc; rep from * three times, MB, 1 sc into next sc, turn. Break off yarn D.

ROW 17: Join yarn A and rep row 1.

ROWS 18 to 21: Rep row 1. Break off yarn A.

ROW 22: Join yarn E, ch 1, 1 sc into next sc, *MB, 1 sc into each of next 5 sc; rep from * three times, MB, 1 sc into next sc, turn. Break off yarn E.

ROW 23: Join yarn A and rep row 1.

ROWS 24 to 27: Rep row 1. Break off yarn A.

ROW 28: Join yarn F, ch 1, 1 sc into next sc, *MB, 1 sc into each of next 5 sc; rep from * three times, MB, 1 sc into next sc, turn. Break off yarn F.

ROW 29: Join yarn A and rep row 1.

ROWS 30 to 32: Rep row 1.

Fasten off yarn.

MIX-AND-MATCH

30 Shell Lace

11

A

FOUNDATION CHAIN: Ch 32.

FOUNDATION ROW: (wrong side) 1 sc into 2nd ch from hook, 1 sc into next ch, *ch 3, skip ch 3, 1 sc into each of next ch 3; rep from * to last 5ch, ch 3, skip ch 3, 1 sc into each of last ch 2, turn.

ROW 1: (right side) Ch 1, 1 sc into first sc, * 5 dc into ch 3 sp, skip 1 sc, 1 sc into next sc; rep from * to end, turn.

ROW 2: Ch 3, 1 sc into 2nd, 3rd and 4th stitches of 5 dc group, ch 3; rep from * to end, ending with 1 sc into 2nd, 3rd and 4th stitches of 5 dc group, ch 2, 1 sc into last st, turn.

ROW 3: Ch 3, 2 dc into ch 2 sp, skip 1 sc, 1 sc into next sc, *5 dc into ch 3 sp, skip 1 sc, 1 sc into next sc; rep from * to end, 3 dc into last ch 3 sp, turn.

ROW 4: Ch 1, 1 sc into each of first 2 dc, *ch 3, 1 sc into 2nd, 3rd and 4th stitches of 5 dc group; rep from * to end, ending with ch 3, 1 sc into 2nd dc, 1 sc into 3rd of ch 3, turn.

Rep rows 1-4 four times, ending with a 4th row.

Fasten off yarn.

MIX-AND-MATCH

31 Primrose Square

11 **A** **B** **C** **D**

Special abbreviations

beg cl = beginning cluster made from 3 dc sts, **cl** = cluster made from 4 dc sts

FOUNDATION RING: Using yarn A, ch 6 and join with sl st to form a ring.

ROUND 1: Ch 5 *(counts as 1 dc, ch 2)*, [1 dc into ring, ch 2] 7 times, join with sl st into 3rd of ch 5. *(8 spaced dc)*

ROUND 2: Ch 3 *(counts as 1 dc)*, beg cl into next ch 2 sp, [ch 5, cl into next ch 2 sp] 7 times, ch 5, join with sl st into top of beg cl. Break off yarn A.

ROUND 3: Join yarn B, ch 1, 1 sc into same place, *ch 2, working over ch 5 sp to enclose it work 1 dc into next dc of round 1, ch 2, 1 sc into top of next cl; rep from * to end omitting last sc, join with sl st into first sc.

ROUND 4: Sl st into next ch, ch 1, 1 sc into same place, *ch 3, 1 sc into next ch 2 sp; rep from * to end omitting last sc, join with sl st into first sc.

ROUND 5: Sl st into next ch, ch 3 *(counts as 1 dc)*, [1 dc, ch 2, 2 dc] into same sp, *ch 2, 1 sc into next ch 3 sp, [ch 3, 1 sc into next ch 3 sp] twice, ch 2, **[2 dc, ch 2, 2 dc] into next ch 3 sp; rep from * twice and from * to ** once again, join with sl st into 3rd of ch 3. Break off yarn B.

ROUND 6: Join yarn C into any ch 2 corner sp, ch 3 *(counts as 1 dc)*, [1 dc, ch 2, 2 dc] into same sp, *ch 2 [1 sc into next ch sp, ch 3] 3 times, 1 sc into next ch sp, ch 2, **[2 dc, ch 2, 2 dc] into ch 2 corner sp; rep from * twice and from * to ** once again, join with sl st into 3rd of ch 3.

ROUND 7: Sl st into next ch 2 corner sp, ch 3 *(counts as 1 dc)*, [1 dc, ch 2, 2 dc] into same sp, *ch 2 [1 sc into next ch sp, ch 3] 4 times, 1 sc into next ch sp, ch 2, **[2 dc, ch 2, 2 dc] into ch 2 corner sp; rep from * twice and from * to ** once again, join with sl st into 3rd of ch 3.

ROUND 8: Sl st into next ch 2 corner sp, ch 3 *(counts as 1 dc)*, [1 dc, ch 2, 2 dc] into same sp, *ch 2 [1 sc into next ch sp, ch 3] 5 times, 1 sc into next ch sp, ch 2, **[2 dc, ch 2, 2 dc] into ch 2 corner sp; rep from * twice and from * to ** once again, join with sl st into 3rd of ch 3.

ROUND 9: Sl st into next ch 2 corner sp, ch 3 *(counts as 1 dc)*, [2 dc, ch 2, 3 dc] into same sp, *3 dc into each ch sp along side of square, **[3 dc, ch 2, 3 dc] into next ch 2 corner sp; rep from * twice and from * to ** once again, join with sl st into 3rd of ch 3. Break off yarn C.

ROUND 10: Join yarn D into any dc along side of square, ch 1, 1 sc into same place, 1 sc into each dc of previous round, working 3 sc into each ch 2 corner sp, join with sl st into first sc. Fasten off yarn.

MIX-AND-MATCH

 137   157   161

32 Oblique Stripe

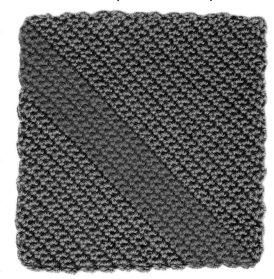

11 ≣ **A** **B**

Special abbreviation

sc3tog = decrease 2 sts by working the next 3 sc together

FOUNDATION CHAIN: Using yarn A, ch 2.

FOUNDATION ROW: *(wrong side)* Work 3 sc into 2nd ch from hook, turn. *(3 sc)*

ROW 1: Ch 1, 2 sc into first sc, 1 sc into next sc, 2 sc into last sc, turn. *(5 sc)*

Begin increase pattern.

ROWS 2 to 4: Ch 1, 2 sc into first sc, 1 sc into each sc along row to last st, 2 sc into last sc, turn.

ROW 5: Ch 1, 1 sc into each sc along row, turn.

Rep rows 2 to 5 three times. *(29 sc)* Break off yarn A. Join yarn B, rep rows 3 to 6 twice. *(41 sc)* Break off yarn B. Join yarn A and begin decrease pattern.

NEXT ROW: Ch 1, 1 sc into each sc along row, turn.

NEXT 3 ROWS: Ch 1, skip first sc, 1 sc into each sc along row to last 2 sts, skip 1 sc, 1 sc into last sc, turn. Rep 4-row decrease pattern five times. *(5 sc)*

NEXT ROW: Ch 1, skip first sc, 1 sc into each of next 2 sc, skip next sc, 1 sc into next sc, turn. *(3 sc)*

NEXT ROW: Ch 1, work sc3tog. Fasten off yarn.

MIX-AND-MATCH

 29   55   156

33 Pretty in Pink

11

Ⓐ Ⓑ Ⓒ
Ⓓ Ⓔ Ⓕ

Special abbreviation

sc3tog = decrease 2 sts by working the next 3 sc together

___

FOUNDATION CHAIN: Using yarn A, ch 58.

FOUNDATION ROW: *(wrong side)* 1 sc into 2nd ch from hook, 1 sc into each ch, turn. *(57 sc)*

ROW 1: Ch 1, 1 sc into each of next 27 sc, sc3tog, 1 sc into each of rem 27 sc, turn. *(55 sc)*

ROW 2: Ch 1, 1 sc into each of next 26 sc, sc3tog, 1 sc into each of rem 26 sc, turn. *(53 sc)*

ROW 3: Ch 1, 1 sc into each of next 25 sc, sc3tog, 1 sc into each of rem 25 sc, turn. *(51 sc)*

ROW 4: Ch 1, 1 sc into each of next 24 sc, sc3tog, 1 sc into each of rem 24 sc, turn. *(49 sc)*

Cont in pattern as set, working sc3tog over 3 center sts on every row. At the same time, change yarn colors in the following color sequence: Work 10 more rows in yarn A, 2 rows in yarn B, 2 rows in yarn C, 2 rows in yarn D, 2 rows in yarn E, 2 rows in yarn F.

Join yarn A and cont in pattern until 3 sc rem.

NEXT ROW: Work sc3tog.

Fasten off yarn.

MIX-AND-MATCH

 77

 119

 148

34 Band of Bobbles

11

Ⓐ

Special abbreviation

MB = make bobble (work 4 open dc in same st leaving 5 loops on hook, draw yarn through all 5 loops at once)

___

FOUNDATION CHAIN: Ch 28.

FOUNDATION ROW: *(wrong side)* Working first sc into 2nd ch from hook, work 1 sc into each ch, turn. *(27 sc)*

ROW 1: Ch 1, 1 sc into each sc, turn. *(27 sc)*

ROW 2: Ch 1, 1 sc into first sc, [MB, 1 sc into each of next 2 sc] 8 times, MB, 1 sc into last sc, turn.

ROWS 3 & 4: Rep row 1.

Rep rows 1 to 4 3 times, then rep row 1 16 times.

Fasten off yarn.

MIX-AND-MATCH

 125 126

 144

35 Tricolor Square

Special abbreviations

beg cl = beginning cluster made from 5 tr sts, **cl** = cluster made from 6 tr sts

FOUNDATION RING: Using yarn A, ch 8 and join with sl st to form a ring.

ROUND 1: Ch 4 *(counts as 1 tr)*, 5 tr, [ch 3, 6 tr into ring] 3 times, ch 3, join with sl st into 4th of ch 4.

ROUND 2: Ch 4 *(counts as 1 tr)*, beg cl into each of next 5 tr, *ch 5, sl st into 2nd of ch 3, ch 5, **cl into next 6 tr; rep from * twice and from * to ** once again, join with sl st into 4th of ch 4. Break off yarn A.

ROUND 3: Join yarn B to top of any cl, *[3 tr, ch 1, 3 tr, ch 2, 3 tr, ch 1, 3 tr] into next ch 3 sp of round 1, sl st into top of next cl; rep from * 3 times, join with sl st into top of first cl. Break off yarn B.

ROUND 4: Join yarn A to sl st at top of any cl, ch 4 *(counts as 1 tr)* 5 tr into same place, *[6 tr, ch 2, 6 tr] into next ch 2 sp, **6 tr to sl st at top of next cl; rep from * twice, and from * to ** once again, join with sl st into 4th of ch 4. Break off yarn A.

ROUND 5: Join yarn C to last sl st of previous round, ch 1, 1 sc into each of next 6 tr, 1 dc into ch 1 sp between groups of tr worked on round 3, *1 sc into each of next 6 tr, 3 sc into ch 2 corner sp, **[1 sc into each of next 6 tr, 1 dc into ch 1 sp between groups of tr worked on round 3] twice; rep from * twice and from * to ** once again, 1 sc into each of next 6 tr, 1 dc into ch 1 sp between groups of tr worked on round 3, join with sl st into first sc.

ROUND 6: Ch 3 *(counts as 1 dc)*, 1 dc into each sc and dc of previous round, working 3 dc into center st of each 3 sc corner group, join with sl st into 3rd of ch 3.

Fasten off yarn.

36 Pink Stripes

FOUNDATION CHAIN: Using yarn A, ch 29.

FOUNDATION ROW: *(wrong side)* 1 hdc into 3rd ch from hook, 1 hdc into each ch, turn. *(27 hdc)*

ROW 1: Ch 2 *(counts as 1 hdc)*, 1 hdc into each hdc, turn. *(27 hdc)*

ROWS 2 & 3: Rep row 1. Break off yarn A.

ROW 4: Join yarn B, ch 1, 1 sc into each hdc, turn. Break off yarn B.

ROW 5: Join yarn C, ch 2 *(counts as 1 hdc)*, 1 hdc into each sc, turn.

ROWS 6 & 7: Rep row 1. Break off yarn C.

ROW 8: Join yarn D, rep row 4. Break off yarn D.

ROW 9: Join yarn A, rep row 5. Rep row 1 11 times.

Fasten off yarn.

MIX-AND-MATCH

MIX-AND-MATCH

37 Pin Stripes

1 A B

FOUNDATION RING: Using yarn A, ch 4 and join with sl st to form a ring.

ROUND 1: Ch 3 *(counts as 1 dc)*, 11 dc into ring, join with sl st into 3rd of ch 3. *(12 dc)*

ROUND 2: Ch 3 *(counts as 1 dc)*, *[2 dc, 1 tr] into next dc, [1 tr, 2 dc] into next dc *(corner made)*, **1 dc into next dc; rep from * twice and from * to ** once again, join with sl st into 3rd of ch 3.

ROUND 3: Ch 3 *(counts as 1 dc)*, 1 dc into each of next 2 dc, *[2 dc, 1 tr] into next tr, [1 tr, 2 dc] into next tr *(corner made)*, **1 dc into each of next 5 dc; rep from * twice and from * to ** once again, 1 dc into each of next 2 dc, join with sl st into 3rd of ch 3. Break off yarn A.

ROUND 4: Join yarn B, ch 1, 1 sc into same place, 1 sc into each of next 4 dc, *2 sc into each of next 2 tr, **1 sc into each of next 9 dc; rep from * twice and from * to ** once again, 1 sc into each of next 4 dc, join with sl st into first sc. Break off yarn B.

ROUND 5: Join yarn A, ch 3 *(counts as 1 dc)*, 1 dc into each of next 5 sc, *[2 dc,1 tr] into next sc, [1 tr, 2 dc] into next sc, **1 dc into each of next 11 sc; rep from * twice and from * to ** once again, 1 dc into each of next 5 sc, join with sl st into 3rd of ch 3. Break off yarn A.

ROUND 6: Join yarn B, ch 1, 1 sc into each dc of previous round, working 2 sc into each tr, join with sl st into first sc. Break off yarn B.

ROUND 7: Join yarn A, ch 3 *(counts as 1 dc)*, 1 dc into each of next 8 sc, *[2 dc,1 tr] into next sc, [1 tr, 2 dc] into next sc, **1 dc into each of next 17 sc; rep from * twice and from * to ** once again, 1 dc into each of next 8 sc, join with sl st into 3rd of ch 3. Break off yarn A.

ROUND 8: Join yarn B and rep round 6. Break off yarn B.

ROUND 9: Join yarn A, ch 1, 1 sc into each sc of previous round, working 2 sc into each of two corner sc, join with sl st into first sc.

Fasten off yarn.

MIX-AND-MATCH

38 Dahlia

11 A B

Special abbreviations

beg pc = beginning popcorn made from ch 3 and 3 dc sts, **pc** = popcorn made from 4 dc sts

FOUNDATION RING: Using yarn A, ch 4 and join with sl st to form a ring.

ROUND 1: Ch 4 *(counts as 1 dc, ch 1)*, [1 dc into ring, ch 1] 11 times, join with sl st into 3rd of ch 4.

ROUND 2: Sl st into next ch 1 sp, beg pc into same sp, ch 3, [pc into next ch 1 sp, ch 3] 11 times, join with sl st into top of beg pc.

ROUND 3: Sl st into next ch 3 sp, [beg pc, ch 3, pc] into same sp, [ch 3, pc into next ch 3 sp] twice, ch 3, *[pc, ch 3, pc] into next ch 3 sp, [ch 3, pc into next ch 3 sp] twice, ch 3; rep from * twice, join with sl st into top of beg pc.

ROUND 4: Sl st into next ch 3 sp, [beg pc, ch 4, pc] into same sp, [ch 3, pc into next ch 3 sp] 3 times, ch 3, *[pc, ch 4, pc] into next ch 3 sp, [ch 3, pc into next ch 3 sp] 3 times, ch 3; rep from * twice, join with sl st into top of beg pc. Break off yarn A.

ROUND 5: Join yarn B to any ch 4 corner sp, ch 7 *(counts as 1 dc, ch 4)*, 1 dc into same sp, [ch 3, 1 dc into next ch 3 sp] 4 times, ch 3, *[1 dc, ch 4, 1 dc] into next ch 4 sp, [ch 3, 1 dc into next ch 3 sp] 4 times, ch 3; rep from * twice, join with sl st into 3rd of ch 7.

ROUND 6: Sl st into next ch 4 sp, ch 3 *(counts as 1 dc)*, [1 dc, 1 tr, 2 dc] into same sp, *[1 dc into next dc, 3 dc into next ch 3 sp] 5 times, 1 dc into next dc, **[2 dc, 1 tr, 2 dc] into next ch 4 sp; rep from * twice and from * to ** once again, join with sl st into 3rd of ch 3.

ROUND 7: Ch 1, 1 sc into each dc of previous round, working 3 hdc into tr at each corner, join with sl st into first sc.

Fasten off yarn.

MIX-AND-MATCH

39 Gavin's Stripes

1 ⊟
Ⓐ Ⓑ Ⓒ
Ⓓ Ⓔ

FOUNDATION CHAIN: Using yarn A, ch 29.

FOUNDATION ROW: *(wrong side)* [1 sc, ch 1, 1 sc] into 2nd ch from hook, *skip ch 1 [1 sc, ch 1, 1 sc] into next ch; rep from * to last ch, 1 sc into last ch, turn.

ROW 1: Ch 1, *[1 sc, ch 1, 1 sc] into first sc of each group of sts on previous row; rep from * to last st, 1 sc into last st, turn.

Rep row 1, working the following color sequence: 2 rows in A , 2 rows in B, 2 rows in C, 2 rows in D, 2 rows in E, 2 rows in A, 4 rows in B, 2 rows in E, 2 rows in C, 2 rows in A, 4 rows in E.

Fasten off yarn.

40 Granny with a Twist

11 ⊡ Ⓐ Ⓑ Ⓒ

Special abbreviations

beg cl = beginning cluster made from 2 dc sts, **cl** = cluster made from 3 dc sts

FOUNDATION RING: Using yarn A, ch 6 and join with sl st to form a ring.

ROUND 1: Ch 3 *(counts as 1 dc)*, beg cl into ring, ch 3, [cl into ring, ch 3] 7 times, join with sl st into top of beg cl. Break off yarn A.

ROUND 2: Join yarn B to any ch 3 sp, ch 3 *(counts as 1 dc)*, [beg cl, ch 3, cl] into same sp, ch 1, *[cl, ch 3, cl] into next ch 3 sp, ch 1; rep from * 6 times, join with sl st into top of beg cl. Break off yarn B.

ROUND 3: Join yarn C to any ch 3 sp, ch 3 *(counts as 1 dc)*, [2 dc, ch 3, 3 dc] into same sp, *ch 1, 3 dc into next ch 3 sp, ch 1, **[3 dc, ch 3, 3 dc] into next ch 3 sp; rep from * twice and from * to ** once again, join with sl st into 3rd of ch 3.

ROUND 4: Sl st in next 2 dc and into next ch 3 sp, ch 3 *(counts as 1 dc)*, [2 dc, ch 3, 3 dc] into same sp, *ch 1, [3 dc into next ch 3 sp, ch 1] twice, **[3 dc, ch 3, 3 dc] into next ch 3 sp; rep from * twice and from * to ** once

again, join with sl st into 3rd of ch 3.

ROUND 5: Sl st in next 2 dc and into next ch 3 sp, ch 3 *(counts as 1 dc)*, [2 dc, ch 3, 3 dc] into same sp, *ch 1, [3 dc into next ch 3 sp, ch 1] 3 times, **[3 dc, ch 3, 3 dc] into next ch 3 sp; rep from * twice and from * to ** once again, join with sl st into 3rd of ch 3.

ROUND 6: Sl st in next 2 dc and into next ch 3 sp, ch 3 *(counts as 1 dc)*, [2 dc, ch 3, 3 dc] into same sp, *ch 1, [3 dc into next ch 3 sp, ch 1] 4 times, **[3 dc, ch 3, 3 dc] into next ch 3 sp; rep from * twice and from * to ** once again, join with sl st into 3rd of ch 3.

ROUND 7: Ch 1, 1 sc into each dc and ch 1 sp of previous round, working [2 sc, ch 1, 2 sc] into each ch 3 corner sp, join with sl st into first sc.

ROUND 8: Ch 1, 1 sc into each sc of previous round, working 3 sc into each ch 1 corner sp, join with sl st into first sc.

Fasten off yarn.

MIX-AND-MATCH

 154 **169** **179**

MIX-AND-MATCH

 93 **135** **150**

41 Bobble Triangle

11  A

Special abbreviation

MB = make bobble (work 4 open dc in same st leaving 5 loops on hook, draw yarn through all 5 loops at once)

FOUNDATION CHAIN: Ch 28.

FOUNDATION ROW: *(wrong side)* Work 1 sc into 2nd ch from hook, 1 sc into each ch to end, turn. *(27 sc)*

ROW 1: Ch 1, 1 sc into each sc, turn. *(27 sc)*

ROW 2: Ch 1, 1 sc into each of next 24 sc, MB, 1 sc into each of next 2 sc, turn.

ROW 3 and every alt row: Rep row 1.

ROW 4: Ch 1, 1 sc into each of next 21 sc, MB, 1 sc into each of next 5 sc, turn.

ROW 6: Ch 1, 1 sc into each of next 18 sc, MB, 1 sc into each of next 5 sc, MB, 1 sc into each of next 2 sc, turn.

ROW 8: Ch 1, 1 sc into each of next 15 sc, MB, 1 sc into each of next 5 sc, MB, 1 sc into each of next 5 sc, turn.

ROW 10: Ch 1, 1 sc into each of next 12 sc, [MB, 1 sc into each of next 5 sc] twice, MB, 1 sc into each of next 2 sc, turn.

ROW 12: Ch 1, 1 sc into each of next 9 sc, [MB, 1 sc into each of next 5 sc] 3 times, turn.

ROW 14: Ch 1, 1 sc into each of next 6 sc, [MB, 1 sc into each of next 5 sc] 3 times, MB, 1 sc into each of next 2 sc, turn.

ROW 16: Ch 1, 1 sc into each of next 3 sc, [MB, 1 sc into each of next 5 sc] 4 times, turn.

ROW 18: Rep row 14.

ROW 20: Rep row 12.

ROW 22: Rep row 10.

ROW 24: Rep row 8.

ROW 26: Rep row 6.

ROW 28: Rep row 4.

ROW 30: Rep row 2.

ROWS 31 & 32: Rep row 1.

Fasten off yarn.

MIX-AND-MATCH

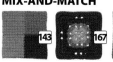

42 Lacy Wheel

1 A B C D

FOUNDATION RING: Using yarn A, ch 8 and join with sl st to form a ring.

ROUND 1: Ch 6 *(counts as 1 dc, ch 3)*, [1 dc into ring, ch 3] 7 times, join with sl st into 3rd of 6 ch. *(8 spaced dc)*

ROUND 2: Sl st into next ch 3 sp, ch 3 *(counts as 1 dc)*, 3 dc into same sp, [ch 2, 4 dc into next ch 3 sp] 7 times, ch 2, join with sl st into 3rd of ch 3. Break off yarn A.

ROUND 3: Join yarn B to any ch 2 sp, ch 3 *(counts as 1 dc)*, 5 dc into same sp, * ch 1, 6 dc into next ch 2 sp, ch 3, **6 dc into next ch 2 sp; rep from * twice and from * to ** once again, join with sl st into 3rd of ch 3. Break off yarn B.

ROUND 4: Join yarn C to any ch 1 sp, 1 sc into same sp, *ch 3, 1 sc between 3rd and 4th dc of next 6 dc group, ch 3, [2 dc, ch 3, 2 dc] into next ch 3 sp to make corner, ch 3, 1 sc between 3rd and 4th dc of next 6 dc group, ch 3, **1 sc into next ch 1 sp; rep from * twice and from * to ** once again, join with sl st into first sc. Break off yarn C.

ROUND 5: Join yarn D to any ch 3 corner sp, ch 3 *(counts as 1 dc)*, [1 dc, ch 3, 2 dc] into same sp, *[ch 3, 1 sc into next ch 3 sp] 4 times, ch 3, **[2 dc, ch 3, 2 dc] into next ch 3 corner sp; rep from * twice and from * to ** once again, join with sl st into 3rd of ch 3.

ROUND 6: Sl st in next dc and into next ch 3 corner sp, ch 3 *(counts as 1 dc)*, [2 dc, ch 3, 3 dc] into same sp, *[ch 3, 1 sc into next ch 3 sp] 5 times, ch 3, **[3 dc, ch 3, 3 dc] into next ch 3 corner sp; rep from * twice and from * to ** once again, join with sl st into 3rd of ch 3.

ROUND 7: Sl st in next 2 dc and into next ch 3 corner sp, ch 3 *(counts as 1 dc)*, [2 dc, ch 3, 3 dc] into same sp, *[ch 3, 1 sc into next ch 3 sp] 6 times, ch 3, **[3 dc, ch 3, 3 dc] into next ch 3 corner sp; rep from * twice and from * to ** once again, join with sl st into 3rd of ch 3.

Fasten off yarn.

MIX-AND-MATCH

43 Four Patch Granny

11

A **B** **C**

44 Subtle Stripes

1

A **B** **C**
D **E** **F**

FOUNDATION RING: Using yarn A, ch 6 and join with sl st to form a ring.

ROUND 1: Ch 3 *(counts as 1 dc)*, 2 dc into ring, ch 3, *3 dc into ring, ch 3; rep from * twice, join with sl st into 3rd of ch 3. Break off yarn A.

ROUND 2: Join yarn B to any ch 3 sp, ch 3 *(counts as 1 dc)*, [2 dc, ch 3, 3 dc] into same sp to make corner, *ch 1, [3 dc, ch 3, 3 dc] into next ch 3 sp to make corner; rep from * twice, ch 1, join with sl st into 3rd of ch 3. Break off yarn B.

ROUND 3: Join yarn C to any ch 3 corner sp, ch 3 *(counts as 1 dc)*, [2 dc, ch 3, 3 dc] into same sp, *ch 1, 3 dc into next ch 1 sp, ch 1, [3 dc, ch 3, 3 dc] into next ch 3 corner sp; rep from * to end, ending with ch 1, join with sl st into 3rd of ch 3.

ROUND 5: Ch 1, 1 sc into every dc and ch 1 sp of previous round, working [2 sc, ch 1, 2 sc] into each ch 3 corner space, join with sl st into first sc.

Fasten off yarn.
Make 1 more patch using this color combination.
Make 2 patches using yarn B instead of yarn A and yarn A instead of yarn B.
Using the photograph as a guide to position, join the patches together into a block of four using yarn B and the slip stitch method of joining shown on page 121.
Fasten off yarn.

FOUNDATION CHAIN: Using yarn A, ch 29.

FOUNDATION ROW: *(wrong side)* 1 sc into 2nd ch from hook, 1 sc into each ch, turn. *(28 sc)*

ROW 1: Ch 1, 1 sc into each sc, turn. *(28 sc)*

Rep row 1, working the following color sequence: 1 more row in A, 3 rows in B, 3 rows in C, 3 rows in D, 3 rows in E, 4 rows in F, 3 rows in E, 3 rows in D, 3 rows in C, 3 rows in B, 3 rows in A.

Fasten off yarn.

MIX-AND-MATCH

8 79 111

MIX-AND-MATCH

160 164 171

45 Steps

11 ≡
Ⓐ Ⓑ

FOUNDATION CHAIN: Using yarn A, ch 29.

WORKING THE PATTERN: When following the chart, read odd-numbered rows (right side rows) from right to left and even-numbered rows (wrong side rows) from left to right.

Starting at the bottom right-hand corner of the chart, work the 34 row pattern from the chart in sc. On the first row, work first sc into 2nd ch from hook, 1 sc into each ch along row. *(28 sc)*

Fasten off yarn.

YARN A
YARN B

MIX-AND-MATCH

166 204 205

46 Meadow

11 🔄 Ⓐ Ⓑ Ⓒ

Special abbreviations

beg pc = popcorn made from ch 3 and 3 dc sts, **pc** = popcorn made from 4 dc sts

FOUNDATION RING: Using yarn A, ch 4 and join with sl st to form a ring.

ROUND 1: Beg pc into ring, [ch 3, pc into ring] 3 times, ch 3, join with sl st into top of beg pc.

ROUND 2: Ch 3 *(counts as 1 dc)*, [2 dc, ch 3, 3 dc] into next ch 3 sp, ch 1, *[3 dc, ch 3, 3 dc] into next ch 3 sp, ch 1; rep from * twice, join with sl st into 3rd of ch 3.

ROUND 3: Ch 1, 1 sc into same place, 1 sc into each of next 2 dc, 5 sc into next ch 3 corner sp, *1 sc into each of next 3 dc, 1 sc into next ch, **1 sc into each of next 3 dc, 5 sc into next ch 3 corner sp; rep from * twice and from * to ** once again, join with sl st into first sc. Break off yarn A.

ROUND 4: Join yarn B to first st of any 5 sc corner group, ch 3 *(counts as 1 dc)*, *1 dc into next sc, [1 dc, ch 2, 1 dc] into next sc, 1 dc into each of next 2 sc, **ch 1, skip 1 sc, 1 dc into next sc] 4 times; rep from * twice and from * to ** once again, [ch 1, skip 1 sc, 1 dc into next sc] 3 times, ch 1, join with sl st into 3rd of ch 3. Break off yarn B.

ROUND 5: Join yarn C, ch 3 *(counts as 1 dc)*, *1 dc into each of next 2 dc, [2 dc, ch 2, 2 dc] into next ch 2 corner sp, 1 dc into each of next 3 dc, **[ch 1, 1 dc into next dc] 4 times; rep from * twice and from * to ** once again, [ch 1, 1 dc into next dc] 3 times, ch 1, join with sl st into 3rd of ch 3. Break off yarn C.

ROUND 6: Join yarn A, ch 3 *(counts as 1 dc)*, *1 dc into each of next 4 dc, [2 dc, ch 2, 2 dc] into next ch 2 corner sp, 1 dc into each of next 5 dc, **[ch 1, 1 dc into next dc] 4 times; rep from * twice and from * to ** once again, [ch 1, 1 dc into next dc] 3 times, ch 1, join with sl st into 3rd of ch 3. Break off yarn A.

ROUND 7: Join yarn C, ch 3 *(counts as 1 dc)*, *1 dc into each of next 6 dc, [2 dc, ch 2, 2 dc] into next ch 2 corner sp, 1 dc into each of next 7 dc, **[ch 1, 1 dc into next dc] 4 times; rep from * twice and from * to ** once again, [ch 1, 1 dc into next dc] 3 times, ch 1, join with sl st into 3rd of ch 3. Break off yarn C.

ROUND 8: Join yarn B, ch 3 *(counts as 1 dc)*, *1 dc into each of next 8 dc, [2 dc, ch 2, 2 dc] into next ch 2 corner sp, 1 dc into each of next 9 dc, **[ch 1, 1 dc into next dc] 4 times; rep from * twice and from * to ** once again, [ch 1, 1 dc into next dc] 3 times, ch 1, join with sl st into 3rd of ch 3.

Fasten off yarn.

MIX-AND-MATCH

 2 19 61

47 Queen Anne's Lace

11 📷 Ⓐ

Special abbreviations

beg cl = beginning cluster made from 3 dc sts, **cl** = cluster made from 4 dc sts

FOUNDATION RING: Using yarn A, ch 6 and join with sl st to form a ring.

ROUND 1: Ch 1, 12 sc into ring, join with sl st into first sc.

ROUND 2: Ch 4 *(counts as 1 dc, ch 1)*, *1 dc into next sc, ch 1; rep from * 10 times, join with sl st into 3rd of ch 4. *(12 spaced dc)*

ROUND 3: Sl st into next ch 1 sp, ch 3 *(counts as 1 dc)*, 2 dc into same sp, ch 1, [3 dc into next ch 1 sp, ch 1] 11 times, join with sl st into 3rd of ch 3.

ROUND 4: Sl st in next 2 dc and into next ch 1 sp, ch 3 *(counts as 1 dc)*, beg cl into same sp, *ch 2, skip 1 dc, 1 dc into next dc, ch 2, **cl into next ch 1 sp; rep from * 10 times and from * to ** once again, join with sl st into top of beg cl.

ROUND 5: Sl st into next ch 2 sp, ch 1, 3 sc into same sp, [3 sc into next ch 2 sp] 23 times, join with sl st into first sc.

ROUND 6: Ch 3 *(counts as 1 dc)*, [1 dc, ch 2, 2 dc] into same place, *[ch 2, skip next 3 sc group, 1 sc into sp between next two 3 sc groups] 5 times, ch 2, **[2 dc, ch 2, 2 dc] into sp above next cl; rep from * twice and from * to ** once again, join with sl st into 3rd of ch 3.

ROUND 7: Ch 3 *(counts as 1 dc)*, 1 dc into next dc, *[2 dc, ch 2, 2 dc] into next ch 2 corner sp, 1 dc into each of next 2 dc, [1 dc, 1 hdc] into next ch 2 sp, 1 hdc into next sc, [2 sc into next ch 2 sp, 1 sc into next sc] 3 times, 2 sc into next ch 2 sp, 1 hdc into next sc, [1 hdc, 1 dc] into next ch 2 sp, **1 dc into each of next 2 dc; rep from * twice and from * to ** once again, join with sl st into 3rd of ch 3.

ROUND 8: Ch 3 *(counts as 1 dc)*, 1 dc into each st of previous round, working [1 dc, 1 tr, 1 dc] into each ch 2 corner sp, join with sl st into 3rd of ch 3.

Fasten off yarn.

MIX-AND-MATCH

 38 94 95

48 Danish Square

11 📷 Ⓐ Ⓑ Ⓒ Ⓓ

FOUNDATION RING: Using yarn A, ch 10 and join with sl st to form a ring.

ROUND 1: Ch 1, 20 sc into ring, join with sl st into first sc. *(20 sc)*

ROUND 2: Ch 9, *skip 4 sc, 1 sc into next sc, ch 8; rep from * twice, join with sl st into first of ch 9.

ROUND 3: Ch 1, 1 sc into same place, [9 sc into next ch 8 sp, 1 sc into next sc] 3 times, 9 sc into next ch 8 sp, join with sl st into first sc. Break off yarn A.

ROUND 4: Join yarn B to 5th st of 9 sc corner group, ch 1, 2 sc into same place, [1 sc into each of next 9 sc, 2 sc into next sc] 3 times, 1 sc into each of next 9 sc, join with sl st into first sc. Break off yarn B.

ROUND 5: Join yarn C, ch 1, 2 sc into same place, [1 sc into each of next 10 sc, 2 sc into next sc] 3 times, 1 sc into each of next 10 sc, join with sl st into first sc. Break off yarn C.

ROUND 6: Join yarn D, ch 4 *(counts as 1 dc, ch 1)*, 1 dc into same place, *ch 1, [1 dc into next sc, ch 1, skip 1 sc] 5 times, 1 dc into next sc, ch 1, **[1 dc, ch 1, 1 dc] into next sc; rep from * twice, and from * to ** once again, join with sl st into 3rd of ch 4.

ROUND 7: Sl st into next ch 1 sp, ch 1, 3 sc into same place, 1 sc into next dc, *[1 sc into ch 1 sp, 1 sc into next dc] 7 times, 3 sc into next ch 1 corner sp, 1 sc into next dc; rep from * twice, [1 sc into ch 1 sp, 1 sc into next dc] 6 times, join with sl st into first sc. Break off yarn D.

ROUND 8: Join yarn A to center st of any 3 sc corner group, ch 1, 3 sc into same place, 1 sc into each sc of previous round, working 3 sc into center st of rem 3 sc corner groups, join with sl st into first sc. Break off yarn A.

ROUND 9: Join yarn C to center st of any 3 sc corner group, ch 4 *(counts as 1 dc, ch 1)*, 1 dc into same place, *[ch 1, skip 1 sc, 1 dc into next sc] 9 times, ch 1, **skip 1 sc, [1 dc, ch 1, 1 dc] into next sc; rep from * twice, and from * to ** once again, join with sl st into 3rd of ch 4.

ROUND 10: Ch 4 *(counts as 1 dc, ch 1)*, *[1 dc, ch 1, 1 dc, ch 1, 1 dc] into next ch 1 corner sp, **[ch 1, 1 dc into next dc] 11 times, ch 1; rep from * twice and from * to ** once again, [ch 1, 1 dc into next dc] 10 times, ch 1, join with sl st into 3rd of 4ch.

ROUND 11: Ch 1, 1 sc into same place, 1 sc into each dc and ch 1 sp of previous round, working 3 sc into center dc of each corner group, join with sl st into first sc.

Fasten off yarn.

MIX-AND-MATCH

 1 74 96

㊾ Rainbow Stripes

11 ⇌
Ⓐ Ⓑ Ⓒ
Ⓓ Ⓔ Ⓕ
Ⓖ

㊿ Seminole

11 ⇌
Ⓐ Ⓑ Ⓒ
Ⓓ Ⓔ Ⓕ
Ⓖ

Special abbreviations

sc3tog = decrease 2 sts by working the next 3 sc together

FOUNDATION CHAIN: Using yarn A, ch 58.

FOUNDATION ROW: *(wrong side)* 1 sc into 2nd ch from hook, 1 sc into each ch, turn. *(57 sc)*

ROW 1: Ch 1, 1 sc into each of next 27 sc, sc3tog, 1 sc into each of rem 27 sc, turn. *(55 sc)*

ROW 2: Ch 1, 1 sc into each of next 26 sc, sc3tog, 1 sc into each of rem 26 sc, turn. *(53 sc)*

ROW 3: Ch 1, 1 sc into each of next 25 sc, sc3tog, 1 sc into each of rem 25 sc, turn. *(51 sc)*

ROW 4: Ch 1, 1 sc into each of next 24 sc, sc3tog, 1 sc into each of rem 24 sc, turn. *(49 sc)* Break off yarn A. Join yarn B. Cont in pattern as set, working sc3tog over 3 center sts on every row. At the same time, change yarn colors in the following color sequence: Work 4 rows in yarn B, 4 rows in yarn C, 4 rows in yarn D, 4 rows in yarn E, 4 rows in yarn F. Join yarn G and cont in pattern until 3 sc rem.

NEXT ROW: Work sc3tog.
Fasten off yarn.

FOUNDATION CHAIN: Using yarn A, ch 29.

WORKING THE PATTERN: When following the chart, read odd-numbered rows (right side rows) from right to left and even-numbered rows (wrong side rows) from left to right.
Starting at the bottom right-hand corner of the chart, work the 34 row pattern from the chart in sc. On the first row, work first sc into 2nd ch from hook, 1 sc into each ch along row. *(28 sc)*
Fasten off yarn.

MIX-AND-MATCH

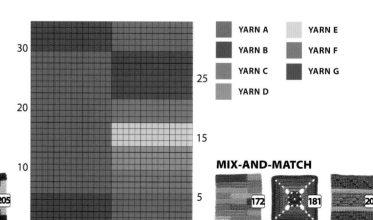

YARN A	YARN E
YARN B	YARN F
YARN C	YARN G
YARN D	

30
25
20
15
10
5

MIX-AND-MATCH

51 Bright Flower

52 Lemon Peel

FOUNDATION RING: Using yarn A, ch 6 and join with sl st to form a ring.

ROUND 1: Ch 3 (counts as 1 dc), 3 dc into ring, ch 3, turn; 1 dc into first dc, 1 dc into each of next 2 dc, 1 dc into 3rd of ch 3 (petal made), ch 3, turn; *working across back of petal just made, 4 dc into ring, ch 3, turn; 1 dc into first dc, 1 dc into each of next 3 dc (petal made), ch 3, turn; rep from * 6 times, join with sl st into 3rd of beg ch 3 of first petal. Break off yarn A.

ROUND 2: Working behind the petals, join yarn B to any ch 3 sp, ch 3 (counts as 1 dc), [2 dc, ch 2, 3 dc] into same sp, 3 dc into next ch 3 sp, *[3 dc, ch 2, 3 dc] into next ch 3 sp, 3 dc into next ch 3 sp; rep from * twice, join with sl st into 3rd of ch 3. Break off yarn B.

ROUND 3: Join yarn C to any ch 2 corner sp, ch 3 (counts as 1 dc), [2 dc, ch 3, 3 dc] into same sp, *1 dc into each of next 9 dc, **[3 dc, ch 3, 3 dc] into next ch 2 corner sp; rep from *

twice and from * to ** once again, join with sl st into 3rd of ch 3.

ROUND 4: Ch 3 (counts as 1 dc), 1 dc into each of next 2 dc, *[3 dc, ch 3, 3 dc] into ch 3 corner sp, **1 dc into each of next 15 dc; rep from * twice and from * to ** once again, 1 dc into each of next 12 dc, join with sl st into 3rd of ch 3.

ROUND 5: Ch 3 (counts as 1 dc), 1 dc into each of next 5 dc, *[3 dc, ch 3, 3 dc] into ch 3 corner sp, **1 dc into each of next 21 dc; rep from * twice and from * to ** once again, 1 dc into each of next 15 dc, join with sl st into 3rd of ch 3.

ROUND 6: Ch 1, 1 sc into each dc of previous round, working 5 sc into each ch 3 corner sp, join with sl st into first sc.

Fasten off yarn.

FOUNDATION CHAIN: Ch 31.

FOUNDATION ROW: (right side) 1 sc into 3rd ch from hook, *1 dc into next ch, 1 sc into next ch; rep from * to end, turn.

ROW 1: Ch 1, 1 sc into first dc, 1 dc into next sc, *1 sc into next dc, 1 dc into next sc; rep from * to end, turn. Rep row 1 21 times.

Fasten off yarn.

MIX-AND-MATCH

52   105   133

MIX-AND-MATCH

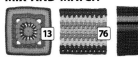

13   76   127

53 Mesh Fantasy

FOUNDATION CHAIN: Using yarn A, ch 12.

FOUNDATION ROW: *(wrong side)* Work 1 dc into 6th ch from hook *(5 skipped ch count as ch 1, 1 dc, ch 1)*, [ch 1, skip next ch, 1 dc into next ch] 3 times, turn.

ROW 1: Ch 4 *(counts as 1 dc, ch 1)*, 1 dc into next dc, [ch 1, 1 dc into next dc] twice, ch 1, skip next ch, 1 dc into next ch, turn.

ROWS 2 & 3: Rep row 1. Break off yarn A.

Change from working rows to working in rounds.

ROUND 1: Holding square with row 3 at the top and right side facing, join yarn B to top right-hand corner sp and begin by working across row 3, ch 3 *(counts as 1 dc)*, [2 dc, ch 2, 3 dc] into same sp *(first corner made)*, 3 dc into each of next 2 ch 3 sps, [3 dc, ch 2, 3 dc] into next sp *(second corner made)*. Working into sps formed by edge dc and turning chs along next side of square, work 3 dc into each of next 2 sps, [3 dc, ch 2, 3 dc] into next sp *(third corner made)*. Working across foundation ch, work 3 dc into each of next 2 sps, [3 dc, ch 2, 3 dc]

into next sp *(fourth corner made)*. Working into sps formed by edge dc and turning chs along last side of square, work 3 dc into each of next 2 sps, join with sl st into 3rd of ch 3. Break off yarn B.

ROUND 2: Join yarn C to any ch 2 corner sp, ch 3 *(counts as 1 dc)*, [2 dc, ch 2, 3 dc] into same sp, *[ch 2, skip next 3 dc, 1 dc between 3 dc groups] 3 times, ch 2, **[3 dc, ch 2, 3 dc] into next ch 2 corner sp; rep from * twice and from * to ** once again, join with sl st into 3rd of ch 3. Break off yarn C.

ROUND 3: Join yarn D to any ch 2 corner sp, ch 3 *(counts as 1 dc)*, [1 dc, ch 2, 2 dc] into same sp, *1 dc into each of next 3 dc, [3 dc into next ch 2 sp] 4 times, 1 dc into each of next 3 dc, **[2 dc, ch 2, 2 dc] into next ch 2 corner sp; rep from * twice and from * to ** once again, join with sl st into 3rd of ch 3. Break off yarn D.

ROUND 4: Join yarn B to any dc, ch 1, 1 sc into each dc of previous round, working 3 sc into each ch 2 corner sp, join with sl st into first sc. Break off yarn B.

ROUND 5: Join yarn A, ch 1, 1 sc into each sc of previous round, working 3 sc into center st of each 3 sc corner group, join with sl st into first sc. Break off yarn A.

ROUND 6: Join yarn B and rep round 5.

Fasten off yarn.

MIX-AND-MATCH

54 Framed Flower

FOUNDATION CHAIN: Using yarn A, ch 7.

ROUND 1: Work [1 dc, ch 3] 3 times into 7th ch from hook *(skipped ch 6 counts as 1dc, ch 3)*, join with sl st into 3rd of ch 3.

ROUND 2: Ch 1, 1 sc into same place, *[1 dc, 5 tr, 1 dc] into next ch 3 sp *(petal made)*, **1 sc into next dc; rep from * twice and from * to ** once again, join with sl st into first sc.

ROUND 3: Ch 1, 1 sc into same place, *1 dc into next dc, 2 dc into each of next 2 tr, 3 dc into next tr, 2 dc into each of next 2 tr, 1 dc into next dc, **1 sc into next sc; rep from * twice and from * to ** once again, join with sl st into first sc. Break off yarn A.

ROUND 4: Join yarn B to 4th dc of any petal, ch 1, 1 sc into same place, *ch 5, skip next 5 sts, 1 sc into next dc, ch 5, **1 sc into 4th dc of next petal; rep from * twice and from * to ** once again, join with sl st into first sc.

ROUND 5: Sl st into next ch 5 sp, ch 3 *(counts as 1 dc)*, [3 dc, ch 3, 4 dc] into same ch 5 sp, *ch 1, 7 hdc into next ch 5 sp, ch 1, **[4 dc, ch 3, 4 dc] into

next ch 5 sp; rep from * twice and from * to ** once again, join with sl st into 3rd of ch 3. Break off yarn B.

ROUND 6: Join yarn A to any ch 3 corner sp, ch 2 *(counts as 1 hdc)*, [1 hdc, ch 2, 2 hdc] into same sp, *1 hdc into each of next 4 dc, skip ch 1 sp, 1 sc into each of next 7 hdc, skip ch 1 sp, 1 hdc into each of next 4 dc, **[2 hdc, ch 2, 2 hdc] into next ch 3 corner sp; rep from * twice and from * to ** once again, join with sl st into 2nd of ch 2. Break off yarn A.

ROUND 7: Join yarn C to any ch 2 corner sp, ch 3 *(counts as 1 dc)*, [1 dc, ch 2, 2 dc] into same sp, *1 dc into each hdc and sc along side of square, **[2 dc, ch 2, 2 dc] into next ch 2 corner sp; rep from * twice and from * to ** once again, join with sl st into 3rd of ch 3.

ROUND 8: Ch 3 *(counts as 1 dc)*, 1 dc into each dc of previous round, working 5 dc into each ch 2 corner sp, join with sl st into 3rd of ch 3. Fasten off yarn.

MIX-AND-MATCH

55 Centered Square

1 📷 Ⓐ Ⓑ Ⓒ

FOUNDATION RING: Using yarn A, ch 4 and join with sl st to form a ring.

ROUND 1: Ch 3 *(counts as 1 dc)*, 2 dc into ring, ch 2, [3 dc into ring, ch 2] 3 times, join with sl st into 3rd of ch 3.

ROUND 2: Sl st in next 2 dc and into next ch 2 sp, ch 3 *(counts as 1 dc)*, [2 dc, ch 2, 3 dc] into same sp, *[3 dc, ch 2, 3 dc] into next ch 2 sp; rep from * twice, join with sl st into 3rd of ch 3.

ROUND 3: Sl st in next 2 dc and into next ch 2 sp, ch 3 *(counts as 1 dc)*, [2 dc, ch 2, 3 dc] into same sp, *3 dc into sp between next two 3 dc groups, **[3 dc, ch 2, 3 dc] into next ch 2 corner sp; rep from * twice and from * to ** once again, join with sl st into 3rd of ch 3. Break off yarn A.

ROUND 4: Join yarn B to any ch 2 corner sp, ch 3 *(counts as 1 dc)*, [1 dc, ch 2, 2 dc] into same sp, *[1 dc into each of next 3 dc, 1 dc into sp between next two 3 dc groups] twice, 1 dc into each of next 3 dc, **[2 dc, ch 2, 2 dc] into next ch 2 corner sp; rep from * twice and from * to ** once again, join with sl st into 3rd of ch 3. Break off yarn B.

ROUND 5: Join yarn A, ch 3 *(counts as 1 dc)*, 1 dc into next dc, *[2 dc, ch 2, 2 dc] into next ch 2 corner sp, **1 dc into each of next 15 dc; rep from * twice and from * to ** once again, 1 dc into each of next 13 dc, join with sl st into 3rd of ch 3. Break off yarn A.

ROUND 6: Join yarn C, ch 1, 1 sc into same place, 1 sc into each of next 3 dc, *3 sc into next ch 2 corner sp, **1 sc into each of next 19 dc; rep from * twice and from * to ** once again, 1 sc into each of next 15 dc, join with sl st into first sc. Break off yarn C.

ROUND 7: Join yarn B, ch 3 *(counts as 1 dc)*, 1 dc into each of next 4 sc, *[2 dc, ch 2, 2 dc] into center st of 3 sc corner group, **1 dc into each of next 21 sc; rep from * twice and from * to ** once again, 1 dc into each of next 16 sc, join with sl st into 3rd of ch 3.

ROUND 8: Ch 1, 1 sc into each dc of previous round, working 5 sc into each ch 2 corner sp, join with sl st into first sc.

Fasten off yarn.

MIX-AND-MATCH

 6   156   203

56 Plain Granny

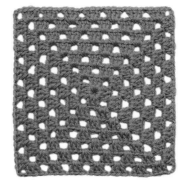

1 📷 Ⓐ

FOUNDATION RING: Ch 4 and join with sl st to form a ring.

ROUND 1: Ch 6 *(counts as 1 dc, ch 3)*, [3 dc into ring, ch 3] 3 times, 2 dc into ring, join with sl st into 3rd of ch 6.

ROUND 2: Sl st into center st of next ch 3 sp, ch 6 *(counts as 1 dc, ch 3)*, 3 dc into same sp, *ch 1, [3 dc, ch 3, 3 dc] into next ch 3 sp; rep from * twice, ch 1, 2 dc into same sp as beg ch 6, join with sl st into 3rd of ch 6.

ROUND 3: Sl st into center st of next ch 3 sp, ch 6 *(counts as 1 dc, ch 3)*, 3 dc into same sp, *ch 1, 3 dc into next ch 1 sp, ch 1, **[3 dc, ch 3, 3 dc] into next ch 3 sp; rep from * twice and from * to ** once again, 2 dc into same sp as beg ch 6, join with sl st into 3rd of ch 6.

ROUND 4: Sl st into center st of next ch 3 sp, ch 6 *(counts as 1 dc, ch 3)*, 3 dc into same sp, *ch 1, [3 dc into next ch 1 sp, ch 1] twice, **[3 dc, ch 3, 3 dc] into next ch 3 sp; rep from * twice and from * to ** once again, 2 dc into same sp as beg ch 6, join with sl st into 3rd of ch 6.

ROUND 5: Sl st into center st of next ch 3 sp, ch 6 *(counts as 1 dc, ch 3)*, 3 dc into same sp, *ch 1, [3 dc into next ch 1 sp, ch 1] 3 times, **[3 dc, ch 3, 3 dc] into next ch 3 sp; rep from * twice and from * to ** once again, 2 dc into same sp as beg ch 6, join with sl st into 3rd of ch 6.

ROUND 6: Sl st into center st of next ch 3 sp, ch 6 *(counts as 1 dc, ch 3)*, 3 dc into same sp, *ch 1, [3 dc into next ch 1 sp, ch 1] 4 times, **[3 dc, ch 3, 3 dc] into next ch 3 sp; rep from * twice and from * to ** once again, 2 dc into same sp as beg ch 6, join with sl st into 3rd of ch 6.

ROUND 7: Sl st into center st of next ch 3 sp, ch 6 *(counts as 1 dc, ch 3)*, 3 dc into same sp, *ch 1, [3 dc into next ch 1 sp, ch 1] 5 times, **[3 dc, ch 3, 3 dc] into next ch 3 sp; rep from * twice and from * to ** once again, 2 dc into same sp as beg ch 6, join with sl st into 3rd of ch 6.

Fasten off yarn.

MIX-AND-MATCH

 138   186   210

57 Arrowhead Bobbles

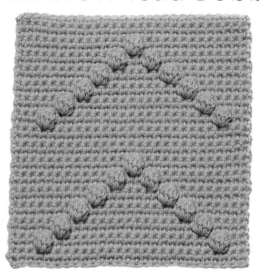

11

Special abbreviation

MB = make bobble (work 4 open dc in same st leaving 5 loops on hook, draw yarn through all 5 loops at once)

FOUNDATION CHAIN: Ch 28.

FOUNDATION ROW: *(right side)* Work 1 sc into 2nd ch from hook, 1 sc into each ch to end, turn. *(27 sc)*

ROW 1: Ch 1, 1 sc into each sc, turn. *(27 sc)*

ROW 2: Rep row 1.

ROW 3: Ch 1, 1 sc into each of next 3 sc, MB, 1 sc into each of next 19 sc, MB, 1 sc into each of next 3 sc, turn.

ROWS 4, 6, 8, 10, 12: Rep row 1.

ROW 5: Ch 1, 1 sc into each of next 5 sc, MB, 1 sc into each of next 15 sc, MB, 1 sc into each of next 5 sc, turn.

ROW 7: Ch 1, 1 sc into each of next 7 sc, MB, 1 sc into each of next 11 sc, MB, 1 sc into each of next 7 sc, turn.

ROW 9: Ch 1, 1 sc into each of next 9 sc, MB, 1 sc into each of next 7 sc, MB, 1 sc into each of next 9 sc, turn.

ROW 11: Ch 1, 1 sc into each of next 11 sc, MB, 1 sc into each of next 3 sc, MB, 1 sc into each of next 11 sc, turn.

ROW 13: Ch 1, 1 sc into each of next 13 sc, MB, 1 sc into each of next 13 sc, turn.

ROWS 14 to 16: Rep row 1. Rep rows 1 to 15 once again.

Fasten off yarn.

MIX-AND-MATCH

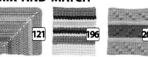

58 Peach Rose

11

FOUNDATION RING: Using yarn A, ch 6 and join with sl st to form a ring.

ROUND 1: Ch 1, 16 sc into ring, join with sl st into first sc. *(16 sc)*

ROUND 2: Ch 6 *(counts as 1 dc, ch 3)*, skip 2 sc, [1 dc into next sc, ch 3, skip 1 sc] 7 times, join with sl st into 3rd of ch 6. *(8 spaced dc)*

ROUND 3: Ch 1 [1 sc, 1 hdc, 3 dc, 1 hdc, 1 sc] into same sp, *[1 sc, 1 hdc, 3 dc, 1 hdc, 1 sc] into next ch 3 sp; rep from * 6 times, join with sl st into first sc. *(8 petals made)* Break off yarn A.

ROUND 4: Join yarn B between any 2 sc, ch 1, 1 sc into same place, ch 6, [1 sc between next 2 sc, ch 6] 7 times, join with sl st into first sc.

ROUND 5: Ch 1 [1 sc, 1 hdc, 5 dc, 1 hdc, 1 sc] into same sp, *[1 sc, 1 hdc, 5 dc, 1 hdc, 1 sc] into next ch 6 sp; rep from * 6 times, join with sl st into first sc. *(8 petals made)* Break off yarn B.

ROUND 6: Join yarn C to 2nd dc of any petal, ch 1, 1 sc into same place, ch 6, skip 2 dc, 1 sc into next dc, [ch 6, 1 sc into 2nd dc of next petal, ch 6, skip 2 dc, 1 sc into next dc] 7 times, join with sl st into first sc.

ROUND 7: Sl st into next ch 6 sp, ch 3 *(counts as 1 dc)*, [3 dc, 4ch, 4 dc] into same sp *(corner made)*, *ch 4, 1 sc into next ch 6 sp, [ch 6, 1 sc into next ch 6 sp] twice, ch 4, **[4 dc, ch 4, 4 dc] into next ch 6 sp *(corner made)*; rep from * twice and from * to ** once again, join with sl st into 3rd of ch 3.

ROUND 8: Ch 3 *(counts as 1 dc)*, 1 dc into each of next 3 dc, *[3 dc, ch 2, 3 dc] into next ch 4 corner sp, 1 dc into each of next 4 dc, ch 1, 2 dc into next ch 4 sp, [ch 1, 3 dc into next ch 6 sp] twice, ch 1, 2 dc into next ch 4 sp, ch 1, **1 dc into each of next 4 dc; rep from * twice and from * to ** once again, join with sl st into 3rd of ch 3.

Fasten off yarn.

MIX-AND-MATCH

59 Coral Quartet

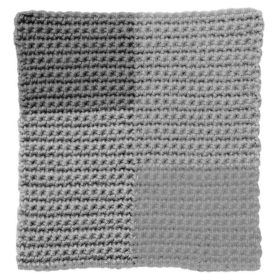

11 ≣
Ⓐ Ⓑ Ⓒ
Ⓓ

FOUNDATION CHAIN: Using yarn A, ch 29.

WORKING THE PATTERN: When following the chart, read odd-numbered rows (right side rows) from right to left and even-numbered rows (wrong side rows) from left to right.

Starting at the bottom right-hand corner of the chart, work the 34 row pattern from the chart in sc. On the first row, work first sc into 2nd ch from hook, 1 sc into each ch along row. *(28 sc)*

Fasten off yarn.

YARN A
YARN B
YARN C
YARN D

MIX-AND-MATCH

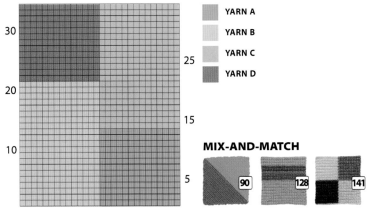

90   128   141

60 Popcorn Corners

11 ◰ Ⓐ Ⓑ Ⓒ Ⓓ

Special abbreviation

pc = popcorn made from 5 dc sts

FOUNDATION RING: Using yarn A, ch 4 and join with sl st to form a ring.

ROUND 1: Ch 3 *(counts as 1 dc)*, 3 dc into ring, ch 1, [4 dc into ring, ch 1] 3 times, join with sl st into 3rd of ch 3. Break off yarn A.

ROUND 2: Join yarn B to any ch 1 sp, ch 3 *(counts as 1 dc)*, [3 dc, ch 1, 4 dc] into same sp, ch 1, *[4 dc, ch 1, 4 dc] into next ch 1 sp, ch 1; rep from * twice, join with sl st into 3rd of ch 3. Break off yarn B.

ROUND 3: Join yarn C to any ch 1 corner sp, ch 3 *(counts as 1 dc)*, [1 dc, pc, 2 dc] into same sp, *skip 1 dc, 1 dc into each of next 3 dc, 1 dc into ch 1 sp, 1 dc into each of next 3 dc, skip 1 dc, **[2 dc, pc, 2 dc] into next ch 1 corner sp; rep from * twice and from * to ** once again, join with sl st into 3rd of ch 3. Break off yarn C.

ROUND 4: Join yarn B to center dc on any side of square, ch 3 *(counts as 1 dc)*, 1 dc into each of next 6 dc, *[1 dc, 2 tr, 1 dc] into top of next pc, **1 dc into each of next 11 dc; rep from * twice and from * to ** once again,

1 dc into each of next 4 dc, join with sl st into 3rd of ch 3. Break off yarn B.

ROUND 5: Join yarn D, ch 3 *(counts as 1 dc)*, 1 dc into each of next 7 dc, *[2 dc, 1 tr] into first tr, [1 tr, 2 dc] into next tr, **1 dc into each of next 13 dc; rep from * twice and from * to ** once again, 1 dc into each of next 5 dc, join with sl st into 3rd of ch 3. Break off yarn D.

ROUND 6: Join yarn C, ch 3 *(counts as 1 dc)*, 1 dc into each of next 9 dc, *2 dc into first tr, pc between this tr and next tr, 2 dc into next tr, **1 dc into each of next 17 dc; rep from * twice and from * to ** once again, 1 dc into each of next 7 dc, join with sl st into 3rd of ch 3. Break off yarn C.

ROUND 7: Join yarn B, ch 1, 1 sc into same place, 1 sc into each of next 12 dc, *ch 2, skip next pc, **1 sc into each of next 21 dc; rep from * twice and from * to ** once again, 1 sc into each of next 8 dc, join with sl st into first sc.

ROUND 8: Ch 1, 1 sc into each sc of previous round, working [2 hdc, 1 tr, 2 hdc] into each ch 2 corner sp, join with sl st into first sc.

Fasten off yarn.

MIX-AND-MATCH

114 132 192

61 Nine Patch Granny

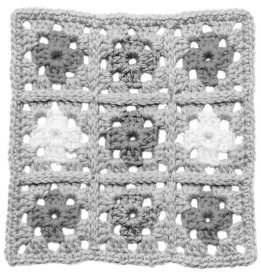

11 A B C D E

62 Edged Square

11 A B

FOUNDATION RING: Using yarn A, ch 6 and join with sl st to form a ring.

ROUND 1: Ch 3 (counts as 1 dc), 2 dc into ring, ch 3, *3 dc into ring, ch 3; rep from * twice more, join with sl st into 3rd of ch 3. Break off yarn A.

ROUND 2: Join yarn B to any ch 3 sp, ch 3 (counts as 1 dc), [2 dc, ch 3, 3 dc] into same sp to make corner, *ch 1, [3 dc, ch 3, 3 dc] into next ch 3 sp to make corner; rep from * twice more, ch 1, join with sl st into 3rd of ch 3. Fasten off yarn.

Make 3 more patches using this color combination.

Make 2 patches using yarn C instead of yarn A.

Make 2 patches using yarn D instead of yarn A.

Make 1 patch using yarn E instead of yarn A.

Using the photograph as a guide to position, join the patches together into a block of nine using yarn B and the slip stitch method of joining shown on page 121.

EDGING ROUND: Join yarn B to any dc along one edge of the block, ch 1, 1 sc into each dc and ch round edge, working 3 sc into center ch at each corner, join with sl st into first sc.

Fasten off yarn.

Special abbreviation

sc3tog = decrease 2 sts by working the next 3 sc together

FOUNDATION CHAIN: Using yarn A, ch 58.

FOUNDATION ROW: (wrong side) 1 sc into 2nd ch from hook, 1 sc into each ch, turn. (57 sc)

ROW 1: Ch 1, 1 sc into each of next 27 sc, sc3tog, 1 sc into each of rem 27 sc, turn. (55 sc)

ROW 2: Ch 1, 1 sc into each of next 26 sc, sc3tog, 1 sc into each of rem 26 sc, turn. (53 sc)

ROW 3: Ch 1, 1 sc into each of next 25 sc, sc3tog, 1 sc into each of rem 25 sc, turn. (51 sc)

ROW 4: Ch 1, 1 sc into each of next 24 sc, sc3tog, 1 sc into each of rem 24 sc, turn. (49 sc) Cont in pattern as set, working sc3tog over 3 center sts on every row.

Work 2 more rows in yarn A. Break off yarn A. Join yarn B and cont in pattern until 3 sc rem.

NEXT ROW: Work sc3tog.

Fasten off yarn.

MIX-AND-MATCH

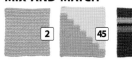 2 45 127

MIX-AND-MATCH

 1 76 96

63 Random Patches

11 ☰
Ⓐ Ⓑ Ⓒ
Ⓓ Ⓔ Ⓕ

64 Sunshine Lace

1 ⬚
Ⓐ

FOUNDATION CHAIN: Using yarn A, ch 29.

WORKING THE PATTERN: When following the chart, read odd-numbered rows (right side rows) from right to left and even-numbered rows (wrong side rows) from left to right.

Starting at the bottom right-hand corner of the chart, work the 34 row pattern from the chart in sc. On the first row, work first sc into 2nd ch from hook, 1 sc into each ch along row. *(28 sc)*

Fasten off yarn.

FOUNDATION RING: Ch 8 and join with sl st to form a ring.

ROUND 1: Ch 1, 12 dc into ring, join with sl st into first dc. *(12 dc)*

ROUND 2: Ch 6 *(counts as 1 tr, ch 2)*, [1 tr into next st, ch 2] 11 times, join with sl st into 4th of ch 6.
(12 spaced tr)

ROUND 3: Ch 5 *(counts as 1 dc, ch 2)*, *[1dc into next ch 2 sp, ch 2] twice, [3 dc, ch 2, 3 dc] into next ch 2 sp, ch 2; rep from *3 times omitting 1 dc, ch 2 at end of last rep, join with sl st into 3rd of ch 5.

ROUND 4: Ch 1, *[1 sc into next ch 2 sp, ch 2] 3 times, [3 dc, ch 2, 3 dc] into ch 2 corner sp, ch 2; rep from *3 times, join with sl st into first sc.

ROUND 5: Sl st into next ch 2 sp, ch 1, 1 sc into same sp, ch 2, [1 sc into next ch 2 sp, ch 2] twice, *[3 dc, ch 2, 3 dc] into next ch 2 corner sp, ch 2, **[1 sc into next ch 2 sp, ch 2] 4 times; rep from * twice and from * to ** once again, 1 sc into next ch 2 sp, ch 2, join with sl st into first sc.

ROUND 6: Sl st into next ch 2 sp, ch 3 *(counts as 1 dc)*, 1 dc into same sp, work 2 dc into each ch 2 sp on previous round, working 1 dc into each dc and [3 dc, ch 2, 3 dc] into each ch 2 corner sp, join with sl st into 3rd of ch 3.

ROUND 7: Ch 3 *(counts as 1 dc)*, work 1 dc into each dc on previous round, working 5 dc into each ch 2 corner sp, join with sl st into 3rd of ch 3.

Fasten off yarn.

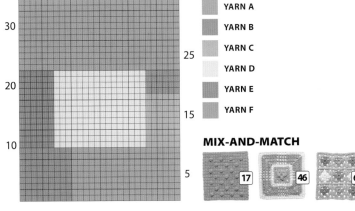

	YARN A
	YARN B
	YARN C
	YARN D
	YARN E
	YARN F

MIX-AND-MATCH

17   **46**   **61**

MIX-AND-MATCH

 3   **74**   **131**

65 Patriotic Sunburst

11 A B C

Special abbreviations

beg cl = beginning cluster made from 1 dc st, **cl** = cluster made from 2 dc sts

---

FOUNDATION RING: Using yarn A, ch 4 and join with sl st to form a ring.

ROUND 1: Ch 1, 6 sc into ring, join with sl st into first sc.

ROUND 2: Ch 1, 2 sc into next sc 6 times, join with sl st into first sc. *(12 sc)*

ROUND 3: Ch 1, 2 sc into next sc 12 times, join with sl st into first sc. *(24 sc)* Break off yarn A.

ROUND 4: Join yarn B to any sc, ch 3 *(counts as 1 dc)*, beg cl into same sc, ch 2, skip next sc, *cl into next sc, ch 2, skip next sc; rep from * 10 times, join with sl st into top of beg cl. Break off yarn B.

ROUND 5: Join yarn C to any ch 2 sp, ch 3 *(counts as 1 dc)*, beg cl into same sp, ch 3, *cl into next ch 2 sp, ch 3; rep from * 10 times, join with sl st into top of beg cl.

ROUND 6: Ch 1, 1 sc into top of beg cl, 3 sc into next ch 3 sp, *1 sc into top of next cl, 3 sc into next ch 3 sp; rep from * 10 times, join with sl st into first sc. Break off yarn C.

ROUND 7: Join yarn A to center st of any

3 sc group, ch 3 *(counts as 1 dc)*, 2 dc into same sc *(corner made)*, *1hdc into each of next 2 sc, 1 sc into each of next 7 sc, 1 hdc into each of next 2 sc, **3 dc into next sc *(corner made)*; rep from * twice and from * to ** once again, join with sl st into 3rd of ch 3. Break off yarn A.

ROUND 8: Join yarn B to center st of any 3 dc corner group, ch 4 *(counts as 1 tr)*, 2 tr into same dc, *1 dc into each of next 2 sts, 1 hdc into each of next 9 sts, 1 dc into each of next 2 sts, **3 tr into next st; rep from * twice and from * to ** once again, join with sl st into 4th of ch 4.

ROUND 9: Ch 1, 1 sc into same place, *3 sc into next tr, 1 sc into each of next 15 sts; rep from * 3 times, ending last rep with 1 sc into each of next 14 sts, join with sl st into first sc. Break off yarn B.

ROUND 10: Join yarn C to any sc along one side of square, ch 1, work 1 sc into each sc of previous round, working 3 sc into center st of each 3 sc corner group, join with sl st into first sc. Break off yarn C.

ROUND 11: Join yarn A, ch 3 *(counts as 1 dc)*, work 1 dc into each sc of previous round, working [2 dc, ch 2, 2 dc] into center st of each 3 sc corner group, join with sl st into 3rd of ch 3. Break off yarn A.

ROUND 12: Join yarn B, ch 1, work 1 sc into each dc of previous round, working 3 sc into each ch 2 corner sp, join with sl st into first sc. Fasten off yarn.

MIX-AND-MATCH

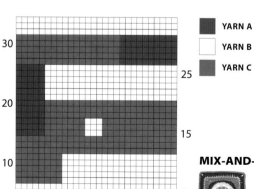

66 Abstract

11
A B C

FOUNDATION CHAIN: Using yarn A, ch 29.

WORKING THE PATTERN: When following the chart, read odd-numbered rows (right side rows) from right to left and even-numbered rows (wrong side rows) from left to right.

Starting at the bottom right-hand corner of the chart, work the 34 row pattern from the chart in sc. On the first row, work first sc into 2nd ch from hook, 1 sc into each ch along row. *(28 sc)*

Fasten off yarn.

	YARN A
	YARN B
	YARN C

MIX-AND-MATCH

67 American Beauty

 Ⓐ B Ⓒ

FOUNDATION RING: Using yarn A, ch 12 and join with sl st to form a ring.

ROUND 1: Ch 1, 18 sc into ring, join with sl st into first sc.

ROUND 2: Ch 1, 1 sc into same place, [ch 3, skip 2 sc, 1 sc into next sc] 5 times, ch 3, skip 2 sc, join with sl st into first sc. *(6 ch 3 loops)*

ROUND 3: Ch 1, [1 sc, ch 3, 5 dc, ch 3, 1 sc] into each of next 6 ch 3 loops, join with sl st into first sc. *(6 petals)*

ROUND 4: Ch 1, 1 sc into same place, [ch 5 behind petal of previous round, 1 sc between 2 sc] 5 times, ch 5 behind petal of previous round, join with sl st into first sc. *(6 ch 5 loops)*

ROUND 5: Ch 1, [1 sc, ch 3, 7 dc, ch 3, 1 sc] into each of next 6 ch 5 loops, join with sl st into first sc. *(6 petals)*

ROUND 6: Ch 1, 1 sc into same place, [ch 7 behind petal of previous round, 1 sc between 2 sc] 5 times, ch 7 behind petal of previous round, join with sl st into first sc. *(6 ch 7 loops)*

ROUND 7: Ch 1, [1 sc, ch 3, 9 dc, ch 3, 1 sc] into each of next 6 ch 7 loops, join with sl st into first sc. *(6 petals)* Break off yarn A.

ROUND 8: Join yarn B between any 2 sc, ch 1, [1 sc between 2 sc, ch 8 behind petal of previous round] 6 times, join with sl st into first sc. *(6 ch 8 loops)*

ROUND 9: Sl st into next ch 8 loop, ch 3 *(counts as 1 dc)*, [7 dc, ch 2, 3 dc] into same loop, *10 dc into next ch 8 loop, [3 dc, ch 2, 8 dc] into next ch 8 loop, **[8 dc, ch 2, 3 dc] into next ch 8 loop; rep from * to ** once, join with sl st into 3rd of ch 3. *(16 dc along each side of square)*

ROUND 10: Ch 3 *(counts as 1 dc)*, 1 dc into each dc of previous round, working [3 dc, ch 2, 3 dc] into each ch 2 corner sp, join with sl st into 3rd of ch 3. Break off yarn B.

ROUND 11: Join yarn C, ch 3 *(counts as 1 dc)*, 1 dc into each dc of previous round, working [2 dc, ch 2, 2 dc] into each ch 2 corner sp, join with sl st to 3rd of ch 3.

ROUND 12: Ch 1, 1 sc into each dc of previous round, working 3 sc into each ch 2 corner sp, join with sl st into first sc.
Fasten off yarn.

MIX-AND-MATCH

68 Red, White & Blue

1 ≡ Ⓐ B Ⓒ

FOUNDATION CHAIN: Using yarn A, ch 6.

ROW 1: *(right side)* Insert hook into 4th ch from hook, work 3 dc, turn.

ROW 2: Ch 3 *(counts as 1 dc)*, 1 dc into each of next 2 dc, 4 dc into loop made by turning ch of previous row, turn.

ROW 3: Ch 3 *(counts as 1 dc)*, 1 dc into each of next 2 dc, [2 dc, ch 2, 2 dc] into next dc, 1 dc into each of next 2 dc, 1 dc into 3rd of 3 ch, turn.

ROW 4: Ch 3 *(counts as 1 dc)*, 1 dc into each of next 4 dc, [2 dc, ch 2, 2 dc] into ch 2 sp, 1 dc into each of next 4 dc, 1 dc into 3rd of ch 3, turn.

ROW 5: Ch 3 *(counts as 1 dc)*, 1 dc into each of next 6 dc, [2 dc, ch 2, 2 dc] into ch 2 sp, 1 dc into each of next 6 dc, 1 dc into 3rd of ch 3, turn. Break off yarn A.

ROW 6: Join yarn B, ch 3 *(counts as 1 dc)*, 1 dc into each of next 8 dc, [2 dc, ch 2, 2 dc] into ch 2 sp, 1 dc into each of next 8 dc, 1 dc into 3rd of ch 3, turn.

ROW 7: Ch 3 *(counts as 1 dc)*, 1 dc into each of next 10 dc, [2 dc, ch 2, 2 dc] into ch 2 sp, 1 dc into each of next 10 dc, 1 dc into 3rd of ch 3, turn.

ROW 8: Ch 3 *(counts as 1 dc)*, 1 dc into each of next 12 dc, [2 dc, ch 2, 2 dc] into ch 2 sp, 1 dc into each of next 12 dc, 1 dc into 3rd of ch 3, turn.

ROW 9: Join yarn A, ch 3 *(counts as 1 dc)*, 1 dc into each of next 14 dc, [2 dc, ch 2, 2 dc] into ch 2 sp, 1 dc into each of next 14 dc, 1 dc into 3rd of ch 3, turn. Break off yarn B.

ROW 10: Join yarn C, ch 3 *(counts as 1 dc)*, 1 dc into each of next 16 dc, [2 dc, ch 2, 2 dc] into ch 2 sp, 1 dc into each of next 16 dc, 1 dc into 3rd of ch 3, turn.

ROW 11: Ch 3 *(counts as 1 dc)*, 1 dc into each of next 18 dc, [2 dc, ch 2, 2 dc] into ch 2 sp, 1 dc into each of next 18 dc, 1 dc into 3rd of ch 3, turn.

ROW 12: Ch 3 *(counts as 1 dc)*, 1 dc into each of next 20 dc, [2 dc, ch 2, 2 dc] into ch 2 sp, 1 dc into each of next 20 dc, 1 dc into 3rd of ch 3, turn.

ROW 13: Ch 3 *(counts as 1 dc)*, 1 dc into each of next 22 dc, [2 dc, ch 2, 2 dc] into ch 2 sp, 1 dc into each of next 22 dc, 1 dc into 3rd of ch 3, turn.

ROW 14: Ch 3 *(counts as 1 dc)*, 1 dc into each of next 24 dc, 5 dc into ch 2 sp, 1 dc into each of next 24 dc, 1 dc into 3rd of ch 3.
Fasten off yarn.

MIX-AND-MATCH

69 Fudge

11 A B C D E

Special abbreviations

beg cl = beginning cluster made from 3 dc sts, **cl** = cluster made from 4 dc sts

FOUNDATION RING: Using yarn A, ch 6 and join with sl st to form a ring.

ROUND 1: Ch 1, 12 sc into ring, join with sl st into first sc. Break off yarn A.

ROUND 2: Join yarn B to any sc, ch 4 *(counts as 1 dc, ch 1)*, *1 dc into next sc, ch 1; rep from * 10 times, join with sl st into 3rd of ch 4. *(12 spaced dc)* Break off yarn B.

ROUND 3: Join yarn C to any ch 1 sp, ch 3 *(counts as 1 dc)*, beg cl into same sp, ch 3, *cl into next ch 1 sp, ch 3; rep from * 10 times, join with sl st into top of beg cl. *(12 clusters)* Break off yarn C.

ROUND 4: Join yarn D to any ch 3 sp, ch 3 *(counts as 1 dc)*, beg cl into same sp, *ch 2, 1 dc into top of next cl, ch 2, **cl into next ch 3 sp; rep from * 10 times and from * to ** once again, join with sl st into top of beg cl. Break off yarn D.

ROUND 5: Join yarn A to any ch 2 sp, ch 1, 3 sc into each ch 2 sp of previous round, join with sl st into first sc. Break off yarn A.

ROUND 6: Join yarn C to top of any cl, ch 3 *(counts as 1 dc)*, [1 dc, ch 2, 2 dc] into same place, * [ch 2, skip next 3 sc group, 1 sc

into sp between next two 3 sc groups] 5 times, ch 2, **[2 dc, ch 2, 2 dc] into sp above next cl; rep from * twice and from * to ** once again, join with sl st into 3rd of ch 3. Break off yarn C.

ROUND 7: Join yarn E into first dc of any corner group, ch 3 *(counts as 1 dc)*, 1 dc into next dc, *[2 dc, ch 2, 2 dc] into ch 2 corner sp, 1 dc into each of next 2 dc, ch 2, 1 dc into next sc, [ch 2, 1 sc into next sc] 3 times, ch 2, 1 dc into next sc, ch 2, **1 dc into each of next 2 dc; rep from * twice and from * to ** once again, join with sl st into 3rd of ch 3. Break off yarn E.

ROUND 8: Join yarn D to any ch 2 corner sp, ch 1, 3 sc into same sp, *1 sc into each of next 4 dc, ch 2, 1 sc into next dc [ch 2, 1 sc into next sc] 3 times, ch 2, 1 sc into next dc, ch 2, 1 sc into each of next 4 dc, **3 sc into ch 2 corner sp; rep from * twice and from * to ** once again, join with a sl st to first sc. Break off yarn D.

ROUND 9: Join yarn B to center st of any 3 sc corner group, ch 1, 3 sc into same place, *1 sc into each of next 5 sc, [ch 2, 1 sc into next sc] 5 times, ch 2, 1 sc into each of next 5 sc; **3 sc into center st of next 3 sc corner group; rep from * twice and from * to ** once again, join with sl st into first sc. Break off yarn B.

ROUND 10: Join yarn C to any sc along side of square, ch 1, 1 sc into each sc of previous round, working 3 sc into center st of each 3 sc corner group and 2 sc into each ch 2 sp, join with sl st into first sc. Fasten off yarn.

MIX-AND-MATCH

 47   94   145

70 ZigZag

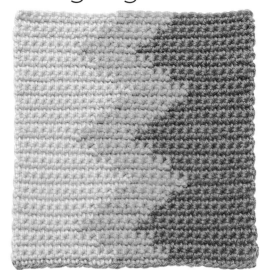

11 ☰
A B C

FOUNDATION CHAIN: Using yarn A, ch 29.

WORKING THE PATTERN: When following the chart, read odd-numbered rows (right side rows) from right to left and even-numbered rows (wrong side rows) from left to right.

Starting at the bottom right-hand corner of the chart, work the 34 row pattern from the chart in sc. On the

first row, work first sc into 2nd ch from hook, 1sc into each ch along row. *(28 sc)*

Fasten off yarn.

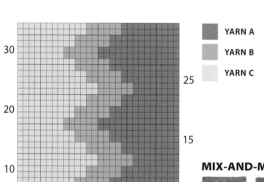

■ YARN A
■ YARN B
▫ YARN C

MIX-AND-MATCH

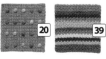 20 39   169

71 StarFlower

11 📷
Ⓐ Ⓑ

FOUNDATION RING: Using yarn A, ch 4 and join with sl st to form a ring.

ROUND 1: Ch 1, 8 sc into ring, join with sl st into first sc.

ROUND 2: *Ch 6, 1 sc into 3rd ch from hook and in next ch, 1 hdc into each of next ch 2, sl st into next sc (*petal made*); rep from * 7 times, join with sl st into first of ch 6. (*8 petals*) Break off yarn A.

ROUND 3: Join yarn B to tip of any petal, ch 5 (*counts as 1 dc, ch 2*), 1 dc into same place (*corner made*), ch 4, sl st into tip of next petal, ch 4, * [1 dc, ch 2, 1 dc] into tip of next petal (*corner made*), ch 4, sl st into tip of next petal, ch 4; rep from * twice, join with sl st into 3rd of ch 5.

ROUND 4: Sl st into next ch 2 corner sp, ch 3 (*counts as 1 dc*), [2 dc, ch 2, 3 dc] into same ch 2 sp, 4 dc into each of next 2 ch 4 sps, *[3 dc, ch 2, 3 dc] into next ch 2 corner sp, 4 dc into each of next 2 ch 4 sps; rep from * twice, join with sl st into 3rd of ch 3.

ROUND 5: Ch 3 (*counts as 1 dc*), 1 dc into each dc of previous round, working [3 dc, ch 2, 3 dc] into each ch 2 corner sp, join with sl st into 3rd of ch 3. Break off yarn B.

ROUND 6: Join yarn A, ch 3 (*counts as 1 dc*), 1 dc into each dc of previous round, working [3 dc, ch 2, 3 dc] into each ch 2 corner sp, join with sl st into 3rd of ch 3. Break off yarn A.

ROUND 7: Join yarn B, ch 3 (*counts as 1 dc*), 1 dc into each dc of previous round, working 5 dc into each ch 2 corner sp, join with sl st into 3rd of ch 3.

Fasten off yarn.

MIX-AND-MATCH

72 Ribbed Square

1 ☰
Ⓐ

FOUNDATION CHAIN: Using yarn A, ch 29.

FOUNDATION ROW: (*wrong side*) 1 sc into 2nd ch from hook, 1 sc into each ch, turn. (*28 sc*)

ROW 1: Ch 1, working only into the back loop of each stitch, 1 sc into each sc, turn. (*28 sc*) Rep row 1 32 times.

Fasten off yarn.

MIX-AND-MATCH

73 Catherine Wheel

11 A B C

FOUNDATION RING: Using yarn A, ch 6 and join with sl st to form a ring.

ROUND 1: Ch 3 *(counts as 1 dc)*, 19 dc into ring, join with sl st into 3rd of ch 3. *(20 dc)* Break off yarn A.

ROUND 2: Join yarn B to any dc, ch 4 *(counts as 1 dc, ch 1)*, [1 dc into next dc, ch 1] 19 times, join with sl st into 3rd of ch 3. *(20 spaced dc)* Break off yarn B.

ROUND 3: Join yarn C to any ch 1 sp, ch 3 *(counts as 1 dc)*, 2 dc into same sp, [3 dc into next ch 1 sp] 3 times, ch 5, *skip next ch 1 sp, [3 dc into next ch 1 sp] 4 times, ch 5; rep from * twice, join with sl st into 3rd of ch 3. Break off yarn C.

ROUND 4: Join yarn A to any dc, 1 dc into each dc of previous round, working [3 dc, ch 2, 3 dc] into each ch 5 corner sp, join with sl st into 3rd of ch 3. Break off yarn A.

ROUND 5: Join yarn B to any ch 2 corner sp, ch 3 *(counts as 1 dc)*, [2 dc, ch 2, 3 dc] into same sp, *[ch 2, skip 2 dc, 1 dc into next dc] 3 times, [1 dc into next dc, ch 2, skip 2 dc] 3 times, **[3 dc, ch 2, 3 dc] into next ch 2 corner sp; rep from * twice and from * to ** once again into 3rd of ch 3.

ROUND 6: Ch 3 *(counts as 1 dc)*, 1 dc into each of next 2 dc, *[3 dc, ch 2, 3 dc] into same sp, 1 dc into each of next 3 dc, [ch 2, 1 dc into next dc] 3 times, [1 dc into next dc, ch 2] 3 times, **1 dc into each of next 3 dc; rep from * twice and from * to ** once again, join with sl st into 3rd of ch 3.

ROUND 7: Ch 1, 1 sc into each dc of previous round, working 2 sc into each ch 2 sp along sides of square and 3 sc into each ch 2 corner sp; join with sl st into first sc.

Fasten off yarn.

MIX-AND-MATCH

 96 151 209

74 Seville

11 A

FOUNDATION RING: Using yarn A, ch 8 and join with sl st to form a ring.

ROUND 1: Ch 3 *(counts as 1 dc)*, 2 dc into ring, ch 7, [3 dc into ring, ch 7] 7 times, join with sl st into 3rd of ch 3.

ROUND 2: Sl st into next ch 7 sp, ch 3 *(counts as 1 dc)*, [2 dc, ch 2, 3 dc] into same sp, *ch 7, skip next ch 7 sp, [3 dc, ch 2, 3 dc] into next ch 7 sp; rep from * twice, ch 7, skip next ch 7 sp, join with sl st into 3rd of ch 3.

ROUND 3: Ch 3 *(counts as 1 dc)*, 1 dc into each of next 2 dc, *[2 dc, ch 2, 2 dc] into ch 2 corner sp, 1 dc into each of next 3 dc, ch 7, **1 dc into each of next 3 dc; rep from * twice and from * to ** once again, join with sl st into 3rd of ch 3.

ROUND 4: Ch 3 *(counts as 1 dc)*, 1 dc into each of next 4 dc, *[2 dc, ch 2, 2 dc] into ch 2 corner sp, 1 dc into each of next 5 dc, ch 4, 1 sc into skipped ch 7 sp of round 1 enclosing ch made on rounds 2 and 3, ch 4, ** 1 dc into each of next 5 dc; rep from * twice and from * to ** once again, join with sl st into 3rd of ch 3.

ROUND 5: Ch 1, 1 sc into same place, 1 sc into each of next 6 dc, *3 sc into next ch 2 corner sp, 1 sc into each of next 7 dc, 1 sc into next ch 4 sp, ch 3, 1 sc into next ch 4 sp, **1 sc into each of next 7 dc; rep from * twice and from * to ** once again, join with sl st into first sc.

ROUND 6: Ch 4 *(counts as 1 dc, ch 1)*, *[skip 1 sc, 1 dc into next sc, ch 1] 3 times, 5 dc into center st of next 3 sc corner group, ch 1, [skip 1 sc, 1 dc into next sc, ch 1] 3 times, skip next sc, 1 dc into each of next 2 sc, 2 dc into next ch 3 sp, **1 dc into each of next 2 sc; rep from * twice and from * to ** once again, 1 dc into next sc, join with sl st into 3rd of ch 4.

ROUND 7: Ch 4 *(counts as 1 dc, ch 1)*, *[1 dc into next dc, ch 1] 3 times, 1 dc into each of next 2 dc, 3 dc into center st of 5 dc corner group, 1 dc into each of next 2 dc, ch 1, [1 dc into next dc, ch 1] 3 times, **1 dc into each of next 6 dc; rep from * twice and from * to ** once again, 1 dc into each of next 5 dc, join with sl st into 3rd of ch 4.

Fasten off yarn.

MIX-AND-MATCH

 166 190 200

75 Half & Half

1 ≣
Ⓐ Ⓑ

FOUNDATION CHAIN: Using yarn A, ch 32.

FOUNDATION ROW: *(wrong side)* 1 dc into 4th ch from hook, 1 dc into each ch to end, turn. (30 dc)

ROW 1: Ch 3 *(counts as 1 dc)*, 1 dc into each dc of previous row, turn. *(30 dc)*
Rep row 1 throughout, working 5 more rows in yarn A and 7 rows in yarn B.

Fasten off yarn.

MIX-AND-MATCH

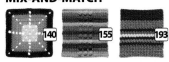

76 Granny Stripes

1 ≣
Ⓐ Ⓑ Ⓒ
Ⓓ

FOUNDATION CHAIN: Using yarn A, ch 32.

FOUNDATION ROW: *(right side)* 1 sc into 2nd ch from hook, 1 sc into each ch to end, turn. *(31 sc)*

ROW 1: Ch 3 *(counts as 1 dc)*, 1 dc into same place, [skip 2 sc, 3 dc into next sc] 9 times, skip 2 sc, 2 dc into next sc, turn.

ROW 2: Ch 3 *(counts as 1 dc)*, [3 dc into next sp between dc groups] 10 times, 1 dc into 3rd of ch 3, turn. Break off yarn A.

ROW 3: Join yarn B, ch 3 *(counts as 1 dc)*, 1 dc into same place, [3 dc into next sp between dc groups] 9 times, 2 dc into 3rd of ch 3, turn.

ROW 4: Ch 3 *(counts as 1 dc)*, [3 dc into next sp between dc groups] 10 times, 1 dc into 3rd of ch 3, turn. Break off yarn B.

Rep rows 3 & 4 5 times changing color every two rows in the following color sequence: 2 rows in yarn C, 2 rows in yarn D, 2 rows in yarn C, 2 rows in yarn B, 2 rows in yarn A.

NEXT ROW: Ch 1, 1 sc into each dc of previous row.

Fasten off yarn.

MIX-AND-MATCH

77 Raspberries & Cream

11 ≡
Ⓐ Ⓑ Ⓒ
Ⓓ Ⓔ

Special abbreviation

sc3tog = decrease 2 sts by working the next 3 sc together

FOUNDATION CHAIN: Using yarn A, ch 58.

FOUNDATION ROW: *(wrong side)* 1 sc into 2nd ch from hook, 1 sc into each ch, turn. *(57 sc)*

ROW 1: Ch 1, 1 sc into each of next 27 sc, sc3tog, 1 sc into each of rem 27 sc, turn. *(55 sc)*

ROW 2: Ch 1, 1 sc into each of next 26 sc, sc3tog, 1 sc into each of rem 26 sc, turn. *(53 sc)* Break off yarn A.

ROW 3: Join yarn B, ch 1, 1 sc into each of next 25 sc, sc3tog, 1 sc into each of rem 25 sc, turn. *(51 sc)*

ROW 4: Ch 1, 1 sc into each of next 24 sc, sc3tog, 1 sc into each of rem 24 sc, turn. *(49 sc)* Break off yarn B. Join yarn C. Cont in pattern as set, working sc3tog over 3 center sts on every row. At the same time, change yarn colors in the following color sequence: Work 2 rows in yarn C,

2 rows in yarn D. Join yarn E and cont in pattern until 3 sc rem.

NEXT ROW: Work sc3tog. Fasten off yarn.

MIX-AND-MATCH

 33
 148
 208

78 Briar Rose

11 📷 Ⓐ Ⓑ Ⓒ Ⓓ

FOUNDATION RING: Using yarn A, ch 6 and join with sl st to form a ring.

ROUND 1: Ch 1, 16 sc into ring, join with sl st into first sc. *(16 sc)*

ROUND 2: Ch 6 *(counts as 1 dc, ch 3)*, skip 2 sc, [1 dc into next sc, ch 3, skip 1 sc] 7 times; join with sl st into 3rd of ch 6. *(8 spaced dc)* Break off yarn A.

ROUND 3: Join yarn B to any ch 3 sp, ch 1 [1 sc, 1 hdc, 1 dc, 1 hdc, 1 sc] into same sp, *[1 sc, 1 hdc, 1 dc, 1 hdc, 1 sc] into next ch 3 sp; rep from * 6 times, join with sl st into first sc. *(8 petals made)*

ROUND 4: Ch 1, 1 sc into each sc and hdc of previous round, working 3 sc into each dc, join with sl st into first sc. Break off yarn B.

ROUND 5: Join yarn C to 2nd sc of any petal, ch 1, 1 sc into same place, *ch 5, skip 3 sc, 1 sc into next sc, ch 7, skip 2 sc, 1 sc into next sc, ch 5, skip 3 sc, 1 sc into next sc, ch 2, skip 2 sc, **1 sc into next sc; rep from * twice and from * to ** once again, join with sl st into first sc.

ROUND 6: Ch 2 *(counts as 1 hdc)*, 3 hdc into next ch 5 sp, * [4 dc, ch 3, 4 dc] into next ch 7 sp, 4 hdc into next

ch 5 sp, 2 hdc into next ch 2 sp, **4 hdc into next ch 5 sp; rep from * twice and from * to ** once again, join with sl st into 2nd of ch 2. Break off yarn C.

ROUND 7: Join yarn D to any ch 3 corner sp, ch 3 *(counts as 1 dc)*, [1 dc, ch 2, 2 dc] into same sp, *1 dc into each of next 4 dc, 1 dc into each of next 3 hdc, ch 1, skip 1 hdc, 1 dc into each of next 2 hdc, ch 1, skip 1 hdc, 1 dc into each of next 3 hdc, 1 dc into each of next 4 dc, **[2 dc, ch 2, 2 dc] into next ch 3 corner sp; rep from * twice and from * to ** once again, join with sl st into 3rd of ch 3.

ROUND 8: Ch 3 *(counts as 1 dc)*, 1 dc into next dc, *[2 dc, ch 2, 2 dc] into next ch 2 corner sp, **1 dc into each of next 20 dc; rep from * twice and from * to ** once again, 1 dc into each of next 18 dc, join with sl st into 3rd of ch 3.

ROUND 9: Ch 1, 1 sc into same place, 1 sc into each dc of previous round, working 3 sc into each ch 2 corner sp, join with sl st into first sc. Fasten off yarn.

MIX-AND-MATCH

 19
 88
 129

79 Baltic Square

11 ✂ A

Special abbreviations

beg pc = beginning popcorn made from ch 3 and 4 dc sts, **pc** = popcorn made from 5 dc sts

FOUNDATION RING: Ch 8 and join with sl st to form a ring.

ROUND 1: Beg pc into ring, [ch 5, pc into ring] 3 times, ch 5, join with sl st into top of beg pc.

ROUND 2: Ch 3 (counts as 1 dc), *[2 dc, ch 2, pc, ch 2, 2 dc] into next ch 5 sp, **1 dc into next pc; rep from * twice and from * to ** again, join with sl st into 3rd of ch 3.

ROUND 3: Ch 3 (counts as 1 dc), 1 dc into each of next 2 sts, *2 dc into next ch 2 sp, ch 2, pc into next pc, ch 2, 2 dc into next ch 2 sp, **1 dc into each of next 5 dc, rep from * twice and from * to ** again, 1 dc into each of last 2 sts, join with sl st into 3rd of ch 3.

ROUND 4: Ch 3 (counts as 1 dc), 1 dc into each of next 4 dc, *2 dc into next ch 2 sp, ch 3, pc into next pc, ch 3, 2 dc into next ch 2 sp, **1 dc into each of next 9 dc, rep from * twice and from * to ** again, 1 dc into each of last 4 dc, join with sl st into

3rd of ch 3.

ROUND 5: Ch 3 (counts as 1 dc), 1 dc into each of next 6 dc, *2 dc into next ch 3 sp, ch 3, pc into next pc, ch 3, 2 dc into next ch 3 sp, **1 dc into each of next 13 dc, rep from * twice and from * to ** again, 1 dc into each of last 6 dc, join with sl st into 3rd of ch 3.

ROUND 6: Ch 3 (counts as 1 dc), 1 dc into each of next 8 dc, *2 dc into next ch 3 sp, ch 3, pc into next pc, ch 3, 2 dc into next ch 3 sp, **1 dc into each of next 17 dc, rep from * twice and from * to ** again, 1 dc into each of last 8 dc, join with sl st into 3rd of ch 3.

ROUND 7: Ch 1, 1 sc into each dc of previous round, working [1 hdc, 1 dc, 1 hdc] into top of each pc, join with sl st into first sc.

Fasten off yarn.

80 Blocks & Shells

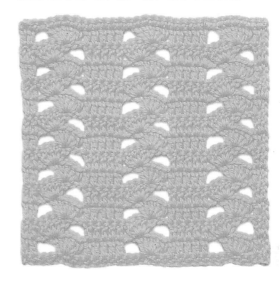

1 ☰

A

FOUNDATION CHAIN: Ch 33.

FOUNDATION ROW: (wrong side) 1 sc into 2nd ch from hook, 1 sc into each ch, turn. (32 sc)

ROW 1: Ch 3 (counts as 1 dc), 1 dc into next sc, *skip 2 sc, 5 dc into next sc, ch 2, skip 3 sc, 1 dc into each of next 5 dc; rep from * ending last rep 1 dc into each of last 2 sc, turn.

ROW 2: Ch 3 (counts as 1 dc), 1 dc into next dc, *skip ch 2, 5 dc into next dc, ch 2, skip 4 dc, 1 dc into each of next 5 dc; rep from * ending last rep 1 dc into each of last 2 dc, turn. Rep row 2 11 times.

NEXT ROW: Ch 1, 1 sc into each dc of previous row, working 1 sc into each ch 2 sp.

Fasten off yarn.

MIX-AND-MATCH

 33 83 111

MIX-AND-MATCH

 36 97 98

81 Sunshine & Showers

FOUNDATION RING: Using yarn A, ch 4 and join with sl st to form a ring.

ROUND 1: Ch 1, [1 sc into ring, ch 3] 8 times, join with sl st into first sc. Break off yarn A.

ROUND 2: Join yarn B to any ch 3 sp, ch 3 *(counts as 1 dc)*, [1 dc, ch 2, 2 dc] into same sp, *2 dc into next ch 3 sp, **[2 dc, ch 2, 2 dc] into next ch 3 sp; rep from * twice and from * to ** once again, join with sl st into 3rd of ch 3. Break off yarn B.

ROUND 3: Join yarn C to any ch 2 corner sp, ch 3 *(counts as 1 dc)*, [2 dc, ch 3, 3 dc] into same sp, *[2 dc in sp between next two 2 sc groups] twice, **[3 dc, ch 3, 3 dc] into next ch 2 corner sp; rep from * twice and from * to ** once again, join with sl st into 3rd of ch 3.

ROUND 4: Ch 1, 1 sc into same place, 1 sc into each dc of previous round, working 3 sc into each ch 3 corner sp, join with sl st into first sc. Break off yarn C.

ROUND 5: Join yarn D, ch 3 *(counts as 1 dc)*, 1 dc into each sc of previous round, working [2 dc, ch 2, 2 dc] into center st of each 3 sc corner group, join with sl st into 3rd of ch 3.

ROUND 6: Ch 1, 1 sc into same place, 1 sc into each dc of previous round, working 3 sc into each ch 2 corner sp, join with sl st into first sc. Break off yarn D.

ROUND 7: Join yarn C, ch 3 *(counts as 1 dc)*, 1 dc into each sc of previous round, working [2 dc, ch 2, 2 dc] into center st of each 3 sc corner group, join with sl st into 3rd of ch 3.

ROUND 8: Ch 1, 1 sc into same place, 1 sc into each dc of previous round, working 3 sc into each ch 2 corner sp, join with sl st into first sc. Break off yarn C.

ROUNDS 9 & 10: Join yarn B, ch 1, 1 sc into same place, 1 sc into each sc of previous round, working 3 sc into center st of each 3 sc corner group, join with sl st into first sc. Fasten off yarn.

82 Webbed Lace

FOUNDATION CHAIN: Ch 33.

FOUNDATION ROW: *(right side)* 1 dc into 4th ch from hook, 1 dc into each ch to end, turn. (31 dc)

ROW 1: Ch 3 *(counts as 1 dc)*, 1 dc into each dc of previous row, turn. *(31 dc)*

ROW 2: Ch 3 *(counts as 1 dc)*, 1 dc into each of next 4 dc, *ch 4, [skip 1 dc, 1 tr into next dc] 4 times, ch 4, skip 1 dc, 1 dc into each of next 3 dc; rep from * once, 1 dc into next dc, 1 dc into 3rd of ch 3, turn.

ROWS 3 & 4: Ch 3 *(counts as 1 dc)*, 1 dc into each of next 4 dc, *ch 4, 1 sc into each of next 4 tr, 4 ch, 1 dc into each of next 3 dc; rep from * once, 1 dc into next dc, 1 dc into 3rd of ch 3, turn.

ROW 5: Ch 3 *(counts as 1 dc)*, 1 dc into each of next 4 dc, *[ch 1, 1 tr into next sc] 4 times, ch 1, 1 dc into each of next 3 dc; rep from * once, 1 dc into next dc, 1 dc into 3rd of ch 3, turn.

ROW 6: Ch 3 *(counts as 1 dc)*, 1 dc into each of next 4 dc, *[1 dc into ch 1 sp, 1 dc into next tr] 4 times, 1 dc into next ch 1 sp, 1 dc into each of next 3 dc; rep from * once, 1 dc into next dc, 1 dc into 3rd of ch 3, turn.

(31 dc) Rep rows 1-6, then rep row 1 once again.
Fasten off yarn.

MIX-AND-MATCH

MIX-AND-MATCH

83 Diamond in a Square

  Ⓐ Ⓑ Ⓒ

FOUNDATION RING: Using yarn A, ch 4 and join with sl st to form a ring.

ROUND 1: Ch 6 *(counts as 1 dc, ch 3)*, [3 dc into ring, ch 3] 3 times, 2 dc into ring, join with sl st into 3rd of 6 ch.

ROUND 2: Sl st into next ch 3 sp, ch 3 *(counts as 1 dc)*, [2 dc, ch 2, 3 dc] into same sp, *1 dc into each of next 3 dc, [3 dc, ch 2, 3 dc] into next ch 3 sp; rep from * twice, 1 dc into each of next 3 dc, join with sl st into 3rd of ch 3. Break off yarn A.

ROUND 3: Join yarn B to any ch 2 sp, *ch 6, skip 4 dc, 1 tr into next dc, ch 6, sl st into next ch 2 sp; rep from * 3 times, join with sl st into first ch.

ROUND 4: Ch 1, *7 sc into next ch 6 sp, [1 hdc, ch 2, 1 hdc] into next tr to make corner, 7 sc into next ch 6 sp, 1 sc into ch 2 sp of round 2; rep from * 3 times, join with sl st into first sc.

ROUND 5: Ch 2 *(counts as 1 hdc)*, 1 hdc into each of next 6 sc, 1 dc into next hdc, *[2 dc, ch 2, 2 dc] into next ch 2 corner sp, 1 dc into next hdc, 1 hdc into each of next 7 sc, 1 dc into next sc, **1 hdc into each of next 7 sc; rep from * twice and from * to ** once again, join with sl st into 2nd of ch 2. Break off yarn B.

ROUND 6: Join yarn C to center dc along one side of square, ch 3 *(counts as 1 dc)*, *1 dc into each of next 7 hdc, 1 hdc into each of next 3 dc, [2 hdc, ch 2, 2 hdc] into next ch 2 corner sp, 1 hdc into each of next 3 dc, 1 dc into next dc; rep from * 3 times, join with sl st into 3rd of ch 3. Break off yarn C.

ROUND 7: Join yarn A to any st along one side of square, ch 1, 1 sc into same place, 1 sc into each hdc and dc of previous round, working 3 sc into each ch 2 corner sp, join with sl st into first sc.

ROUND 8: Ch 1, 1 sc into same place, 1 sc into each sc of previous round, working 3 sc into center st of each 3 sc corner group, join with sl st into first sc.

Fasten off yarn.

MIX-AND-MATCH

84 Combination Stripes

 ≋ Ⓐ Ⓑ Ⓒ Ⓓ Ⓔ

FOUNDATION CHAIN: Using yarn A, ch 2.

FOUNDATION ROW: *(right side)* Work 5 sc into 2nd ch from hook, turn. *(5 sc)*

ROW 1: Ch 1, 1 sc into each of next 2 sc, [1 sc, ch 2, 1 sc] into next sc *(center st)*, 1 sc into each of next 2 sc, turn.

ROW 2: Ch 1, 1 sc into each of next 3 sc, [1 sc, ch 2, 1 sc] into ch 2 corner sp, 1 sc into each of next 3 sc, turn.

ROW 3: Ch 1, 1 sc into each of next 4 sc, [1 sc, ch 2, 1 sc] into ch 2 corner sp, 1 sc into each of next 4 sc, turn.

Cont in pattern as set, working 1 more sc at each side of corner until 4 more rows have been worked in A. Break off yarn A. Join yarn B and work 2 rows. Break off yarn B. Join yarn C and work 2 rows. Break off yarn C. Join yarn D and work 2 rows. Break off yarn D. Join yarn E and work 2 rows. Break off yarn E.

ROW 16: Join yarn A, ch 3 *(counts as 1 dc)*, 1 dc into each of next 16 sc, [2 dc, ch 2, 2 dc] into ch 2 corner sp, 1 dc into each of next 17 sc, turn.

ROW 17: Ch 3 *(counts as 1 dc)*, 1 dc into each of next 18 dc, [2 dc, ch 2, 2 dc] into ch 2 corner sp, 1 dc into

each of next 19 dc, turn.

ROW 18: Ch 3 *(counts as 1 dc)*, 1 dc into each of next 20 dc, [2 dc, ch 2, 2 dc] into ch 2 corner sp, 1 dc into each of next 21 dc, turn.

ROW 19: Ch 3 *(counts as 1 dc)*, 1 dc into each of next 22 dc, [2 dc, ch 2, 2 dc] into ch 2 corner sp, 1 dc into each of next 23 dc, turn. Break off yarn A.

ROW 20: Join yarn B, ch 1, 1 sc into first dc, 1 sc into each of next 24 dc, [1 sc, ch 2, 1 sc] into ch 2 corner sp, 1 sc into each of next 25 dc, turn.

ROW 21: Ch 1, 1 sc into each of next 26 sc, [1 sc, ch 2, 1 sc] into ch 2 corner sp, 1 sc into each of next 26 sc, turn. Break off yarn B.

ROW 22: Join yarn C, ch 1, 1 sc into each of next 27 sc, [1 sc, ch 2, 1 sc] into ch 2 corner sp, 1 sc into each of next 27 sc, turn.

ROW 23: Ch 1, 1 sc into each of next 28 sc, 3 sc into ch 2 corner sp, 1 sc into each of next 28 sc.

Fasten off yarn.

MIX-AND-MATCH

85 Lemon Stripe

11 📷 Ⓐ Ⓑ

Special abbreviations

beg pc = beginning popcorn made from ch 3 and 4 dc sts, **pc** = popcorn made from 5 dc sts

FOUNDATION RING: Using yarn A, ch 6 and join with sl st to form a ring.

ROUND 1: Ch 3 *(counts as 1 dc)*, [1 dc, pc, 2 dc] into ring, ch 2, *[2 dc, pc, 2 dc] into ring, ch 2; rep from * twice, join with sl st into 3rd of ch 3.

ROUND 2: Ch 3 *(counts as 1 dc)*, 1 dc into each of next 4 sts, [1 dc, ch 3, 1 dc] into next ch 2 sp *(corner made)*, *1 dc into each of next 5 sts, [1 dc, ch 3, 1 dc] into next ch 2 sp *(corner made)*; rep from * twice, join with sl st into 3rd of ch 3.

ROUND 3: Ch 3 *(counts as 1 dc)*, pc into next dc, 1 dc into next dc, pc into next dc, 1 dc into each of next 2 dc, *[1 dc, ch 3, 1 dc] into next ch 3 corner sp, **1 dc into each of next 2 dc, pc into next dc, 1 dc into next dc, pc into next dc, 1 dc into each of next 2 dc; rep from * twice and from * to ** once again, 1 dc into next dc, join with sl st into 3rd of ch 3.

ROUND 4: Ch 3 *(counts as 1 dc)*, 1 dc into each of next 6 sts, [1 dc, ch 4, 1 dc] into next ch 3 corner sp, *1 dc into each of next 9 sts, [1 dc, ch 4, 1 dc] into next ch 3 corner sp; rep from * twice, 1 dc into each of next 2 sts, join with sl st into 3rd of ch 3.

ROUND 5: Beg pc into same ch, 1 dc into each of next 3 dc, pc into next dc, 1 dc into each of next 3 dc, *[1 dc, ch 3, 1 dc] into next ch 4 corner sp, **1 dc into each of next 3 dc, [pc into next dc, 1 dc into each of next 3 dc] twice; rep from * twice and from * to ** once again, 1 dc into each of next 3 dc, join with sl st into 3rd of ch 3. Break off yarn A.

ROUND 6: Join yarn B, ch 3 *(counts as 1 dc)*, 1 dc into each of next 8 sts, *[3 dc, ch 3, 3 dc] into next ch 4 corner sp, **1 dc into each of next 13 sts; rep from * twice and from * to ** once again, 1 dc into each of next 4 sts, join with sl st into 3rd of ch 3. Break off yarn B.

ROUND 7: Join yarn A, ch 3 *(counts as 1 dc)*, 1 dc into each of next 11 dc, *5 dc into next ch 3 corner sp, **1 dc into each of next 19 dc; rep from * twice and from * to ** once again, 1 dc into each of next 7 dc, join with sl st into 3rd of ch 3.

Fasten off yarn.

MIX-AND-MATCH

 30   156   199

86 Sunray

11 📷 Ⓐ Ⓑ

FOUNDATION RING: Using yarn A, ch 6 and join with sl st to form a ring.

ROUND 1: Ch 4 *(counts as 1 tr)*, 1 tr into ring, ch 2, [2 tr into ring, ch 2] 7 times, join with sl st into 4th of ch 4.

ROUND 2: Ch 3 *(counts as 1 dc)*, 2 dc into next tr, ch 2, [1 dc into next tr, 2 dc into next tr, ch 2] 7 times, join with sl st into 3rd of ch 3.

ROUND 3: Ch 3 *(counts as 1 dc)*, 3 dc into next dc, 1 dc into next dc, ch 2, *1 dc into next dc, 3 dc into next dc, 1 dc into next dc, ch 2; rep from * 6 times, join with sl st into 3rd of ch 3.

ROUND 4: Ch 3 *(counts as 1 dc)*, 2 hdc into next dc, 1 sc into each of next 3 dc, 1 sc into next ch 2 sp, 1 sc into each of next 3 dc, 2 hdc into next dc, 1 dc into next dc, *ch 3 *(corner sp made)*, 1 dc into next dc, 2 hdc into next dc, 1 sc into each of next 3 dc, 1 sc into next ch 2 sp, 1 sc into each of next 3 dc, 2 hdc into next dc, 1 dc into next dc; rep from * twice, ch 3 *(corner sp made)*, join with sl st into 3rd of ch 3.

ROUND 5: Ch 3 *(counts as 1 dc)*, 2 dc into same place, *1 hdc into each of next 5 sts, skip 1 st, ch 2, 1 dc into each of next 5 sts, 3 dc into next st, ch 3, **3 dc into next st; rep from * twice and from * to ** once again, join with sl st into 3rd of ch 3.

ROUND 6: Ch 3 *(counts as 1 dc)*, 1 dc into each of next 7 sts, *2 dc into next ch 2 sp, 1 dc into each of next 8 sts, 5 dc into next ch 3 corner sp, **1 dc into each of next 8 sts; rep from * twice and from * to ** once again, join with sl st into 3rd of ch 3. Break off yarn A.

ROUND 7: Join yarn B to any dc along side of square, ch 2 *(counts as 1 hdc)*, 1 hdc into each dc of previous round, working 3 hdc into center st of each 5 dc corner group, join with sl st into 2nd of ch 2.

Fasten off yarn.

MIX-AND-MATCH

 125   185   197

87 Peony

FOUNDATION CHAIN: Using yarn A, ch 2.

FOUNDATION RING: Work 8 sc into 2nd ch from hook, join with sl st into first sc. Break off yarn A.

ROUND 1: Join yarn B to any sc, ch 1, 1 sc into same place, ch 2, [1 sc into next sc, ch 2] 7 times, join with sl st into first sc.

ROUND 2: Sl st into first ch 2 sp, ch 1, [1 sc, 1 hdc, 1 sc] into same sp, [1 sc, 1 hdc, 1 sc] into next ch 2 sp 7 times, join with sl st into back of first sc. (8 petals made)

ROUND 3: Working behind petals, [ch 3, sl st behind first sc of next petal] 7 times, ch 3, join with sl st into first of ch 3.

ROUND 4: Working behind petals, sl st into first ch 3 sp, ch 1, [1 sc, 3 hdc, 1 sc] into same sp, [1 sc, 3 hdc, 1 sc] into next ch 3 sp 7 times, join with sl st into back of first sc. (8 petals made)

ROUND 5: Working behind petals, [ch 5, sl st behind first sc of next petal] 7 times, ch 5, join with sl st into first of ch 5.

ROUND 6: Working behind petals, sl st into first ch 5 sp, ch 1, [1 sc, 2 hdc, 3 dc, 2 hdc, 1 sc] into same sp, [1 sc, 2 hdc, 3 dc, 2 hdc, 1 sc] into next ch 5 sp 7 times, join with sl st into back of first sc. (8 petals made)

ROUND 7: Working behind petals, [ch 6, sl st behind first sc of next petal] 7 times,

ch 6, join with sl st into first of ch 6.

ROUND 8: Working behind petals, sl st into first ch 6 sp, ch 1, [1 sc, 2 hdc, 5 dc, 2 hdc, 1 sc] into same sp, [1 sc, 2 hdc, 5 dc, 2 hdc, 1 sc] into next ch 6 sp 7 times, join with sl st into back of first sc. (8 petals made) Break off yarn B.

ROUND 9: Working behind petals, join yarn C to back of first sc on any petal, [ch 8, sl st behind first sc of next petal] 7 times, ch 8, join with sl st into first of ch 3.

ROUND 10: Sl st into next ch 8 sp, ch 1, 8 sc into same sp, *[4 dc, ch 2, 4 dc] into next ch 8 sp (corner made), **8 sc into next ch 8 sp; rep from * twice and from * to ** once again, join with sl st into first sc.

ROUND 11: Ch 3 (counts as 1 dc), 1 dc into each sc and dc of previous round, working [2 dc, ch 2, 2 dc] into each ch 2 corner sp, join with sl st into 3rd of ch 3.

ROUND 12: Ch 1, 1 sc into same place, 1 sc into each dc of previous round, working 3 sc into each ch 2 corner sp, join with sl st into first sc. Break off yarn C.

ROUND 13: Join yarn B to any sc along side of square, ch 1, 1 sc into each sc of previous round, working 3 sc into center st of each 3 sc corner group, join with sl st into first sc.

ROUNDS 14 & 15: Ch 1, 1 sc into each sc of previous round, working 3 sc into center st of each 3 sc corner group, join with sl st into first sc.

Fasten off yarn.

MIX-AND-MATCH

 86 129 144

88 Edwardian Fancy

FOUNDATION RING: Using yarn A, ch 4 and join with sl st to form a ring.

ROUND 1: Ch 3 (counts as 1 dc), 11 dc into ring, join with sl st into 3rd of ch 3. (12 dc) Break off yarn A.

ROUND 2: Join yarn B to any dc, ch 5 (counts as 1 dc, ch 2), *1 dc into next dc, ch 2; rep from * 10 times, join with sl st into 3rd of ch 5. (12 spaced dc)

ROUND 3: Sl st into next ch 2 sp, ch 1, 3 sc into same sp, *3 sc into next ch 2 sp; rep from * to end, join with sl st into first sc. Break off yarn B.

ROUND 4: Join yarn C to last st of any 3 sc group, ch 1, 1 sc into same place, 1 sc into next sc, *2 sc into next sc, 1 sc into each of next 2 sc; rep from * 10 times, 2 sc into next sc, join with sl st into first sc.

ROUND 5: Ch 1, [1 sc, 1 dc] into same place, ch 1, [1 dc, 1 sc] into next sc, * sl st into each of next 2 sc, [1 sc, 1 dc] into next sc, ch 1, [1 dc, 1 sc] into next sc; rep from * 10 times, sl st into next 2 sc, join with sl st into first sc.

ROUND 6: Sl st into next ch 1 sp, ch 1, 1 sc into same sp, ch 5, *1 sc into next ch 1 sp, ch 5; rep from * 10

times, join with sl st into first sc.

ROUND 7: Sl st into next ch 5 sp, ch 1, [1 sc, 1 hdc, 2 dc, ch 2, 2 dc, 1 hdc, 1 sc] into same sp (corner made), *1 sc into next sc, [4 sc into next ch 5 sp, 1 sc into next sc] twice, **[1 sc, 1 hdc, 2 dc, ch 2, 2 dc, 1 hdc, 1 sc] into next ch 5 sp (corner made); rep from * twice and from * to ** once again, join with sl st into first sc.

ROUND 8: Ch 1, 1 sc into each st of previous round, working 3 sc into each ch 2 corner sp, join with sl st into first sc. Break off yarn C.

ROUND 9: Join yarn D to center st of any 3 sc corner group, ch 3 (counts as 1 dc), [1 dc, ch 2, 2 dc] into same place, *1 dc into next sc, ch 1, skip 1 sc, [1 dc into next sc, ch 1, skip 1 sc] 9 times, 1 dc into next sc, **[2 dc, ch 2, 2 dc] into next sc; rep from * twice and from * to ** once again, join with sl st into 3rd of ch 3. Break off yarn D.

ROUND 10: Join yarn A to any dc along side of square, ch 1, 1 sc into each dc and ch of previous round, working 3 sc into each ch 2 corner sp, join with sl st into first sc. Break off yarn A.

ROUND 11: Join yarn D to any sc along side of square, ch 1, 1 sc into each sc of previous round, working 3 sc into center st of each 3 sc corner group, join with sl st into first sc. Break off yarn A.

Fasten off yarn.

MIX-AND-MATCH

 19 133 137

89 Spinner

11 A B C

FOUNDATION RING: Using yarn A, ch 4 and join with sl st to form a ring.

ROUND 1: Ch 3 *(counts as 1 dc)*, 15 dc into ring, join with sl st into 3rd of ch 3. *(16 dc)* Break off yarn A.

ROUND 2: Join yarn B into sp between any 2 dc, ch 3 *(counts as 1 dc)*, 1 dc into same sp, 2 dc into each rem sp between dc, join with sl st into 3rd of ch 3. *(32 dc)*

ROUND 3: Ch 3 *(counts as 1 dc)*, 1 dc into same place, 1 dc into next dc, [2 dc into next dc, 1 dc into next dc] 15 times, join with sl st into 3rd of ch 3. *(48 dc)* Break off yarn B.

ROUND 4: Join yarn C to any dc, ch 4 *(counts as 1 tr)*, [2 dc, ch 2, 2 dc, 1 tr] into same place, *skip next 2 dc, 1 hdc into each of next 2 dc, 1 sc into each of next 3 dc, 1 hdc into each of next 2 dc, skip next 2 dc, **[1 tr, 2 dc, ch 2, 2 dc, 1 tr] into next dc; rep from * twice and from * to ** once again, join with sl st into 4th of ch 4. Break off yarn C.

ROUND 5: Join yarn A to any ch 2 corner sp, ch 3 *(counts as 1 dc)*, [1 dc, 2 tr, ch 2, 2 tr, 1 dc] into same sp, *1 dc into each st along side of square, **[1 dc, 2 tr, ch 2, 2 tr, 1 dc] into next ch 2 corner sp; rep from * twice and from * to ** once again, join with sl st into 3rd of ch 3. Break off yarn A.

ROUND 6: Join yarn B to any ch 2 corner sp, ch 3 *(counts as 1 dc)*, [1 dc, ch 2, 2 dc] into same sp, *1 dc into each st along side of square, **[2 dc, ch 2, 2 dc into next ch 2 corner sp; rep from * twice and from * to ** once again, join with sl st into 3rd of ch 3.

ROUND 7: Ch 3 *(counts as 1 dc)*, 1 dc into each dc of previous round, working 5 dc into each ch 2 corner sp, join with sl st into 3rd of ch 3. Fasten off yarn.

MIX-AND-MATCH

 10 117 173

90 Bright Triangles

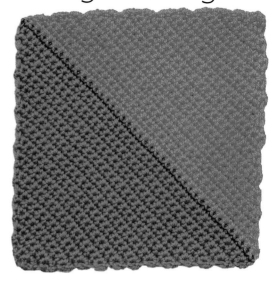

11 A B

Special abbreviation

sc3tog = decrease 2 sts by working the next 3 sc together

FOUNDATION CHAIN: Using yarn A, ch 2.

FOUNDATION ROW: *(wrong side)* Work 3 sc into 2nd ch from hook, turn. *(3 sc)*

ROW 1: Ch 1, 2 sc into first sc, 1 sc into next sc, 2 sc into last sc, turn. *(5 sc)*

Begin increase pattern.

ROW 2 to 4: Ch 1, 2 sc into first sc, 1 sc into each sc along row to last st, 2 sc into last sc, turn.

ROW 5: Ch 1, 1 sc into each sc along row, turn.

Rep rows 2 to 5 five times. *(41 sc)* Break off yarn A. Join yarn B and begin decrease pattern.

NEXT ROW: Ch 1, 1 sc into each sc along row, turn.

NEXT 3 ROWS: Ch 1, skip first sc, 1 sc into each sc along row to last 2 sts, skip 1 sc, 1 sc into last sc, turn.

Rep 4-row decrease pattern five times. *(5 sc)*

NEXT ROW: Ch 1, skip first sc, 1 sc into each of next 2 sc, skip next sc, 1 sc into next sc, turn. *(3 sc)*

NEXT ROW: Ch 1, work sc3tog. Fasten off yarn.

MIX-AND-MATCH

 59 132 172

91 Terraces

111 ☰
Ⓐ Ⓑ Ⓒ
Ⓓ Ⓔ

FOUNDATION CHAIN: Using yarn A, ch 31.

FOUNDATION ROW: *(right side)* 1 sc into 2nd ch from hook, 1 sc into each ch, turn. *(30 sc)*

ROW 1: Ch 1, 1 sc into each sc, turn. Break off yarn A.

ROW 2: Join yarn B, ch 3 *(counts as 1 dc)*, skip first sc, 1 dc into next sc, *ch 2, skip 2 sc, 1 dc into each of next 2 sc; rep from * to end, turn.

ROW 3: Ch 1, 1 sc into each of next 2 dc, *ch 2, 1 sc into each of next 2 dc; rep from * to end, turn. Break off yarn B.

ROW 4: Join yarn C, ch 1, 1 sc into each of first 2 sc, *1 tr into each of next 2 skipped sc 3 rows below, 1 sc into each of next 2 sc; rep from * to end, turn.

ROW 5: Ch 1, 1 sc into each sc and tr of previous row, turn. Break off yarn C.

ROW 6: Join yarn A, ch 3 *(counts as 1 dc)*, 1 dc into each sc of previous row, turn.

ROW 7: Ch 1, 1 sc into each dc of previous row, turn. Break off yarn A. Join yarn D and rep rows 2 & 3. Break off yarn D. Join yarn E and rep rows 4 & 5. Break off yarn E. Join yarn A and rep rows 6 & 7. Break off yarn A. Join yarn C and rep rows 2 & 3. Break off yarn C. Join yarn B and rep rows 4 & 5. Break off yarn B. Join yarn A and rep rows 6 & 7. Break off yarn A. Join yarn E and rep rows 2 & 3. Break off yarn E. Join yarn D and rep rows 4 & 5. Break off yarn D. Join yarn A and rep row 1 twice.

Fasten off yarn.

MIX-AND-MATCH

47 **104** **121**

92 Victorian Lace

11 📷 Ⓐ

Special abbreviations

tr2tog = work 2 tr together, **beg cl** = beginning cluster made from 2 dc sts, **cl** = cluster made from 3 dc sts

FOUNDATION RING: Ch 10 and join with sl st to form a ring.

ROUND 1: Ch 4 *(counts as 1 tr)*, 1 dc into ring, 2 ch, [tr2tog into ring, ch 2] 11 times, join with sl st into 4th of ch 4.

ROUND 2: Sl st into next ch 2 sp, ch 3 *(counts as 1 dc)*, beg cl into same sp, ch 3, [cl into next ch 2 sp, ch 3] 11 times, join with sl st into top of beg cl.

ROUND 3: Ch 5 *(counts as 1 hdc, ch 3)*, skip next ch 3 sp, [cl, ch 2, cl, ch 4, cl, ch 2, cl] into next ch 3 sp, ch 3, *skip next ch 3 sp, 1 hdc into top of next cl, ch 3, skip next ch 3 sp, [cl, ch 2, cl, ch 4, cl, ch 2, cl] into next ch 3 sp, ch 3; rep from * twice, join with sl st into 2nd of ch 5.

ROUND 4: Sl st into next ch 3 sp, ch 4 *(counts as 1 dc, ch 1)*, 1 dc into same sp, *ch 1, 1 dc into top of next cl, ch 1, 1 dc into next ch 2 sp, ch 1, [cl, ch 2, cl, ch 4, cl, ch 2, cl] into next ch 4 sp, ch 1, 1 dc into next ch 2 sp, ch 1,

1 dc into top of next cl, ch 1, 1 dc into next ch 3 sp, ch 1, **1 dc into next hdc, ch 1, 1 dc into next ch 2 sp; rep from * twice and from * to ** once again, join with sl st into 3rd of ch 4.

ROUND 5: Ch 4 *(counts as 1 dc, ch 1)*, [1 dc into next dc, ch 1] 3 times, *1 dc into top of next cl, ch 1, 1 dc into next ch 2 sp, ch 1, [cl, ch 2, cl, ch 4, cl, ch 2, cl] into next ch 4 corner sp, ch 1, 1 dc into next ch 2 sp, ch 1, 1 dc into top of next cl, ch 1, **[1 dc into next dc, ch 1] 7 times; rep from * twice and from * to ** once again, [1 dc into next dc, ch 1] 3 times, join with sl st into 3rd of ch 4.

ROUND 6: Ch 4 *(counts as 1 dc, ch 2)*, [1 dc into next dc, ch 1] 5 times, *1 dc into top of next cl, ch 1, 1 dc into next ch 2 sp, ch 1, 5 dc into next ch 4 corner sp, ch 1, 1 dc into next ch 2 sp, ch 1, 1 dc into top of next cl, ch 1, **[1 dc into next dc, ch 1] 11 times; rep from * twice and from * to ** once again, [1 dc into next dc, ch 1] 5 times, join with sl st into 3rd of ch 4.

Fasten off yarn.

MIX-AND-MATCH

9 **57** **192**

93 Sequenced Stripes

1 ≣
A B C
D E

FOUNDATION CHAIN: Using yarn A, ch 30.

FOUNDATION ROW: *(right side)* 1 sc into 2nd ch from hook, 1 sc into each ch to end, turn. *(29 sc)*

ROW 1: Ch 1, 1 sc into each st of previous row, turn. *(29 sc)*

ROWS 2, 3, 4 & 5: Rep row 1. Break off yarn A.

ROW 6: Join yarn B, ch 1, 1 sc into each of next 2 sc, *ch 1, skip 1 sc, 1 sc into next sc; rep from * to last 3 sts, ch 1, skip 1 sc, ch 1 into each of next 2 sc, turn.

ROW 7: Ch 1, 1 sc into each sc and 1 ch sp of previous row, turn. *(29 sc)* Break off yarn B.

Rep rows 6 and 7 eleven more times, changing yarn color every two rows and using the following sequence: C, D, E, A, B, A, E, D, C, B, A. Cont with yarn A and rep row 1 three times.

Fasten off yarn.

MIX-AND-MATCH

94 Gothic Square

11 ⌂ A B C D

Special abbreviations
beg cl = beginning cluster of dc2tog, **cl** = cluster of dc3tog

FOUNDATION RING: Using yarn A, ch 4 and join with sl st to form a ring.

ROUND 1: Ch 4 *(counts as 1 dc, ch 1)*, [1 dc into ring, ch 1] 11 times, join with sl st into 3rd of ch 4. *(12 spaced dc)* Break off yarn A.

ROUND 2: Join yarn B to any ch 1 sp, ch 3 *(counts as 1 dc)*, beg cl in same sp, [ch 3, cl into next ch 1 sp] 11 times, ch 3, join with sl st into top of beg cl.

ROUND 3: Sl st into center st of next ch 3 sp, ch 1, 1 sc into same sp, [ch 5, 1 sc into next ch 3 sp] 11 times, join with sl st into first sc. Break off yarn B.

ROUND 4: Join yarn C to center st of any ch 5 sp, ch 3 *(counts as 1 dc)*, 4 dc into same sp, *ch 1, 1 sc into next ch 5 sp, ch 5, 1 sc into next ch 5 sp, ch 1, **[5 dc, ch 3, 5 dc] into next ch 5 sp; rep from * twice and from * to ** once again, 5 dc into next ch 5 sp, ch 3, join with sl st into 3rd of ch 3. Break off yarn C.

ROUND 5: Join yarn D to any ch 3 sp, ch 3 *(counts as 1 dc)*, [1 dc, ch 2, 2 dc] into same sp, *1 dc into each of next 4 dc, ch 4, 1 sc into next ch 5 sp, ch 4, skip next dc, 1 dc into each of next 4 dc, **[2 dc, ch 2, 2 dc] into next ch 3 sp; rep from * twice and from * to ** once again, join with sl st into 3rd of ch 3.

ROUND 6: Sl st in next dc and into next ch 2 sp, ch 3 *(counts as 1 dc)*, [1 dc, ch 2, 2 dc] into same sp, *1 dc into each of next 4 dc, [ch 4, 1 sc into next ch 4 sp] twice, ch 4, skip next 2 dc, 1 dc into each of next 4 dc, **[2 dc, ch 2, 2 dc] into next ch 2 sp; rep from * twice and from * to ** once again, join with sl st into 3rd of ch 3.

ROUND 7: Ch 3 *(counts as 1 dc)*, 1 dc into next dc, *5 dc into next ch 2 corner sp, 1 dc into each of next 6 dc, 4 dc into next ch 4 sp, 3 dc into next ch 4 sp, 4 dc into next ch 4 sp, **1 dc into each of next 6 dc; rep from * twice and from * to ** once again, 1 dc into each of next 4 dc, join with sl st into 3rd of ch 3.

Fasten off yarn.

MIX-AND-MATCH

95 Kingcup

111 Ⓐ Ⓑ Ⓒ

Special abbreviation

bpsc = back post single crochet

FOUNDATION RING: Using yarn A, ch 6 and join with sl st to form a ring.

ROUND 1: Ch 3 *(counts as 1 dc)*, 11 dc into ring, join with sl st into 3rd of ch 3. *(12 dc)*

ROUND 2: Ch 2 *(counts as 1 hdc)*, 1 hdc into same place, 2 hdc into each of next 11 dc, join with sl st into 2nd of ch 2. *(24 hdc)*

ROUND 3: Ch 1, 1 sc into same place, *ch 5, skip next 2 hdc, 1 sc into next hdc; rep from * 6 times, ch 5, join with sl st into first sc. Break off yarn A.

ROUND 4: Join yarn B to any ch 5 sp, ch 1, [1 sc, 1 hdc, 5 dc, 1 hdc, 1 sc] into same ch 5 sp *(petal made)*, [1 sc, 1 hdc, 5 dc, 1 hdc, 1 sc] into next ch 5 sp 7 times, join with sl st into back loop of first sc. *(8 petals)*

ROUND 5: Working behind petals of previous round, [ch 5, bpsc round next sc] 8 times, do not join round. *(8 5ch sps)*

ROUND 6: Sl st into next ch 5 sp, [1 sc, 1 hdc, 7 dc, 1 hdc, 1 sc] into same ch 5 sp *(petal made)*, [1 sc, 1 hdc,

7 dc, 1 hdc, 1 sc] into next ch 5 sp 7 times, join with sl st into back loop of first sc. Break off yarn B.

ROUND 7: Join yarn C to 3rd dc of any petal of previous round, ch 1, 1 sc into same place, 1 sc into each of next 2 dc, *ch 5, 1 sc into each of center 3 dc of next petal, ch 8, **1 sc into each of center 3 dc of next petal; rep from * twice and from * to ** once again, join with sl st into first sc.

ROUND 8: Ch 3 *(counts as 1 dc)*, 1 dc into each sc of previous round, working 5 dc into each ch 5 sp and [5 dc, ch 3, 5 dc] into each ch 8 sp to make corner, join with sl st into 3rd of ch 3.

ROUND 9: Ch 3 *(counts as 1 dc)*, 1 dc into each dc of previous round, working [2 dc, ch 2, 2 dc] into each ch 3 corner sp, join with sl st into 3rd of ch 3. Break off yarn C.

ROUND 10: Join yarn B, ch 1, 1 sc into same place, 1 sc into each dc of previous round, working 3 sc into each ch 2 corner sp, join with sl st into first sc.

Fasten off yarn.

MIX-AND-MATCH

96 Light & Shade

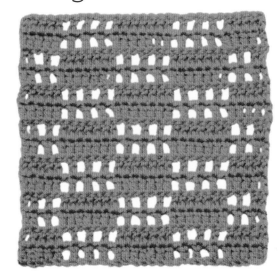

11
Ⓐ

FOUNDATION CHAIN: Ch 33.

FOUNDATION ROW: *(right side)* 1 dc into 4th ch from hook, 1 dc into each of next ch 2, [1 dc into next ch, ch 1, skip ch 1] 4 times, 1 dc into each of next ch 6, [1 dc into next ch, ch 1, skip ch 1] 4 times, 1 dc into each of next ch 5, turn.

ROW 1: Ch 3 *(counts as 1 dc)*, 1 dc into each of next 3 dc, [1 dc into next dc, ch 1, skip 1 dc] 4 times, 1 dc into each of next 6 dc, [1 dc into next dc, ch 1, skip 1 dc] 4 times, 1 dc into each of next 5 dc, turn.

ROWS 2 & 3: Ch 3 *(counts as 1 dc)*, [1 dc into next dc, ch 1, skip 1 dc] twice, 1 dc into each of next 6 dc, [1 dc into next dc, ch 1, skip 1 dc] 4 times, 1 dc into each of next 6 dc, [1 dc into next dc, ch 1, skip 1 dc] twice, 1 dc into each of next 2 dc, turn.

ROWS 4 & 5: Ch 3 *(counts as 1 dc)*, 1 dc into each of next 3 dc, [1 dc into next dc, ch 1, skip 1 dc] 4 times, 1 dc into each of next 6 dc, [1 dc into

next dc, ch 1, skip 1 dc] 4 times, 1 dc into each of next 5 dc, turn. Rep rows 2 to 5 twice.

Fasten off yarn.

MIX-AND-MATCH

97 Eyelet Lace

1

Ⓐ Ⓑ Ⓒ
Ⓓ Ⓔ

98 Old Vienna

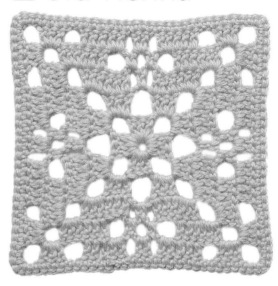

1

Ⓐ

FOUNDATION CHAIN: Using yarn A, ch 32.

FOUNDATION ROW: *(right side)* 1 dc into 4th ch from hook, 1 dc into each ch to end, turn. *(30 dc)*

ROW 1: Ch 3 *(counts as 1 dc)*, 1 dc into each of next 2 dc, *ch 2, skip 2 dc, 1 dc into each of next 6 dc; rep from * twice, ch 2, skip 2 dc, 1 dc into 3rd of ch 3, turn. Break off yarn A.

ROW 2: Join yarn B, ch 3 *(counts as 1 dc)*, *1 dc into each of next ch 2, 1 dc into each of next 4 dc, ch 2, skip 2 dc; rep from * twice, 1 dc into each of next ch 2, 1 dc into each of next 2 dc, 1 dc into 3rd of ch 3, turn.

ROW 3: Ch 3 *(counts as 1 dc)*, *1 dc into each of next 4 dc, 1 dc into each of next ch 2, ch 2, skip 2 dc; rep from * twice, 1 dc into each of next 4 dc, 1 dc into 3rd of ch 3, turn. Break off yarn B.

ROW 4: Join yarn C, ch 3 *(counts as 1 dc)*, 1 dc into each of next 2 dc, *ch 2, skip 2 dc, 1 dc into each of next ch 2, 1 dc into each of next 4 dc; rep

from * twice, ch 2, skip 2 dc, 1 dc into 3rd of ch 3, turn. Break off yarn A.

ROW 5: Rep row 1. Break off yarn C.

ROW 6: Join yarn D, rep row 2.

ROW 7: Rep row 3. Break off yarn D.

ROW 8: Join yarn E, rep row 4.

ROW 9: Rep row 1. Break off yarn E.

ROW 10: Join yarn B, rep row 2.

ROW 11: Rep row 3. Break off yarn B.

ROW 12: Join yarn A, rep row 4.

ROW 13: Ch 3 *(counts as 1 dc)*, 1 dc into each dc and ch of previous row. *(30 dc)*

Fasten off yarn.

FOUNDATION RING: Ch 8 and join with sl st to form a ring.

ROUND 1: Ch 3 *(counts as 1 dc)*, 2 dc into ring, ch 5, *3 dc into ring, ch 5; rep from * twice, join with sl st into 3rd of ch 3.

ROUND 2: Sl st in next 2 dc and into next ch 5 sp, ch 3 *(counts as 1 dc)*, [2 dc, ch 5, 3 dc] into same sp, *ch 3, [3 dc, ch 5, 3 dc] into next ch 5 sp; rep from * twice, ch 3, join with sl st into 3rd of ch 3.

ROUND 3: Ch 3 *(counts as 1 dc)*, 1 dc into each of next 2 dc, *[3 dc, ch 5, 3 dc] into next ch 5 sp, 1 dc into each of next 3 dc, ch 3, 1 sc into next ch 3 sp, ch 3, **1 dc into each of next 3 dc; rep from * twice and from * to ** once again, join with sl st into 3rd of ch 3.

ROUND 4: Sl st in each of next 3 dc, ch 3 *(counts as 1 dc)*, 1 dc into each of next 2 dc, *[3 dc, ch 5, 3 dc] into next ch 5 sp, 1 dc into each of next 3 dc, ch 3, [1 sc into next ch 3 sp, ch 3] twice, **skip next 3 dc, 1 dc into

each of next 3 dc; rep from * twice and from * to ** once again, join with sl st into 3rd of ch 3.

ROUND 5: Ch 3 *(counts as 1 dc)*, 1 dc into each of next 2 dc, ch 2, skip 3 dc *[3 dc, ch 5, 3 dc] into next ch 5 sp, ch 2, skip next 3 dc, 1 dc into each of next 3 dc, [2 dc into next ch 3 sp, ch 1] twice, 2 dc into next ch 3 sp, **1 dc into each of next 3 dc, ch 2; rep from * twice and from * to ** once again, join with sl st into 3rd of ch 3.

ROUND 6: Ch 1, 1 sc into each dc and ch of previous round, working 3 sc into 3rd of ch 5 at each corner, join with sl st into first sc.

Fasten off yarn.

MIX-AND-MATCH

 121 162 194

MIX-AND-MATCH

 125 129 174

99 Baby Bow

Special abbreviation

MB = make bobble (work 4 open dc in same st leaving 5 loops on hook, draw yarn through all 5 loops at once)

FOUNDATION CHAIN: Ch 28.

FOUNDATION ROW: *(wrong side)* Work 1 sc into 2nd ch from hook, 1 sc into each ch to end, turn. *(27 sc)*

ROW 1: Ch 1, 1 sc into each sc, turn. *(27 sc)*

ROWS 2 to 5: Rep row 1.

ROW 6: *(wrong side)* Ch 1, [1 sc into each of next 3 sc, MB] twice, 1 sc into each of next 11 sc, [MB, 1 sc into each of next 3 sc] twice, turn.

ROW 7 and every alt row: Rep row 1.

ROW 8: Ch 1, 1 sc into each of next 5 sc, *MB, 1 sc into next sc, MB, *1 sc into each of next 11 sc; rep from * to * once, 1 sc into each of next 5 sc, turn.

ROW 10: Ch 1, 1 sc into each of next 6 sc, *MB, 1 sc into next sc, MB, *1 sc into each of next 9 sc; rep from * to * once, 1 sc into each of next 6 sc, turn.

ROW 12: Ch 1, 1 sc into each of next 7 sc, *MB, 1 sc into next sc, MB, *1 sc into each of next 7 sc; rep from * to * once, 1 sc into each of next 7 sc, turn.

ROW 14: Ch 1, 1 sc into each of next 8 sc, *MB, 1 sc into next sc, MB, *1 sc into each of next 5 sc; rep from * to * once, 1 sc into each of next 8 sc, turn.

ROW 16: Ch 1, 1 sc into each of next 9 sc, *MB, 1 sc into next sc, MB, *1 sc into each of next 3 sc; rep from * to * once, 1 sc into each of next 9 sc, turn.

ROW 18: Ch 1, 1 sc into each of next 6 sc, *MB, [1 sc into next sc, MB] twice, *1 sc into each of next 2 sc, MB, 1 sc into each of next 2 sc; rep from * to * once, 1 sc into each of next 6 sc, turn.

ROW 20: Ch 1, *1 sc into each of next 4 sc, MB, 1 sc into next sc, MB, *1 sc into each of next 4 sc, *[MB, [1 sc into next sc, MB] twice; rep from * to * once, turn.

ROW 22: Ch 1, 1 sc into each of next 3 sc, *MB, 1 sc into next sc, MB, *1 sc into each of next 7 sc, MB, 1 sc into each of next 7 sc; rep from * to * once, 1 sc into each of next 3 sc, turn.

ROW 24: Ch 1, 1 sc into each of next 3 sc, *MB, 1 sc into next sc, MB, *1 sc into each of next 5 sc, MB, 1 sc into each of next 5 sc; rep from * to * once, 1 sc into each of next 3 sc, turn.

ROW 26: Ch 1, 1 sc into each of next 5 sc, *MB, [1 sc into next sc, MB] twice, *1 sc into each of next 7 dc; rep from * to * once, 1 sc into each of next 5 sc, turn.

ROWS 27 to 32: Rep row 1.

Fasten off yarn.

MIX-AND-MATCH

100 Pastel Delight

FOUNDATION RING: Using yarn A, ch 4 and join with sl st to form a ring.

ROUND 1: Ch 3 *(counts as 1 dc)*, 2 dc into ring, ch 2, [3 dc into ring, ch 2] 3 times, join with sl st into 3rd of ch 3. Break off yarn A.

ROUND 2: Join yarn B to any ch 2 sp, ch 3 *(counts as 1 dc)*, [2 dc, ch 2, 3 dc] into same sp, [3 dc, ch 2, 3 dc into next ch 2 sp] 3 times, join with sl st into 3rd of ch 3.

ROUND 3: Sl st in each of next 2 dc and into next ch 2 sp, ch 3 *(counts as 1 dc)*, [2 dc, ch 2, 3 dc] into same sp, *ch 1, skip next 2 dc, 1 dc into each of next 2 dc, ch 1, skip next 2 dc, **[3 dc, ch 2, 3 dc] into next ch 2 sp; rep from * twice and from * to ** once again, join with sl st into 3rd of ch 3.

ROUND 4: Sl st in each of next 2 dc and into next ch 2 sp, ch 3 *(counts as 1 dc)*, [2 dc, ch 2, 3 dc] into same sp, *ch 1, skip next 2 dc, 1 dc into next dc, 1 dc into next ch, 1 dc into each of next 2 dc, 1 dc into next ch, 1 dc into next dc, ch 1, skip next 2 dc, **[3 dc, ch 2, 3 dc] into next ch 2 sp; rep from * twice and from * to ** once again, join with sl st into 3rd of ch 3. Break off yarn B.

ROUND 5: Join yarn C to any ch 2 corner sp, ch 3 *(counts as 1 dc)*, [2 dc, ch 2, 3 dc] into same sp, * ch 1, skip 2 dc, 1 dc into next dc, ch 1, 1 dc into each of next 6 dc, ch 1, 1 dc into next dc, ch 1, skip 2 dc, **[3 dc, ch 2, 3 dc] into next ch 2 corner sp; rep from * twice and from * to ** once again, join with sl st into 3rd of ch 3.

ROUND 6: Sl st in each of next 2 dc and into next ch 2 sp, ch 3 *(counts as 1 dc)*, [2 dc, ch 3, 3 dc] into same sp, *ch 1, skip next 2 dc, 1 dc into next dc, [ch 1, 1 dc into next dc] twice, ch 1, skip 1 dc, 1 dc into each of next 2 dc, ch 1, skip 1 dc, 1 dc in next dc, [ch 1, 1 dc in next dc] twice, ch 1, skip 2 dc, **[3 dc, ch 3, 3 dc] in next ch 3 sp; rep from * twice, and from * to ** once again, join with sl st into 3rd of ch 3.

ROUND 7: Join yarn B to any ch 3 corner sp, ch 3 *(counts as 1 dc)*, [2 dc, ch 3, 3 dc] into same sp, *1 dc into each of next 3 dc, [ch 1, 1 dc into next dc] 4 times, [1 dc into next dc, ch 1] 4 times, 1 dc into each of next 3 dc, **[3 dc, ch 3, 3 dc] into next ch 3 corner sp; rep from * twice and from * to ** once again, join with sl st into 3rd of ch 3.

ROUND 8: Ch 1, 1 sc into same place, 1 sc into each dc and ch 1 sp of previous round, working 3 sc into each ch 3 corner sp, join with sl st into first sc.

Fasten off yarn.

MIX-AND-MATCH

101

Into the Blue

1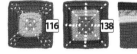

MIX-AND-MATCH

116   138   186

FOUNDATION RING: Using yarn A, ch 5 and join with sl st to form a ring.

ROUND 1: Ch 3 *(counts as 1 dc)*, 15 dc into ring, join with sl st into 3rd of ch 3. *(16 dc)* Break off yarn A.

ROUND 2: Join yarn B to any st. Ch 3 *(counts as 1 dc)*, 4 dc into base of ch 3, *1 dc into each of next 3 dc, 5 dc into next dc; rep from * to last 3 sts, 1 dc into each of next 3 dc, join with sl st to 3rd of ch 3. *(Four corners made)* Break off yarn B.

ROUND 3: Join yarn C to center st of corner group. Ch 3 *(counts as 1 dc)*, 4 dc into base of ch 3, *1 dc into each of next 7 dc, 5 dc into next dc; rep from * to last 7 sts, 1dc into each of next 7 dc, join with sl st to 3rd of ch 3. Break off yarn C.

ROUND 4: Join yarn A to center st of corner group. Ch 3 *(counts as 1 dc)*, [1 dc, ch 2, 2 dc] into base of ch 3, *1 dc into each of next 11 dc, [2 dc, ch 2, 2 dc] into next dc; rep from * to last 11

sts, 1 dc into each of next 11 dc, join with sl st to 3rd of ch 3. Break off yarn C.

ROUND 5: Join yarn D to ch 2 sp at corner. Ch 3 *(counts as 1 dc)*, [1 dc, ch 2, 2 dc] into ch 2 sp, *1 dc into each of next 15 dc, [2 dc, ch 2, 2 dc] into next dc; rep from * to last 15 sts, 1 dc into each of next 15 dc, join with sl st to 3rd of ch 3. Break off yarn D.

ROUND 6: Join yarn A to ch 2 sp at corner. Ch 3 *(counts as 1 dc)*, [1 dc, ch 4, 2 dc] into ch 2 sp, *1 dc into each of next 19 dc, [2 dc, ch 4, 2 dc] into next dc; rep from * to last 19 sts, 1 dc into each of next 19 dc, join with sl st to 3rd of ch 3.

ROUND 7: Ch 1, 1 sc into each dc in previous round, working [2 sc, ch 1, 2 sc] into each ch 4 corner sp, join with sl st into first sc.

ROUND 8: Ch 1, 1 sc into each sc in previous round, working ch 2 at each corner, join with sl st into first sc. Fasten off yarn.

102 COLOR SCHEME Brown, oatmeal and other colors derived from nature are perennial favorites for home furnishings.

103 COLOR SCHEME: Changing the yarn colors to bright pastel shades surrounded by cream makes the perfect block for a baby afghan.

104 COLOR SCHEME: Two stripes worked in shades of dark blue show up well against the main turquoise yarn and add an extra zing to the pattern.

OTHER COLOR SCHEMES

102

103

104

OTHER COLOR SCHEMES

106 Ⓐ Ⓑ Ⓒ Ⓓ

107 Ⓐ Ⓑ Ⓒ Ⓓ

108 Ⓐ Ⓑ Ⓒ Ⓓ

FOUNDATION CHAIN: Using yarn A, ch 29.

ROW 1: *(wrong side)* Work 1 sc into 2nd ch from hook, work 1 sc into each chain along row, turn. *(28 sc)*

ROW 2: Ch 1, work 1 sc into each st along row, turn.

Rep row 2 7 times. Break off yarn A. Join yarn B and rep row 2 twice. Break off yarn B.

Join yarn C and rep row 2 twice. Break off yarn C.

Join yarn D and rep row 2 21 times. Break off yarn D.

Fasten off yarn.

106 COLOR SCHEME: Soft, neutral shades combine well in this block which would look good displayed against pine or other light wood furniture.

107 COLOR SCHEME: Change the color balance of the original block by using a dark color to work the lower section of the block.

108 COLOR SCHEME: Pastel shades of pink, mauve and blue show up well against the deep band of cream at the top of the block.

105

Double Stripes

1 ≣

Ⓐ Ⓑ Ⓒ Ⓓ

MIX-AND-MATCH

23 **142** **210**

OTHER COLOR SCHEMES

109

110

Four Square

1 📷

MIX-AND-MATCH

FOUNDATION RING: Using yarn A, ch 4 and join with sl st to form a ring.

ROUND 1: Ch 1, 12 sc into ring, join with sl st into first sc.

ROUND 2: Ch 1, 1 sc into first sc, *3 sc into next sc, 1 sc into each of next 2 sc; rep from * ending last rep with 1 sc, join with sl st to first sc. *(Four corners made)*

ROUND 3: Ch 1, 1 sc into each of next 2 sc, *3 sc into next sc, 1 sc into each of next 4 sc; rep from * ending last rep with 2 sc, join with sl st to first sc.

ROUND 4: Ch 1, 1 sc into each of next 3 sc, *3 sc into next sc, 1 sc into each of next 6 sc; rep from * ending last rep with 3 sc, join with sl st to first sc.

Cont working rounds in the same way, working 2 more sc along each side of the square. After 3 more rounds have been worked, break off yarn A. *(12 sc along each side)*

Join yarn B and work one round. *(14 sc along each side)* Break off yarn B.

Join yarn C and work two rounds. *(18 sc along each side)* Break off yarn C.

Join yarn D and work five rounds. *(28 sc along each side)*

Fasten off yarn.

110 COLOR SCHEME: Warm shades of coral and eggplant combine well with cool shades of green and oatmeal with the darkest color placed at the center.

111 COLOR SCHEME: The large area of soft turquoise worked at the start of this block draws the eye immediately towards the center of the block.

112 COLOR SCHEME: A single stripe of bright yellow provides a strong contrast to the rather ordinary color scheme of three shades of blue.

111

112

OTHER COLOR SCHEMES

114

115

116

Special abbreviations

beg cl = beginning cluster made from 2 dc sts, **cl** = cluster made from 3 dc sts

FOUNDATION RING: Using yarn A, ch 4 and join with sl st to form a ring.

ROUND 1: Ch 3 *(counts as 1 dc)*, beg cl into ring, ch 5, *cl into ring, ch 2, **cl into ring, ch 5; rep from * twice and from * to ** once again, join with sl st into 3rd of ch 3. Break off yarn A.

ROUND 2: Join yarn B to any ch 5 corner sp, ch 3 *(counts as 1 dc)*, [beg cl, ch 2, cl] into same sp, *ch 2, 3 dc into next ch 2 sp, ch 2, **[cl, ch 2, cl] into next ch 5 sp; rep from * twice and from * to ** once again, join with sl st into 3rd of ch 3.

ROUND 3: Sl st into next ch 2 corner sp, ch 3 *(counts as 1 dc)*, [beg cl, ch 2, cl] into same sp, *ch 2, 2 dc into next ch 2 sp, 1 dc into each of next 3 dc, 2 dc into next ch 2 sp, ch 2, **[cl, ch 2, cl] into next ch 2 sp; rep from * twice and from * to ** once again, join with sl st into 3rd of ch 3. Break off yarn B.

ROUND 4: Join yarn C into any ch 2 corner sp, ch 3 *(counts as 1 dc)*, [beg cl, ch 2, cl] into same sp, *ch 2, 2 dc into next ch 2 sp, 1 dc into each of next 7 dc, 2 dc into next ch 2 sp, ch 2, **[cl, ch 2, cl] into next ch 2 sp; rep from * twice and from * to ** once again, join with sl st into 3rd of ch 3. Break off yarn C.

ROUND 5: Join yarn D into any ch 2 corner sp, ch 3 *(counts as 1 dc)*, [beg cl, ch 3, cl] into same sp, *ch 2, 2 dc into next ch 2 sp, 1 dc into each of next 11 dc, 2 dc into next ch 2 sp, ch 2, **[cl, ch 3, cl] into next ch 2 sp; rep from * twice and from * to ** once again, join with sl

st into 3rd of ch 3.

ROUND 6: Sl st into next ch 3 corner sp, ch 3 *(counts as 1 dc)*, [beg cl, ch 3, cl] into same sp, *ch 2, 2 dc into next ch 2 sp, 1 dc into each of next 15 dc, 2 dc into next ch 2 sp, ch 2, ** [cl, ch 3, cl] into next ch 3 sp; rep from * twice and from * to ** once again, join with sl st into 3rd of ch 3.

ROUND 7: Ch 1, 1 sc into same place, work 1 sc into each dc and the top of each cl of previous round, working 2 sc into each ch 2 sp and [2 sc, ch 1, 2 sc] into each ch 3 corner sp, join with sl st into first sc.
Fasten off yarn.

113

Wisteria

11

MIX-AND-MATCH

 37 40   88

115 COLOR SCHEME: Purples and a dusky pink work well together in this block while the single stripe of soft, cool green adds a welcome note of contrast.

116 COLOR SCHEME: The pale blue flower motif draws the eye inwards toward the center of this strongly patterned block.

114 COLOR SCHEME: This block features an unusual colorway, combining coral and aubergine with vibrant lime green and pale oatmeal.

117

Granny in the Middle

1

MIX-AND-MATCH

57 59 92

FOUNDATION RING: Using yarn A, ch 6 and join with sl st to form a ring.

ROUND 1: Ch 3 *(counts as 1 dc)*, 2 dc into ring, ch 3, *3 dc into ring, ch 3; rep from * twice more, join with sl st into 3rd of ch 3. Break off yarn A.

ROUND 2: Join yarn B to any ch 3 sp, ch 3, [2 dc, ch 3, 3 dc] into same sp to make corner, *ch 1, [3 dc, ch 3, 3 dc] into next ch 3 sp to make corner; rep from * twice more, ch 1, join with sl st into 3rd of ch 3. Break off yarn B.

ROUND 3: Join yarn C to any ch 3 corner sp, ch 3, [2 dc, ch 3, 3 dc] into same sp, *ch 1, 3 dc into ch sp, ch 1, [3 dc, ch 3, 3 dc] into corner sp; rep from * to end, ending with ch 1, join with sl st into 3rd of ch 3. Break off yarn C.

ROUND 4: Join yarn D to any ch 3 corner sp, ch 3, [2 dc, ch 3, 3 dc] into same sp, *[ch 1, 3 dc into each ch sp] along side of square, ch 1, [3 dc, ch 3, 3 dc] into corner sp; rep from * to end, ending with ch 1, sl st into

3rd of ch 3. Break off yarn D.

ROUND 5: Join yarn E to any ch 3 corner sp, ch 3, [2 dc, ch 3, 3 dc] into same sp, *[ch 1, 3 dc into each ch sp] along side of square, ch 1, [3 dc, ch 3, 3 dc] into corner sp; rep from * to end, ending with ch 1, sl st into 3rd of ch 3.

ROUND 6: Ch 1, work 1 sc into each dc of previous round, working 5 sc into each ch 3 corner sp and 1 sc into each ch 1 sp, join with sl st into first sc.

ROUND 7: Ch 1, 1 sc into each sc of previous round, working 3 sc into center st of each 5 sc corner group, join with sl st into first sc. Break off yarn E.

ROUND 8: Join yarn D, ch 1, 1 sc into each sc of previous round, working 3 sc into center st of each 3 sc corner group, join with sl st into first sc. Break off yarn D.

ROUND 9: Join yarn C and rep round 8. Fasten off yarn.

118 COLOR SCHEME: Cool colors such as turquoise and lavender combine well with a cool blue-toned gray and the result is very easy on the eye.

119 COLOR SCHEME: This variation on the classic granny square uses a palette of colors graduating outwards from pale pink to dark purple.

120 COLOR SCHEME: Unlike those used in the blocks 118 and 119, the colors in this scheme are of a similar mid-tone and this gives a different effect to the pattern.

OTHER COLOR SCHEMES

118 A B C D E

119 A B C D E

120 A B C D E

OTHER COLOR SCHEMES

122 Ⓐ Ⓑ Ⓒ Ⓓ

123 Ⓐ Ⓑ Ⓒ Ⓓ

124 Ⓐ Ⓑ Ⓒ Ⓓ

FOUNDATION ROW: Using yarn A, ch 6.

ROW 1: Insert hook into 4th ch from hook, work 3 dc, turn.

ROW 2: Ch 3 *(counts as 1 dc)*, 1 dc into each of next 2 dc, 4 dc into loop made by turning ch of previous row, turn.

ROW 3: Ch 3 *(counts as 1 dc)*, 1 dc into each of next 2 dc, [2 dc, ch 2, 2 dc into next dc, 1 dc into each of next 2 dc, 1 dc into 3rd of ch 3, turn.

ROW 4: Ch 3 *(counts as 1 dc)*, 1 dc into each of next 4 dc, [2 dc, ch 2, 2 dc] into ch 2 sp, 1 dc into each of next 4 dc, 1 dc into 3rd of ch 3, turn. Break off yarn A.

ROW 5: Join yarn B, ch 3 *(counts as 1 dc)*, 1 dc into each of next 6 dc, [2 dc, ch 2, 2 dc] into ch 2 sp, 1 dc into each of next 6 dc, 1 dc into 3rd of ch 3, turn. Break off yarn B.

ROW 6: Join yarn A, ch 3 *(counts as 1 dc)*, 1 dc into each of next 8 dc, [2 dc, ch 2, 2 dc] into ch 2 sp, 1 dc into each of next 8 dc, 1 dc into 3rd of ch 3, turn.

ROW 7: Ch 3 *(counts as 1 dc)*, 1 dc into each of next 10 dc, [2 dc, ch 2, 2 dc] into ch 2 sp, 1 dc into each of next 10 dc, 1 dc into 3rd of ch 3, turn. Break off yarn A.

ROW 8: Join yarn C, ch 3 *(counts as 1 dc)*, 1 dc into each of next 12 dc, [2 dc, ch 2, 2 dc] into ch 2 sp, 1 dc into each of next 12 dc, 1 dc into 3rd of ch 3, turn. Break off yarn C.

ROW 9: Join yarn A, ch 3 *(counts as 1 dc)*, 1 dc into each of next 14 dc, [2 dc, ch 2, 2 dc] into ch 2 sp, 1 dc into each of next 14 dc, 1 dc into 3rd of ch 3, turn.

ROW 10: Ch 3 *(counts as 1 dc)*, 1 dc into each of next 16 dc, [2 dc, ch 2, 2 dc] into ch 2 sp, 1 dc into each of next 16 dc, 1

121

dc into 3rd of ch 3, turn. Break off yarn A.

ROW 11: Join yarn D, ch 3 *(counts as 1 dc)*, 1 dc into each of next 18 dc, [2 dc, ch 2, 2 dc] into ch 2 sp, 1 dc into each of next 18 dc, 1 dc into 3rd of ch 3. Break off yarn D.

ROW 12: Join yarn A, ch 3 *(counts as 1 dc)*, 1 dc into each of next 20 dc, [2 dc, ch 2, 2 dc] into ch 2 sp, 1 dc into each of next 20 dc, 1 dc into 3rd of ch 3, turn.

ROW 13: Ch 3 *(counts as 1 dc)*, 1 dc into each of next 22 dc, [2 dc, ch 2, 2 dc] into ch 2 sp, 1 dc into each of next 22 dc, 1 dc into 3rd of ch 3, turn.

ROW 14: Ch 3 *(counts as 1 dc)*, 1 dc into each of next 24 dc, 5 dc into ch 2 sp, 1 dc into each of next 24 dc, 1 dc into 3rd of ch 3.

Fasten off yarn.

122 **COLOR SCHEME:** Most neutral shades, including pale grays and beige, look best when combined with a selection of stronger, brighter colors.

Coral Seas

1 ⊜

Ⓐ Ⓑ Ⓒ Ⓓ

MIX-AND-MATCH

 9 **11** **89**

123 **COLOR SCHEME:** A single stripe worked in bright pink close to one corner adds a note of crisp contrast to the subtle, rather sombre shades used for this color scheme.

124 **COLOR SCHEME:** Changing the position of the strongly colored stripe changes the emphasis of the striped pattern.

125

Triple Stripes

1

MIX-AND-MATCH

 119 **148** **197**

FOUNDATION CHAIN: Using yarn A, ch 29.

ROW 1: *(wrong side)* Work 1 sc into 2nd ch from hook, work 1 sc into each chain along row, turn. *(28 sc)*

ROW 2: Ch 1, work 1 sc into each st along row, turn.

Rep row 2 15 times. Break off yarn A. Join yarn B and rep row 2 four times. Break off yarn B.

Join yarn C and rep row 2 twice. Break off yarn C.

Join yarn D and rep row 2 four times. Break off yarn D.

Join yarn A and rep row 2 seven times. Fasten off yarn.

126 **COLOR SCHEME:** This color scheme combined with the crisp pattern of contrasting horizontal stripes makes a bold, modern statement.

127 **COLOR SCHEME:** Change the appearance of the block by choosing dark colors for the background and thin middle stripe and warm colors for the wider stripes.

128 **COLOR SCHEME:** Soft, pretty and very feminine, this color combination would also look good used to make an unusual baby afghan.

OTHER COLOR SCHEMES

126

127

128

OTHER COLOR SCHEMES

130 Ⓐ Ⓑ Ⓒ Ⓓ Ⓔ

131 Ⓐ Ⓑ Ⓒ Ⓓ Ⓔ

132 Ⓐ Ⓑ Ⓒ Ⓓ Ⓔ

FOUNDATION RING: Using yarn A, ch 4 and join with sl st to form a ring.

ROUND 1: Ch 3 *(counts as 1 dc)*, 3 dc into ring, ch 1, *4 dc into ring, ch 1; rep from * twice, join with sl st into 3rd of ch 3. Break off yarn A.

ROUND 2: Join yarn B to any ch 1 sp, ch 3 *(counts as 1 dc)*, [3 dc, ch 1, 4 dc] into next ch 1 sp *(corner made)*, ch 1, *[4 dc, ch 1, 4 dc into next ch 1 sp, ch 1; rep from * twice, join with sl st into 3rd of ch 3. *(Four corners made)* Break off yarn B.

ROUND 3: Join yarn C, ch 1, 1 sc into same place, 1 sc into each dc and ch 1 sp of previous round, join with sl st into first sc. Break off yarn C.

ROUND 4: Join yarn D into any corner sc, ch 3 *(counts as 1 dc)*, [3 dc, ch 1, 4 dc] into same sc, ch 1, *skip 4 sc, [2 dc, ch 1, 2 dc] into next sc, ch 1, skip 4 sc, **[4 dc, ch 1, 4 dc] into next sc, ch 1; rep from * twice and from * to ** once again, join with sl st into 3rd of ch 3. Break off yarn D.

ROUND 5: Join yarn E to first dc of any corner group, ch 3 *(counts as 1 dc)*, work 1 dc into each dc of previous round, working 1 dc into each ch 1 sp along sides of square and [2 dc, ch 1, 2 dc] into each ch 1 corner sp, join with sl st into 3rd of ch 3.

ROUNDS 6 & 7: Ch 3 *(counts as 1 dc)*, work 1 dc into each dc of previous round, working [2 dc, ch 1, 2 dc] into each ch 1 corner sp, join with sl st into 3rd of ch 3.
Fasten off yarn.

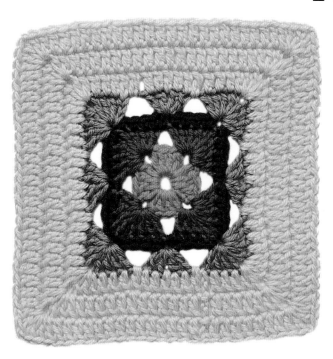

129

Anemone

1 📷
Ⓐ Ⓑ **Ⓒ** Ⓓ Ⓔ

130 COLOR SCHEME: The dark background color makes the bright tones of the flower motif stand out and show off the pattern of the block.

131 COLOR SCHEME: The rather masculine colors of this block would be perfect for the study, set against leather or tweed upholstery.

132 COLOR SCHEME: An afghan worked in corals and soft green would look pretty thrown over a rocking chair in a Victorian-style bedroom.

MIX-AND-MATCH

103 **111** **185**

OTHER COLOR SCHEMES

Sunshine Stripes

MIX-AND-MATCH

Special abbreviation

sc3tog = decrease 2 sts by working the next 3 sc together

FOUNDATION CHAIN: Using yarn A, ch 58.

FOUNDATION ROW: *(wrong side)* 1 sc into 2nd ch from hook, 1 sc into each ch, turn. *(57 sc)*

ROW 1: Ch 1, 1 sc into each of next 27 sc, sc3tog, 1 sc into each of rem 27 sc, turn. *(55 sc)*

ROW 2: Ch 1, 1 sc into each of next 26 sc, sc3tog, 1 sc into each of rem 26 sc, turn. *(53 sc)*

ROW 3: Ch 1, 1 sc into each of next 25 sc, sc3tog, 1 sc into each of rem 25 sc, turn. *(51 sc)*

ROW 4: Ch 1, 1 sc into each of next 24 sc, sc3tog, 1 sc into each of rem 24 sc, turn. *(49 sc)* Break off yarn A.

Join yarn B. Cont in pattern as set, working sc3tog over 3 center sts on every row. At the same time, change yarn colors in the following color sequence: Work 2 rows in yarn B, 4 rows in yarn A, 2 rows in yarn B. Join yarn A and cont in pattern until 3 sc rem.

NEXT ROW: Work sc3tog.
Fasten off yarn.

134 **COLOR SCHEME:** Mid and light blue are a good color combination for a baby boy's afghan. For a girl, substitute mid and light shades of pink.

135 **COLOR SCHEME:** Changing the colors to simple mid gray stripes contrasting with a plain cream background gives this block an almost minimalist style.

136 **COLOR SCHEME:** Art Deco colors of hot orange and creamy yellow work well on this block decorated with twin L-shaped stripes.

137

OTHER COLOR SCHEMES

138 Ⓐ Ⓑ Ⓒ Ⓓ

139 Ⓐ Ⓑ Ⓒ Ⓓ

140 Ⓐ Ⓑ Ⓒ Ⓓ

FOUNDATION RING: Using yarn A, ch 6, and join with sl st to form a ring.

ROUND 1: Ch 3 *(counts as 1 dc)*, 3 dc into ring, ch 3, [4 dc into ring, ch 3] 3 times, join with sl st into 3rd of ch 3.

ROUND 2: Ch 5 *(counts as 1 dc, ch 2)*, *skip next 2 dc, 1 dc into next dc, [2 dc, ch 3, 2 dc] into next ch 3 sp, **1 dc into next dc; rep from * twice and from * to ** once again, join with sl st into 3rd of ch 5. Break off yarn A.

ROUND 3: Join yarn B to dc before ch 2 sp, ch 5 *(counts as 1 dc, ch 2)*, *1 dc into each of next 3 dc, [2 dc, ch 3, 2 dc] into next ch 3 sp, **1 dc into each of next 3 dc, ch 2; rep from * twice and from * to ** once again, 1 dc into each of next 2 dc, join with sl st into 3rd of ch 5.

ROUND 4: Ch 5 *(counts as 1 dc, ch 2)*, *1 dc into each of next 5 dc, [2 dc, ch 3, 2 dc] into next ch 3 sp, **1 dc into each of next 5 dc, ch 2; rep from * twice and from * to ** once again, 1 dc into each of next 4 dc, join with sl st into 3rd of ch 5. Break off yarn B.

ROUND 5: Join yarn C to dc before ch 2 sp, ch 5 *(counts as 1 dc, ch 2)*, *1 dc into each of next 7 dc, [2 dc, ch 3, 2 dc] into next ch 3 sp, **1 dc into each of next 7 dc, ch 2; rep from * twice and from * to ** once again, 1 dc into each of next 6 dc, join with sl st into 3rd of ch 3. Break off yarn C.

ROUND 6: Join yarn D to dc before ch 2 sp, ch 5 *(counts as 1 dc, ch 2)*, *1 dc into each of next 9 dc, [2 dc, ch 3, 2 dc] into next ch 3 sp, **1 dc into each of next 9 dc, ch 2; rep from * twice and from * to ** once again, 1 dc into each of next 8 dc, join with sl st into 3rd of ch 3.

ROUND 7: Ch 1, 1 sc into same place, work 1 sc into each dc of previous round, working 2 sc into each ch 2 sp and [2 sc, ch 2, 2 sc] into each ch 3 corner sp.

Fasten off yarn.

Criss Cross

1

Ⓐ Ⓑ Ⓒ Ⓓ

138 **COLOR SCHEME:** This color scheme uses cool shades of blue, turquoise and purple to make a calm and restful visual statement.

139 **COLOR SCHEME:** Cream, oatmeal and gray are a classic color combination, which enhances the simple striped pattern of this easy-to-crochet block.

140 **COLOR SCHEME:** Warm shades of yellow, orange and fuchsia pink framed with dark red combine well to make a bright, modern block.

MIX-AND-MATCH

 46

 63

 203

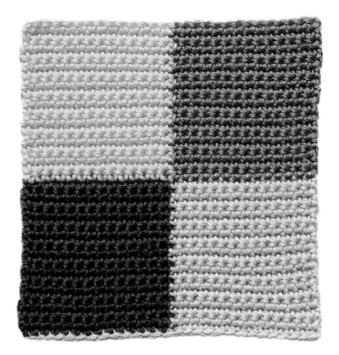

141

142

Quartet

11

A B C D

143

MIX-AND-MATCH

11 **207** **211**

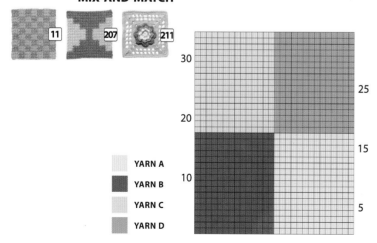

YARN A
YARN B
YARN C
YARN D

FOUNDATION CHAIN: Using yarn A, ch 29.

WORKING THE PATTERN: When following the chart, read odd-numbered rows (right side rows) from right to left and even-numbered rows (wrong side rows) from left to right.
Starting at the bottom right-hand corner of the chart, work the 34 row

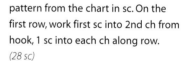

pattern from the chart in sc. On the first row, work first sc into 2nd ch from hook, 1 sc into each ch along row.
(28 sc)

Fasten off yarn.

142 COLOR SCHEME: Another symmetrical arrangement of two dark squares set diagonally opposite each other and combined with two paler squares.

143 COLOR SCHEME: The symmetrical appearance of the block changes here, by simply contrasting one dark square against three squares worked in mid tones.

144 COLOR SCHEME: Squares worked in variegated yarns look good when set next to squares of matching solid color. The four squares are arranged symmetrically in this block.

144

OTHER COLOR SCHEMES

146

147

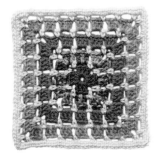

148

FOUNDATION RING: Using yarn A, ch 4, and join with sl st to form a ring.

ROUND 1: Ch 3 *(counts as 1 dc)*, 2 dc into ring, ch 2, *3 dc into ring, ch 2; rep from * twice, join with sl st into 3rd of ch 3. Break off yarn A.

ROUND 2: Join yarn B to any ch 2 sp, ch 1, [1 sc, ch 3, 1 sc] into same sp, ch 3, *[1 sc, ch 3, 1 sc] into next ch 2 sp, ch 3; rep from * twice, join with sl st to first sc. *(Four corners made)* Break off yarn B.

ROUND 3: Join yarn C to any ch 3 corner sp, ch 3 *(counts as 1 dc)*, [2 dc, ch 3, 3 dc] into same sp, ch 1, 3 dc into next 3 ch sp, ch 1, *[3 dc, ch 3, 3 dc] into next ch 3 corner sp, ch 1, 3 dc into next ch 3 sp, ch 1; rep from * twice, join with sl st into 3rd of ch 3. Break off yarn C.

ROUND 4: Join yarn B to any ch 3 corner sp, ch 1, [1 sc, ch 3, 1 sc] into same sp, ch 3, [1 sc into next ch 1 sp, ch 3] twice, *[1 sc, ch 3, 1 sc] into next ch 3 corner sp, ch 3, [1 sc into next ch 1 sp, ch 3] twice; rep from * twice, join with sl st into first sc. Break off yarn B.

ROUND 5: Join yarn D to any ch 3 corner sp, ch 3 *(counts as 1 dc)*, [2 dc, ch 3, 3 dc] into same sp, ch 1, [3 dc into next ch 3 sp, ch 1] 3 times, *[3 dc, ch 3, 3 dc] into next ch 3 corner sp, ch 1, [3 dc into next ch 3 sp, ch 1] 3 times; rep from * twice, join with sl st into 3rd of ch 3. Break off yarn D.

ROUND 6: Join yarn B to any ch 3 corner sp, ch 1, [1 sc, ch 3, 1 sc] into same sp, ch 3, [1 sc into next ch 1 sp, ch 3] 4 times, *[1 sc, ch 3, 1 sc] into next ch 3 corner sp, ch 3, [1 sc into next ch 1 sp, ch 3] 4 times; rep from * twice, join with sl st into first sc. Break off yarn B.

ROUND 7: Join yarn E to any ch 3 corner sp, ch 3 *(counts as 1 dc)*, [2dc, ch 3, 3 dc] into same sp, ch 1, [3 dc into

next 3 ch sp, ch 1] 5 times, *[3 dc, ch 3, 3 dc] into next ch 3 corner sp, ch 1, [3 dc into next ch 3 sp, ch 1] 5 times; rep from * twice, join with sl st into 3rd of ch 3. Break off yarn E.

ROUND 8: Join yarn B to any ch 3 corner sp, ch 1, [1 sc, ch 3, 1 sc] into same sp, ch 3, [1 sc into next ch 1 sp, ch 3] 6 times, *[1 sc, ch 3, 1 sc] into next ch 3 corner sp, ch 3, [1 sc into next ch 1 sp, ch 3] 6 times; rep from * twice, join with sl st into first sc.

ROUND 9: Ch 1, 1 sc in same place, work 1 sc into each sc of previous round and 3 sc into each ch 3 sp along sides of square, working 5 sc into each ch 3 corner sp, join with sl st to first sc. Fasten off yarn.

146 **COLOR SCHEME:** An unusual color scheme of blues, greens and pale turquoise shows the block's pattern off to great effect.

145

Chocolate Box

1

MIX-AND-MATCH

 58 92 192

147 **COLOR SCHEME:** Strong, jewel tones zing when surrounded with the very dark berry color used as the main contrast.

148 **COLOR SCHEME:** The main contrast has been changed completely from a very dark color to pale cream.

149

Solid Square

1

FOUNDATION RING: Using yarn A, ch 4 and join with sl st to form a ring.

ROUND 1: Ch 3 *(counts as 1 dc)*, 11 dc into ring, join with sl st into 3rd of ch 3. *(12 dc)*

ROUND 2: Ch 3 *(counts as 1 dc)*, *[2 dc, 1 tr] into next dc, [1 tr, 2 dc] into next dc, **1dc into next dc; rep from * twice and from * to ** once again, join with sl st into 3rd of ch 3. Break off yarn A.

ROUND 3: Join yarn B, ch 3 *(counts as 1 dc)*, 1 dc into each of next 2 dc, *[2 dc, 1 tr] into next tr, [1 tr, 2 dc] into next tr, **1dc into each of next 5 dc; rep from * twice and from * to ** once again, 1 dc into each of next 2 dc, join with sl st into 3rd of ch 3. Break off yarn B.

ROUND 4: Join yarn C, ch 3 *(counts as 1 dc)*, 1 dc into each of next 4 dc, *[2 dc, 1 tr] into next tr, [1 tr, 2 dc] into next tr, **1dc into each of next 9 dc; rep from * twice and from * to ** once again, 1dc into each of next 4 dc, join with sl st into 3rd of ch 3. Break off yarn C.

ROUND 5: Join yarn B, ch 3 *(counts as 1 dc)*, 1 dc into each of next 6 dc, *[2 dc, 1 tr] into next tr, [1 tr, 2 dc] into next tr, **1dc into each of next 13 dc; rep from * twice and from * to ** once again, 1 dc into each of next 6 dc, join with sl st into 3rd of ch 3. Break off yarn B.

ROUND 6: Join yarn A, ch 3 *(counts as 1 dc)*, 1 dc into each of next 8 dc, *[2 dc, 1 tr] into next tr, [1 tr, 2 dc] into next tr, **1 dc into each of next 17 dc; rep from * twice and from * to ** once again, 1 dc into each of next 8 dc, join with sl st into 3rd of ch 3.

ROUND 7: Ch 1, 1 sc into same place, 1 sc into each dc of previous round, working [2 sc, 1 hdc] into first tr of each corner group and [1 hdc, 2 sc] into last tr of each corner group, join with sl st into first dc.

Fasten off yarn.

MIX-AND-MATCH

13 **73** **185**

OTHER COLOR SCHEMES

150 A B C

151 A B C

152 A B C

150 COLOR SCHEME: Neutral shades of gray and camel are always a popular color choice but look even better when combined with a light color such as cream or white.

151 COLOR SCHEME: Bright, clashing colors make a strong statement in this block, with the striped pattern showing off the color arrangement well.

152 COLOR SCHEME: Strong shades of blue and green work well together in this easy-to-make block featuring a strong pattern of stripes.

OTHER COLOR SCHEMES

154

155

156

Special abbreviation

MB = make bobble (work 4 open dc in same st leaving 5 loops on hook, draw yarn through all 5 loops at once)

FOUNDATION CHAIN: Using yarn A, ch 28.

FOUNDATION ROW: *(wrong side)* Working first sc into 2nd ch from hook, work 1 sc into each ch, turn. *(27 sc)*

ROW 1: Ch 1, 1 sc into each sc, turn.

ROW 2: Ch 1, 1 sc into each of next 10 sc, *MB, 1 sc into each of next 2 sc; rep from * once, MB, 1 sc into each of next 10 sc, turn. Break off yarn A.

Join yarn B, rep row 1 3 times. Break off yarn B.

Join yarn C, rep row 2, then rep row 1 twice. Break off yarn C.

Join yarn D, rep row 1, then rep row 2, then rep row 1. Break off yarn D.

Join yarn B, rep row 1 twice, then rep row 2. Break off yarn B.

Join yarn C, rep row 1 3 times. Break off yarn C.

Join yarn B, rep row 2, then rep row 1 twice. Break off yarn B.

Join yarn D, rep row 1, then rep row 2, then rep row 1. Break off yarn D.

Join yarn C, rep row 1 twice, then rep row 2. Break off yarn C.

Join yarn B, rep row 1 3 times. Break off yarn B.

Join yarn A, rep row 2, then rep row 1 twice.

Fasten off yarn.

153

Candy Stripe Bobbles

MIX-AND-MATCH

 15 **33** **34**

154 **COLOR SCHEME:** Another color scheme based on the neutral palette features in this block where rows of bobbles offer a change of texture at the center.

155 **COLOR SCHEME:** Lots of texture from the regimented rows of bobbles running down the center of the block contrasts strongly with the bright colors.

156 **COLOR SCHEME:** Bright shades of royal blue and jade combine well with softer shades of blue and green to make this lovely color scheme.

157

Boxed Square

1

MIX-AND-MATCH

170 **184** **203**

FOUNDATION RING: Using yarn A, ch 4 and join with sl st to form a ring.

ROUND 1: Ch 1, 12 sc into ring, join with sl st into first sc.

ROUND 2: Ch 1, 1 sc into first sc, *3 sc into next sc, 1 sc into each of next 2 sc; rep from * ending last rep with 1 sc, join with sl st to first sc. *(Four corners made)*

ROUND 3: Ch 1, 1 sc into each of next 2 sc, *3 sc into next sc, 1 sc into each of next 4 sc; rep from * ending last rep with 2 sc, join with sl st to first sc.

ROUND 4: Ch 1, 1 sc into each of next 3 sc, *3 sc into next sc, 1 sc into each of next 6 sc; rep from * ending last rep with 3 sc, join with sl st to first sc. Cont working rounds in the same way, working 2 more sc along each side of the square. After 6 more rounds have been worked, break off yarn A. *(18 sc along each side)*

Join yarn B and work two rounds. *(22 sc along each side)* Break off yarn B.

Join yarn C and work three rounds. *(28 sc along each side)*

Fasten off yarn.

158 COLOR SCHEME: Soft, subtle shades of green combined with pale turquoise make an unusual color scheme for a baby's room.

159 COLOR SCHEME: Three shades of the same color look good when the darkest shade is used to frame the block.

160 COLOR SCHEME: Change the effect of this block by using the darkest shade at the centre, graduating to the lightest shade round the outside.

OTHER COLOR SCHEMES

158

159

160

OTHER COLOR SCHEMES

 A B C

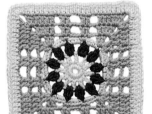

 A B C

 A B C

Special abbreviations

beg cl = beginning cluster made from 2 dc sts, **cl** = cluster made from 3 dc sts

FOUNDATION RING: Using yarn A, ch 6 and join with sl st to form a ring.

ROUND 1: Ch 1, 12 sc into ring, join with sl st into first sc.

ROUND 2: Ch 4 *(counts as 1 dc, ch 1)*, *1 dc into next sc, ch 1; rep from * 10 times, join with sl st into 3rd of ch 4. *(12 spaced dc)* Break off yarn A.

ROUND 3: Join yarn B to any ch 1 sp, ch 3 *(counts as 1 dc)*, beg cl into same sp, ch 3, *cl into next ch 1 sp, ch 3; rep from * 10 times, join with sl st into top of beg cl. *(12 clusters)* Break off yarn B.

ROUND 4: Join yarn A to any ch 3 sp, ch 1, 4 sc into same sp, 4 sc into each rem ch 3 sp, join with sl st into first sc. Break off yarn A.

ROUND 5: Join yarn C into top of any cl, ch 3 *(counts as 1 dc)*, [1 dc, ch 2, 2 dc] into same place, *ch 2, skip next 4 sc group, 2 sc into sp above next cl, ch 3, skip next 4 sc group, 2 sc into sp above next cl, skip next 4 sc group, **[2 dc, ch 2, 2 dc] into sp above next cl; rep from * twice and from * to ** once again, join with sl st into 3rd of ch 3.

ROUND 6: Ch 3 *(counts as 1 dc)*, 1 dc into next dc, *[2 dc, ch 2, 2 dc] into ch 2 corner sp, 1 dc into each of next 2 dc, ch 2, 1 dc into each of next 2 sc, ch 3, 1 dc into each of next 2 sc, ch 2, **1 dc into each of next 2 dc; rep from * twice and from * to ** once again, join with sl st into 3rd of ch 3.

ROUND 7: Ch 3 *(counts as 1 dc)*, 1 dc into each of next 3 dc, *[2 dc, ch 3, 2 dc] into ch 2 corner sp, 1 dc into each of next 4 dc, ch 2, 1 dc into each of next 2 dc, ch 3, 1 dc into each of next 2 dc, ch 2, **1 dc into each of next 4 dc; rep from * twice and from * to ** once again, join with sl st into 3rd of ch 3. Break off yarn C.

ROUND 8: Join yarn A, ch 3 *(counts as 1 dc)*, work 1 dc into each dc and ch of previous round, working 5 dc into each ch 3 corner sp, join with sl st into 3rd of ch 3.

Fasten off yarn.

161

Daisy Chain

11

A B C

MIX-AND-MATCH

 18 **31** **137**

162 COLOR SCHEME: The two lightest colors from block 158 are enhanced by a strong turquoise to make a good choice for the nursery.

163 COLOR SCHEME: Two shades of blue combine well with a soft, buttery yellow to show off the intricate center of this block.

164 COLOR SCHEME: Amethyst and lavender are highlighted with a variegated yarn to make the perfect color choice for a bed throw in a pretty, feminine bedroom.

Coffee & Cream

11

MIX-AND-MATCH

47 94 95

FOUNDATION RING: Using yarn A, ch 6, and join with sl st to form a ring.

ROUND 1: Ch 3 *(counts as 1 dc)*, 3 dc into ring, *ch 2, 4 dc into ring; rep from * twice, ch 2, join with sl st into 3rd of ch 3.

ROUND 2: Sl st in next dc and then between same dc and next dc, ch 1, 1 sc into same place, 9 dc into next ch 2 sp *(corner made)*, *skip next dc,

1 sc between next 2 dc, 9 dc into next ch 2 sp; rep from * twice, join with sl st into first sc. Break off yarn A.

ROUND 3: Join yarn B to any sc, ch 3 *(counts as 1 dc)*, 1 dc into same place, * ch 2, skip 2 dc, 1 hdc into each of next 2 dc, 3 dc into next dc, 1 hdc into each of next 2 dc, ch 2, **skip next 2 dc, 2 dc into next sc; rep from * twice and from * to ** once again, ch 2, skip 2 dc, join with sl st into 3rd of ch 3.

ROUND 4: Ch 1, 1 sc into same place, 1 sc into next dc, *2 sc into next ch 2 sp, 1 sc into each of next 2 hdc, 1 sc into next dc, ch 4, skip 1 dc, 1 sc into next dc, 1 sc into each of next 2 hdc, 2 sc into ch 2 sp; **1 dc into each of next 2 dc; rep from * twice and from * to ** once again, join with sl st into first sc. Break off yarn B.

ROUND 5: Join yarn C to any ch 4 sp, ch 3 *(counts as 1 dc)*, 8 dc into same sp, * skip 2 sc, 1 sc into next sc, ch 2, skip 2 sc, 1 sc into each of next 2 sc, ch 2, skip

2 sc, 1 sc into next sc, skip 2 sc, **9 dc into next ch 4 sp; rep from * twice and from * to ** once again, join with sl st into 3rd of ch 3.

ROUND 6: Ch 1, 1 sc into same place, 1 sc into each of next 3 dc, [1 hdc, 1 dc, 1 hdc] into next dc, 1 sc into each of next 4 dc, *1 sc into next sc, ch 2, 1 sc into each of next 2 dc, ch 2, 1 sc into next sc, **1 sc into each of next 4 dc, [1 hdc, 1 dc, 1 hdc] into next dc, 1 sc into each of next 4 dc; rep from * twice and from * to ** once again, join with sl st into first sc.

ROUND 7: Ch 1, 1 sc into same place, 1 sc into each of next 4 sc, *1 sc into next hdc, 3 sc into next dc, 1 sc into next hdc, 1 sc into each of next 5 sc, ch 2, 1 sc into each of next 2 sc, ch 2, **1 sc into each of next 5 sc; rep from * twice and from * to ** once again, 1 sc into next sc, join with sl st into first sc.

ROUND 8: Ch 3 *(counts as 1 dc)*, 1 dc into each of next 5 sc, *5 dc into next sc, 1 dc into each of next 7 sc, ch 2, 1 dc into each of next 2 sc, ch 2, **1 dc into each of next 7 sc; rep from * twice and from * to ** once again, 1 dc into next sc, join with sl st into 3rd of ch 3.

ROUND 9: Ch 3 *(counts as 1 dc)*, 1 dc into each dc and ch of previous round, working 5 dc into center st of each 5 dc corner group, join with sl st into 3rd of ch 3.

Fasten off yarn.

166 COLOR SCHEME: Warm colors are perfect with natural pine furniture.

167 COLOR SCHEME: A dark background shade enhances the paler motif at the center of the block.

168 COLOR SCHEME: Three bright colors display the block's intricacy.

OTHER COLOR SCHEMES

166

167

168

169

OTHER COLOR SCHEMES

170 Ⓐ Ⓑ Ⓒ Ⓓ Ⓔ Ⓕ Ⓖ Ⓗ

171 Ⓐ Ⓑ Ⓒ Ⓓ Ⓔ Ⓕ Ⓖ Ⓗ

172 Ⓐ Ⓑ Ⓒ Ⓓ Ⓔ Ⓕ Ⓖ Ⓗ

FOUNDATION CHAIN: Using yarn A, ch 29.

WORKING THE PATTERN: When following the chart, read odd-numbered rows (right side rows) from right to left and even-numbered rows (wrong side rows) from left to right. Starting at the bottom right-hand corner of the chart, work the 34 row pattern from the chart in sc. On the first row, work first sc into 2nd ch from hook, 1 sc into each ch along row. *(28 sc)*

Fasten off yarn.

170 COLOR SCHEME: Autumn leaf colors are always pleasing to look at— the different shades combine well in this block.

171 COLOR SCHEME: Solid and variegated shades of one single color change the appearance of this block and make the stripes blend together and look more harmonious.

172 COLOR SCHEME: Eight strong, clashing colors makes each stripe stand out against its neighbors. This colorway would make a cheerful throw for a child's bedroom.

Interlocking Stripes

11 ⊟

Ⓐ Ⓑ Ⓒ Ⓓ Ⓔ Ⓕ Ⓖ Ⓗ

MIX-AND-MATCH

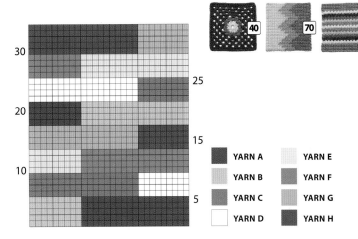

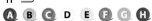

		YARN A			YARN E
		YARN B			YARN F
		YARN C			YARN G
		YARN D			YARN H

173

Big Round

11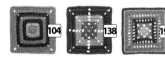

MIX-AND-MATCH

104 138 199

Special abbreviations

beg cl = beginning cluster made from 3 dc sts, **cl** = cluster made from 4 dc sts

FOUNDATION RING: Using yarn A, ch 6 and join with sl st to form a ring.

ROUND 1: Ch 1, 12 sc into ring, join with sl st into first sc.

ROUND 2: Ch 4 (counts as 1 dc, ch 1), *1 dc into next sc, ch 1; rep from * 10 times, join with sl st into 3rd of ch 4. (12 spaced dc)

ROUND 3: Sl st into next ch 1 sp, ch 3 (counts as 1 dc), beg cl into same sp, ch 3, *cl into next ch 1 sp, ch 3; rep from * 10 times, join with sl st into top of beg cl. (12 clusters)

ROUND 4: Sl st into next ch 3 sp, ch 3 (counts as 1 dc), beg cl into same sp, *ch 2, 1 dc into top of next cl, ch 2, **cl into next ch 3 sp; rep from * 10 times and from * to ** once again, join with sl st into top of beg cl.

ROUND 5: Ch 1, 3 sc into each ch 2 sp of previous round, join with sl st into first sc. Break off yarn A.

ROUND 6: Join yarn B into top of any cl, ch 3 (counts as 1 dc), [1 dc, ch 2, 2 dc] into same place, *[ch 2, skip next 3 sc group, 1 sc into sp between next two 3 sc groups] 5 times, ch 2, **[2 dc, ch 2, 2 dc] into sp above next cl; rep from * twice and from * to ** once again, join

with sl st into 3rd of ch 3.

ROUND 7: Ch 3 (counts as 1 dc), 1 dc into next dc, *[2 dc, ch 3, 2 dc] into ch 2 corner sp, 1 dc into each of next 2 dc, ch 2, 1 dc into next sc, [ch 2, 1 sc into next sc] 3 times, ch 2, 1 dc into next sc, ch 2, **1 dc into each of next 2 dc; rep from * twice and from * to ** once again, join with sl st into 3rd of ch 3.

ROUND 8: Ch 3 (counts as 1 dc), 1 dc into each of next 3 dc, *[2 dc, ch 3, 2 dc] into ch 2 corner sp, 1 dc into each of next 4 dc, ch 2, 1 dc into next dc, [ch 2, 1 dc into next sc] 3 times, ch 2, 1 dc into next dc, ch 2, **1 dc into each of next 4 dc; rep from * twice and from * to ** once again, join with sl st into 3rd of ch 3.

ROUND 9: Ch 1, 1 sc into same place, 1 sc into each of next 5 dc, *5 sc into ch 3 corner sp, 1 sc into each of next 6 dc, [2 sc into next ch 2 sp] 6 times, **1 sc into each of next 6 dc; rep from * twice and from * to ** once again, join with sl st into first sc.

Fasten off yarn.

---

174 COLOR SCHEME: This is such a pretty block to use for making a baby girl's afghan. You can use the same pattern to make one for a baby boy, but substitute a variegated blue yarn for the center motif.

---

175 COLOR SCHEME: This subtle, rather sophisticated color scheme of earth tones will look good displayed with natural materials such as natural wood, leather and terracotta.

---

176 COLOR SCHEME: By contrasting a pale center motif against a dark background, the appearance of this block changes drastically.

OTHER COLOR SCHEMES

174 A B

175 A B

176 A B

OTHER COLOR SCHEMES

178

179 Ⓐ Ⓑ Ⓒ Ⓓ

180 Ⓐ Ⓑ Ⓒ Ⓓ

FOUNDATION CHAIN: Using yarn A, ch 29.

WORKING THE PATTERN: When following the chart, read odd-numbered rows (right side rows) from right to left and even-numbered rows (wrong side rows) from left to right.

Starting at the bottom right-hand corner of the chart, work the 34 row pattern from the chart in sc. On the first row, work first sc into 2nd ch from hook, 1 sc into each ch along row. *(28 sc)*

Fasten off yarn.

178 **COLOR SCHEME:** Pale shades of pink and cream are used to work the pattern of rectangles so they contrast strongly against the hot pink background.

179 **COLOR SCHEME:** Change the tonal balance of the original block by using a light color to work the background and contrasting darker shades for the rectangles.

180 **COLOR SCHEME:** This really attractive color scheme contrasts rectangles worked in berry and wine shades set on a lavender colored background.

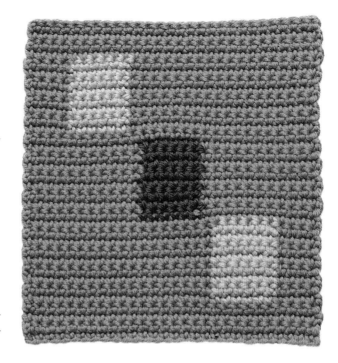

177

Trio

11 ▤

Ⓐ Ⓑ Ⓒ Ⓓ

MIX-AND-MATCH

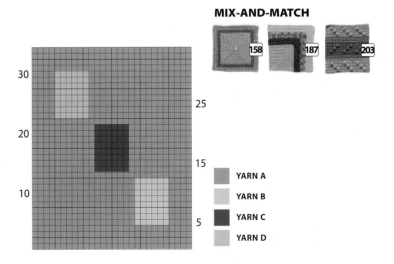

158   187   203

	YARN A
	YARN B
	YARN C
	YARN D

30 / 25 / 20 / 15 / 10 / 5

181

Begonia

11

MIX-AND-MATCH

14   130   144

Special abbreviations

beg cl = beginning cluster made from 3 tr sts, **cl** = cluster made from 4 tr sts

FOUNDATION RING: Using yarn A, ch 8 and join with sl st to form a ring.

ROUND 1: Ch 4 *(counts as 1 tr)*, beg cl, *ch 4, cl; rep from * 6 times, ch 4, join with sl st into 4th of ch 4. Break off yarn A.

ROUND 2: Join yarn B to any ch 4 sp, ch 3 *(counts as 1 dc)*, 3 dc into same ch 4 sp, *4 dc into next ch 4 sp, ch 6, **4 dc into next ch 4 sp; rep from * twice and from * to ** once again, join with sl st into 3rd of ch 3.

ROUND 3: Ch 3 *(counts as 1 dc)*, 1 dc into each of next 7 dc, *[3 dc, ch 3, 3 dc] into next ch 6 sp, **1 dc into each of next 8 dc; rep from * twice and from * to ** once again, join with sl st into 3rd of ch 3. Break off yarn B.

ROUND 4: Join yarn C to any ch 3 sp, ch 3 *(counts as 1 dc)*, [1 dc, ch 3, 2 dc] into same ch 3 sp, *1 dc into each of next 14 dc, **[2 dc, ch 3, 2 dc] into next ch 3 sp; rep from * twice and from * to ** once again, join with sl st into 3rd of ch 3. Break off yarn C.

ROUND 5: Join yarn D to any ch 3 sp, ch 3 *(counts as 1 dc)*, [1 dc, ch 3, 2 dc] into same ch 3 sp, *1 dc into each of next 18 dc, **[2 dc, ch 3, 2 dc] into next ch 3 sp; rep from * twice and from * to ** once again, join with sl st into 3rd of ch 3. Break off yarn D.

ROUND 6: Join yarn E, ch 1, 1 sc into each dc of previous round, working [2 sc, ch 1, 2 sc] into each ch 3 sp, join with sl st into first sc.

ROUND 7: Ch 1, 1 sc into each sc of previous round, working 3 sc into each ch 1 corner sp, join with sl st into first sc.

Fasten off yarn.

182 COLOR SCHEME: A light color such as cream used to crochet the first part of a block worked in rounds will take your eye straight to the center of the pattern.

183 COLOR SCHEME: Bright yellow adds interest to this colorway worked mainly in shades of dark-toned blues and light-toned turquoises.

184 COLOR SCHEME: Greens and browns are a very masculine color scheme, particularly when used for a throw displayed against leather or dark wood furniture.

OTHER COLOR SCHEMES

182

183

184

OTHER COLOR SCHEMES

186

187

188

Special abbreviation

sc3tog = decrease 2 sts by working the next 3 sc together

FOUNDATION CHAIN: Using yarn A, ch 58.

FOUNDATION ROW: *(right side)* 1 sc into 2nd ch from hook, 1 sc into each ch, turn. *(57 sc)*

ROW 1: Ch 1, 1 sc into each of next 27 sc, skip 1 sc, 1 sc into next sc, skip 1 sc, 1 sc into each of rem 27 sc, turn. *(55 sc)*

ROW 2: Ch 1, 1 sc into each of next 26 sc, skip 1 sc, 1 sc into next sc, skip 1 sc, 1 sc into each of rem 26 sc, turn. *(53 sc)*

ROW 3: Ch 1, 1 sc into each of next 25 sc, skip 1 sc, 1 sc into next sc, skip 1 sc, 1 sc into each of rem 25 sc, turn. *(51 sc)*

ROW 4: Ch 1, 1 sc into each of next 24 sc, skip 1 sc, 1 sc into next sc, skip 1 sc, 1 sc into each of rem 24 sc, turn. *(49 sc)*
Break off yarn A.
Join yarn B. Cont in pattern as set, dec 1 st at each side of center st on every row. At the same time, change yarn colors in the following color sequence: Work 4 rows in yarn B, 4 rows in yarn C. Join yarn D and cont in pattern until 3 sc rem.

NEXT ROW: Work sc3tog.
Fasten off yarn.

185

In the Pink

11

186 **COLOR SCHEME:** A bright, hot shade of yellow is used to give this block a strongly-defined outside edge as it contrasts well with the other colors which are cool in tone.

187 **COLOR SCHEME:** This choice of colors would be perfect for making a small, strongly patterned afghan for a baby boy.

188 **COLOR SCHEME:** The variegated yarn used in this block shades from green to brown through beige and adds interest to the striped pattern.

MIX-AND-MATCH

 35

 77

97

189

Willow

11 📷

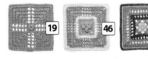

MIX-AND-MATCH

19 46 199

FOUNDATION RING: Using yarn A, ch 6 and join with sl st to form a ring.

ROUND 1: Ch 3 *(counts as 1 dc)*, 15 dc into ring, join with sl st into 3rd of ch 3. *(16 dc)*

ROUND 2: Ch 4 *(counts as 1 dc, ch 1)*, [1 dc into next dc, ch 1] 15 times, join with sl st into 3rd of ch 4. Break off yarn A.

ROUND 3: Join yarn B to any dc of previous round, ch 3 *(counts as 1 dc)*, [2 dc into next ch 1 sp, 1 dc into next dc] 15 times, join with sl st into 3rd of ch 3. *(48 dc)*

ROUND 4: Ch 1, 1 sc into same place, * ch 5, sl st into 5th ch from hook, skip next 2 dc, 1 sc into next dc, ch 2, skip next 2 dc, 1 sc into next dc, ch 3, skip next 2 dc, 1 sc into next dc, ch 2, skip next 2 dc, **1 sc into next dc; rep from * twice and from * to ** once again, join with sl st into first sc.

ROUND 5: Sl st into next ch 5 sp, ch 3 *(counts as 1 dc)*, [4 dc, ch 3, 5 dc] into same sp, *1 sc into next ch 2 sp, 5 dc into next ch 3 sp, 1 sc into next ch 2 sp, **[5 dc, ch 3, 5 dc] into next ch 5 sp; rep from * twice and from * to ** once more, join with sl st into 3rd of ch 3. Break off yarn B.

ROUND 6: Join yarn C to any corner ch 3 sp, ch 1, [1 sc, ch 3, 1 sc] into same place, *ch 5, 1 dc into next sc, ch 3, skip next 2 dc, 1 sc into next dc, ch 3, skip next 2 dc, 1 dc into next sc, ch 5, **[1 sc, ch 3, 1 sc] into next ch 3 sp; rep from * twice and from * to ** once again, join with sl st into first sc.

ROUND 7: Sl st into next ch 3 sp, ch 3 *(counts as 1 dc)*, [2 dc, ch 2, 3 dc] into same ch 3 sp, *5 dc into next ch 5 sp, 3 dc into each of next 2 ch 3 sps, 5 dc into next ch 5 sp, **[3 dc, ch 2, 3 dc] into next ch 3 sp; rep from * twice and from * to ** once again, join with sl st into 3rd of ch 3. Break off yarn C.

ROUND 8: Join yarn A, ch 1, 1 sc into each dc of previous round, working [2 sc, ch 2, 2 sc] into each ch 2 corner sp, join with sl st into first sc.

ROUND 9: Ch 1, 1 sc into each sc of previous round, working 3 sc into each ch 2 corner sp, join with sl st into first sc.

Fasten off yarn.

190 COLOR SCHEME: A soft, warm amber shade combines well with bright shades of yellow and orange to work this intricately patterned block.

191 COLOR SCHEME: The center motif graduates outward from a light center to dark outside band, then the lightest color is used to frame the block.

192 COLOR SCHEME: To give a different effect from the previous block, the three colors used here graduate outward from dark to light, then the dark color is repeated round the edge.

OTHER COLOR SCHEMES

190

191

192

OTHER COLOR SCHEMES

194

195

196 Ⓐ Ⓑ Ⓒ Ⓓ Ⓔ

FOUNDATION CHAIN: Using yarn A, ch 32, turn.

FOUNDATION ROW: *(right side)* 2 sc into 4th ch from hook, *skip ch 1, 2 sc into next ch; rep from * to end, turn. *(30 sc)*

ROW 1: Ch 2, *skip 1 sc, 2 sc into next sc; rep from * to end, turn.

Rep row 1 four times. Break off yarn A.

Join yarn B and rep row 1 twice. Break off yarn B.

Join yarn C and rep row 1 twice. Break off yarn C.

Join yarn D and rep row 1 twice. Break off yarn D.

Join yarn C and rep row 1 twice. Break off yarn C.

Join yarn E and rep row 1 twice. Break off yarn E.

Join yarn B and rep row 1 twice. Break off yarn B.

Join yarn C and rep row 1 twice. Break off yarn C.

Join yarn A and rep row 1 six times. Break off yarn A.

Join yarn C and rep row 1 eight times. Fasten off yarn.

193

Textured Stripes

1 ☰

Ⓐ Ⓑ Ⓒ Ⓓ Ⓔ

MIX-AND-MATCH

 4 **18** **64**

194 COLOR SCHEME: A textured surface plus stripes of color work well in this lively color scheme of shades of yellow highlighted with soft turquoise.

195 COLOR SCHEME: Variegated yarns add extra surface interest to stripes worked in a textured stitch. Cool colors of purple and dull pink come to life with the addition of two stripes of bright lime green.

196 COLOR SCHEME: A small amount of Capri blue, a deep, vibrant shade of kingfisher blue, looks good combined with stripes worked in pale, ice cream colors.

197

Fretwork

A B C D

MIX-AND-MATCH

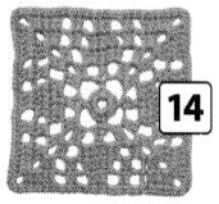
14

35

212

FOUNDATION RING: Using yarn A, ch 6 and join with sl st to form a ring.

ROUND 1: Ch 3 *(counts as 1 dc)*, 2 dc into ring, ch 3, *3 dc into ring, ch 3; rep from * twice more, join with sl st into 3rd of ch 3. Break off yarn A.

ROUND 2: Join yarn B to any ch 3 sp, ch 3, [2 dc, ch 3, 3 dc] into same sp to make corner, *ch 1, [3 dc, ch 3, 3 dc] into next ch 3 sp to make corner; rep from * twice more, ch 1, join with sl st into 3rd of ch 3. Break off yarn B.

ROUND 3: Join yarn C to any ch 1 sp, ch 1, 1 sc into same sp, 1 sc into each dc and ch 1 sp of previous round, working 5 sc into each ch 3 corner sp, join with sl st into first sc.

ROUND 4: Ch 4 *(counts as 1 dc, ch 1)*, skip 1 sc, [1 dc into next sc, ch 1, skip 1 sc] twice, *[1 dc, ch 1, 1 dc, ch 1, 1 dc] into next sc to form corner, ch 1, skip 1 sc, **[1 dc into next sc, ch 1, skip 1 sc] 5 times; rep from * twice and from * to ** once again, [1 dc into next sc, ch 1, skip 1 sc] twice, join with sl st into 3rd of ch 4. Break off yarn C.

ROUND 5: Join yarn D into any dc along one side of square, ch 1, 1 sc into same place, 1 sc into each dc and ch 1 sp of previous round, working 3 sc into center dc of each corner group, join with sl st into first sc.

ROUND 6: Ch 4 *(counts as 1 dc, ch 1)*, skip 1 sc, [1 dc into next sc, ch 1, skip 1 sc] 3 times, 1 dc into next sc, ch 1, *[1 dc, ch 1, 1 dc, ch 1, 1 dc] into next sc to form corner, ch 1, **[1 dc into next sc, ch 1, skip 1 sc] 8 times, 1 dc into next sc, ch 1; rep from * twice and from * to ** once again, [1 dc into next sc, ch 1, skip 1 sc] 4 times, join with sl st into 3rd of ch 4.

ROUND 7: Ch 1, 1 sc into same place, 1 sc into each dc and ch 1 sp of previous round, working 3 sc into center dc of each corner group, join with sl st into first sc. Break off yarn D.

ROUND 8: Join yarn B into any sc along one side of square, ch 1, 1 sc into same place, 1 sc into each sc of previous round, working 3 sc into center st of each 3 sc corner group, join with sl st into first sc. Break off yarn B.

ROUND 9: Join yarn A and rep round 8. Break off yarn A.

ROUND 10: Join yarn C, ch 1, 1 sc into same place, 1 sc into each sc of previous round, working 2 sc into center st of each 3 sc corner group, join with sl st into first sc.

Fasten off yarn.

198 **COLOR SCHEME:** Change the color balance of this block by contrasting salmon and coral shades with a clear, mid-toned blue.

199 **COLOR SCHEME:** Bright turquoise enlivens a subtle color combination of three soft greens with a wide band of contrast.

200 **COLOR SCHEME:** An afghan worked in bright, cheerful colors such as yellow and orange will add life and warmth to any neutral decorating scheme.

OTHER COLOR SCHEMES

198 A B C D

199 A B C D

200 A B C D

201

Zigzag Bobbles

11

A B C

MIX-AND-MATCH

41

44

180

Special abbreviation

MB = make bobble (work 4 open dc in same st leaving 5 loops on hook, draw yarn through all 5 loops at once)

FOUNDATION CHAIN: Using yarn A, ch 28.

FOUNDATION ROW: *(wrong side)* Working first sc into 2nd ch from hook, work 1 sc into each ch, turn. *(27 sc)*

ROW 1: Ch 1, 1 sc into each sc, turn.

ROW 2: Ch 1, 1 sc into each of next 7 sc, *MB, 1 sc into each of next 7 sc; rep from *, ending last rep with 1 sc into each of next 3 sc, turn.

ROWS 3 & 5: Rep row 1.

ROW 4: Ch 1, 1 sc into each of next 5 sc, MB, 1 sc into each of next 7 sc; rep from *, ending last rep with 1 sc into each of next 5 sc , turn.

ROW 6: Ch 1, 1 sc into each of next 3 sc, MB, 1 sc into each of next 7 sc; rep from *, ending last rep with 1 sc into each of next 7 sc, turn.

ROWS 7 & 8: Rep row 1. Break off yarn A.

Join yarn B and rep row 1 three times. Break off yarn B.

ROWS 12 & 13: Join yarn C and rep row 1.

ROW 14: Rep row 6.

ROWS 15 & 17: Rep row 1.

ROW 16: Rep row 4.

ROW 18: Rep row 2.

ROWS 19 & 20: Rep row 1. Break off yarn C.

Join yarn B and rep row 1 three times. Break off yarn B.

Join yarn A and rep row 1 twice, then rep rows 2 to 8.

Fasten off yarn.

OTHER COLOR SCHEMES

202 A B C

203 A B C

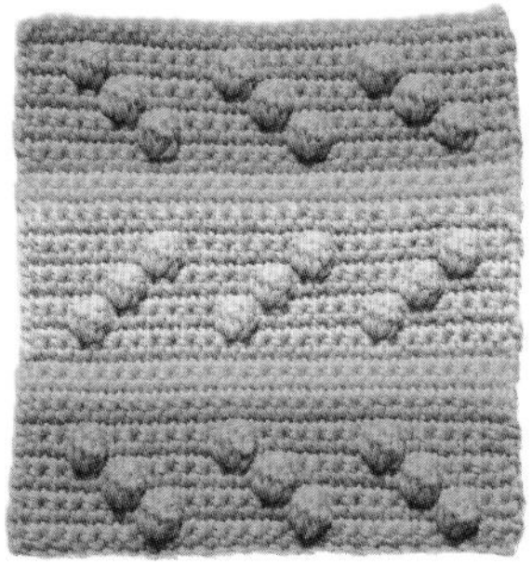

204 A B C

202 **COLOR SCHEME:** Bobbles make an interesting texture, especially when contrasted with smooth stripes of color in blue and coral.

203 **COLOR SCHEME:** Many shades of green and turquoise look good together, particularly this clear asparagus green and deep, blue-toned turquoise.

203 **COLOR SCHEME:** This block would be a good choice for making cushions and a small throw for a rocking chair in a sunny breakfast room.

205

Hourglass

MIX-AND-MATCH

45 127 136

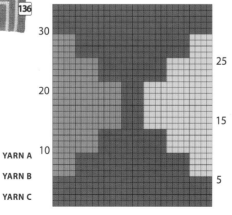

YARN A
YARN B
YARN C

FOUNDATION CHAIN: Using yarn A, ch 29.

WORKING THE PATTERN: When following the chart, read odd-numbered rows (right side rows) from right to left and even-numbered rows (wrong side rows) from left to right.
Starting at the bottom right-hand corner of the chart, work the 34 row pattern from the chart in sc. On the first row, work first sc into 2nd ch from hook, 1 sc into each ch along row.
(28 sc)

Fasten off yarn.

206 COLOR SCHEME: Variegated blue and cream yarn used for the hourglass shape makes a striking contrast to the plain areas of mid and dark shades of blue.

207 COLOR SCHEME: Use a dark color to accentuate the hourglass shape and set it against two paler contrasts which have a similar tone.

208 COLOR SCHEME: Two strong but harmonious colors show up well against cream, a versatile color which looks as good with bright colors as with neutral shades.

OTHER COLOR SCHEMES

206

207

208

OTHER COLOR SCHEMES

210 Ⓐ Ⓑ Ⓒ Ⓓ

211 Ⓐ Ⓑ Ⓒ Ⓓ

212 Ⓐ Ⓑ Ⓒ Ⓓ

FOUNDATION RING: Using yarn A, ch 6 and join with sl st to form a ring.

ROUND 1: Ch 5 *(counts as 1 dc, ch 2)*, [1 dc into ring, ch 2] 7 times, join with sl st into 3rd of ch 5.

ROUND 2: Sl st into next ch 2 sp, ch 1, [1 sc, 1 hdc, 1 dc, 1 hdc, 1 sc] into same sp *(petal made)*, [1 sc, 1 hdc, 1 dc, 1 hdc, 1 sc] into each rem ch 2 sp, join with sl st into first sc. Break off yarn A.

ROUND 3: Working behind petals of previous round, join yarn B between two petals, ch 3, [sl st into back of first sc of next petal, ch 3] 7 times, join with sl st into first of ch 3.

ROUND 4: Sl st into next ch 3 sp, ch 1, [1 sc, 2 hdc, 1 dc, 2 hdc, 1 sc] into same sp, [1 sc, 2 hdc, 1 dc, 2 hdc, 1 sc] into each rem ch 3 sp, join with sl st into first sc. Break off yarn B.

ROUND 5: Working behind petals of previous round, join yarn C between two petals, ch 4, [sl st into back of first sc of next petal, ch 4] 7 times, join with sl st into first of ch 4.

ROUND 6: Sl st into next ch 4 sp, ch 1, [1 sc, 2 hdc, 3 dc, 2 hdc, 1 sc] into same sp, [1 sc, 2 hdc, 3 dc, 2 hdc, 1 sc] into each rem ch 4 sp, join with sl st into first sc. Break off yarn C.

ROUND 7: Working behind petals of previous round, join yarn D between two petals, ch 5, [sl st into back of first sc of next petal, ch 5] 7 times, join with sl st into first of ch 5.

ROUND 8: Sl st into next ch 5 sp, ch 1, 6 sc into same sp, *[3 dc, ch 2, 3 dc] into next ch 5 sp (corner made), **6 sc into next ch 5 sp; rep from * twice and from * to ** once again, join with sl st into first sc.

ROUND 9: Ch 3 *(counts as 1 dc)*, 1 dc into each sc and dc of previous round, working [2 dc, ch 2, 2 dc] into each ch 2 corner sp, join with sl st into 3rd of ch 3.

ROUND 10: Sl st into next dc, ch 5 *(counts as 1 dc, ch 2)*, skip 2 dc, 1 dc into next dc, [ch 2, skip 2 dc, 1 dc into next dc] twice, *[3 dc, ch 2, 3 dc] into next ch 2 corner sp, **[1 dc into next dc, ch 2, skip 2 dc] 5 times, 1 dc into next dc; rep from * twice and from * to ** once again, 1 dc into next dc, ch 2, skip 2 dc, 1 dc into next dc, ch 2, join with sl st into 3rd of ch 5.

ROUND 11: Ch 5 *(counts as 1 dc, ch 2)*, [1 dc into next dc, ch 2] 3 times, skip 2 dc, 1 dc into next dc, *[3 dc, ch 2, 3 dc] into next ch 2 corner sp, 1 dc into next dc, ch 2, skip 2 dc, **[1 dc into next dc, ch 2] 6 times, skip 2 dc, 1 dc into next dc; rep from * twice and from * to ** once again, [1 dc into next dc, ch 2] twice, join with sl st into 3rd of ch 5.

ROUND 12: Ch 1, 1 sc into same place, 1 sc into each dc of previous round, working 2 sc into each ch 2 sp along sides of square and 3 sc into each ch 2 corner sp, join with sl st into first sc.

209

Marigold

111 📷

Ⓐ Ⓑ Ⓒ Ⓓ

MIX-AND-MATCH

 140   155   166

ROUND 13: Ch 1, 1 sc into same place, 1 sc into each sc of previous round, working 3 sc into center st of each 3 sc corner group, join with sl st into first sc. Fasten off yarn.

210 **COLOR SCHEME:** Variety of blues.

211 **COLOR SCHEME:** Coral and cream.

212 **COLOR SCHEME:** Amethyst, pinks.

Techniques

In this chapter, you'll find a refresher course to help you make and join the blocks shown in the directory, including tips on joining yarns and working a colored pattern from a chart. There are also patterns for making a variety of pretty edgings and details of the actual yarns used to work the blocks.

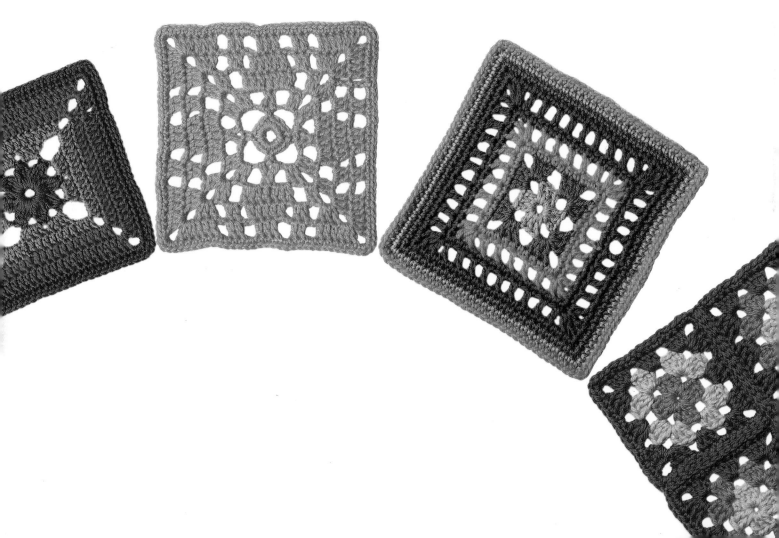

How to start

Holding the hook and yarn

1 Holding the hook as if it was a pen is the most widely used method. Center the tips of your right thumb and forefinger over the flat section of the hook.

2 An alternative way to hold the hook is to grasp the flat section of the hook between your right thumb and forefinger as if you were holding a knife.

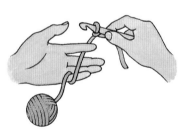

3 To control the supply and keep an even tension on the yarn, loop the short end of the yarn over your left forefinger and take the yarn coming from the ball loosely around the little finger on the same hand. Use the middle finger on the same hand to help hold the work. If left-handed, hold the hook in the left hand and the yarn in the right.

Working a foundation chain (ch)

The foundation chain is the equivalent of casting on in knitting and it's important to make sure that you have made the required number of chains for the pattern you are going to work. Count each V-shaped loop on the front of the chain as one chain stitch, except for the loop on the hook which is not counted. You may find it easier to turn the chain over and count the stitches on the back of the chain. When working the first row of stitches (usually called the foundation row) into the chain, insert the hook under one thread or two, depending on your preference.

1 Holding the hook with the slip knot in your right hand and the yarn in your left, wrap the yarn over the hook. Draw the yarn through to make a new loop and complete the first chain stitch.

2 Repeat this step, drawing a new loop of yarn through the loop already on the hook until the chain is the required length. Move the thumb and forefinger that are grasping the chain upward after every few stitches to keep the tension even. When working into the chain, insert the hook under one thread (for a looser edge) or two (for a firmer edge), depending on your preference.

Making a slip knot

1 Loop the yarn as shown, insert the hook into the loop, catch the yarn with the hook and pull it through to make a loop over the hook.

2 Gently pull the yarn to tighten the loop around the hook and complete the slip knot.

Turning chains

When working crochet in rows or rounds, you will need to work a specific number of extra chains at the beginning of each row or round. The extra chains are needed to bring the hook up to the correct height for the particular stitch you will be working next. When the work is turned at the end of a straight row, the extra chains are called a turning chain, and when they are worked at the beginning of a round, they are called a starting chain.

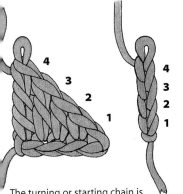

The turning or starting chain is usually counted as the first stitch of the row, except when working single crochet where the single turning chain is ignored. For example, *ch 3 (counts as 1 dc)* at the beginning of a row or round means that the turning or starting chain contains three chain stitches and these are counted as the equivalent of one double crochet stitch. A chain may be longer than the number required for the stitch and in that case, counts as one stitch plus a number of chains. For example, *ch 5 (counts as 1 dc, ch 2)* means that the chain is the equivalent of one double crochet stitch plus two chain stitches.

At the end of the row or round, the final stitch is usually worked into the turning or starting chain worked on the previous row or round. The final stitch may be worked into the top chain of the turning or starting chain or into another specified stitch of the chain. For example, *1 dc into 3rd of ch 5* means that the final stitch is a double crochet stitch and is worked into the 3rd stitch of the turning or starting chain.

The box below shows the correct number of chain stitches needed to make a turn for each stitch.

SINGLE CROCHET STITCH (sc) - 1 CHAIN TO TURN

HALF DOUBLE CROCHET STITCH (hdc) - 2 CHAINS TO TURN

DOUBLE CROCHET STITCH (dc) - 3 CHAINS TO TURN

TREBLE CROCHET STITCH (tr) - 4 CHAINS TO TURN.

Stitches

Working a slip stitch (sl st)

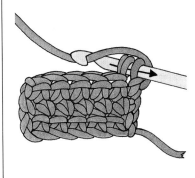

Slip stitch is the shortest of all the crochet stitches and its main uses are for joining rounds, making seams, and carrying the hook and yarn from one place to another. Insert the hook from front to back into the required stitch. Wrap the yarn over the hook (*yarn over*) and draw it through both the work and the loop on the hook. One loop remains on the hook and one slip stitch has been worked.

Working a single crochet (sc)

1 Begin with a foundation chain and insert the hook from front to back into the second chain from the hook. Wrap the yarn over the hook (*yarn over*) and draw it through the first loop, leaving two loops on the hook.

2 To complete the stitch, yarn over and draw it through both loops on the hook, leaving one loop on the hook. Continue in this way, working one single crochet into each chain.

3 At the end of the row, turn, work one chain for the turning chain (remember that this chain does not count as a stitch). Insert the hook into the first single crochet at the beginning of the row. Work a single crochet into each stitch of the previous row, being careful to work the final stitch into the last stitch of the row, but not into the turning chain.

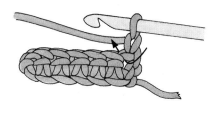

Working a half double crochet (hdc)

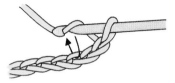 

1 Begin with a foundation chain, wrap the yarn over the hook (*yarn over*) and insert the hook into the third chain from the hook.

2 Draw the yarn through the chain, leaving three loops on the hook. Yarn over and draw through all three loops on the hook, leaving one loop on the hook. One half double stitch complete.

3 Continue along the row, working one half double crochet into each chain. At the end of the row, work two chains to turn. Skip the first stitch and work a half double crochet into each stitch made on the previous row. At the end of the row, work the last stitch into the top of the turning chain.

Working a double crochet (dc)

1 Begin with a foundation chain, wrap the yarn over the hook and insert the hook into the fourth chain from the hook.

2 Draw the yarn through the chain, leaving three loops on the hook. Yarn over again and draw the yarn through the first two loops on the hook, leaving two loops on the hook.

3 Yarn over and draw the yarn through the two loops on the hook leaving one loop on the hook. One double crochet complete. Continue along the row, working one double crochet stitch into each chain. At the end of the row, work three chains to turn. Skip the first stitch and work a double crochet into each stitch made on the previous row. At the end of the row, work the last stitch into the top of the turning chain.

Working a treble crochet (tr)

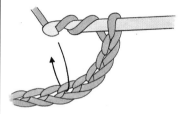 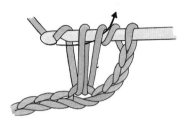

1 Begin with a foundation chain, wrap the yarn over the hook twice (*yarn over twice*) and insert the hook into the fifth chain from the hook.

2 Draw the yarn through the chain, leaving four loops on the hook. Yarn over again and draw the yarn through the first two loops on the hook, leaving three loops on the hook.

3 Yarn over again and draw through the first two loops on the hook leaving two loops on the hook.

4 Yarn over again and draw through the two remaining loops, leaving one loop on the hook. Treble crochet complete.

5 Continue along the row, working one treble crochet stitch into each chain. At the end of the row, work four chains to turn. Skip the first stitch and work a treble crochet into each stitch made on the previous row. At the end of the row, work the last stitch into the top of the turning chain.

Working into the front and back of stitches

Unless pattern details instruct you otherwise, it's usual to work crochet stitches under both loops of the stitches made on the previous row.

WORKING INTO FRONT

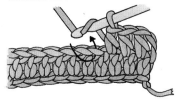

WORKING INTO BACK

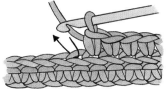

When instructions tell you to work into the front of the stitches, insert the hook only under the front loops of stitches on the previous row.

Likewise, to work into the back of the stitches, insert the hook only under the back loops of stitches on the previous row.

Gauge

Each of the blocks shown in the book measures 6" (15cm) across after blocking. They were all worked using the same weight of yarn (DK) and the same hook (4mm Inox hook). No two people will crochet to exactly the same gauge, even working with the identical hook and yarn. How you hold the hook and the rate at which the yarn flows through your fingers will affect the gauge you produce.

To check your own gauge, make a sample block using the recommended weight of yarn and the same size hook. Measure the block. It should be slightly smaller than 6" (15cm) across so that when it is blocked it will be exactly 6" (15cm) square. As a rule, if your block is smaller than required, make another sample using a hook one size larger. Also do this when the crochet fabric feels tight and hard. If your block is larger than required, make another sample using a hook one size smaller. Also do this if the crochet fabric feels loose and floppy. Gauge can also be affected by the color and fiber composition of the yarn and the size and brand of the crochet hook, so you may need to make several blocks using different hooks until you're happy with the size and feel of your crochet fabric.

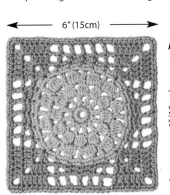

6" (15cm)

6" (15cm)

Joining yarns

Some of the instructions in the book, especially for those blocks worked in rounds, will tell you exactly where to join the next yarn. For example, *Join yarn B to any dc* along one side of the block means you should join the next yarn color to any of the double crochet stitches along one side of the block worked on the previous row.

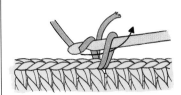

To do this, insert the hook in the work as instructed and draw up a loop of the new color, leaving a tail of about 4" (10cm). Work one chain and continue with the new yarn. When instructed to *Join yarn B* without being given a specific position, you should join the new yarn where the old ends.

Changing colors

1 To make a neat join between colors, leave the last stitch of the old color incomplete so there are two loops on the hook and wrap the new color around the hook.

2 Draw the new color through to complete the stitch and continue working in the new color. The illustrations show a color change in a row of double crochet stitches—the method is the same for single crochet and other stitches.

Fastening off yarn

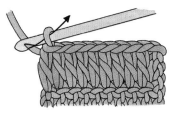

To fasten off the yarn at the end of the block, cut the yarn 6" (15cm) from the last stitch and pull the yarn end through the loop on the hook. Gently pull the yarn end to tighten the loop. To finish off yarn ends, thread the end in a large tapestry needle. Weave the end through several stitches on the wrong side of the work. Trim the remaining yarn.

Textured stitches

Working clusters (cl)

Multiples of half double, double and treble crochet stitches can be joined into clusters by leaving the last loop of each stitch on the hook as it is made, then securing the loops together at the end. When working a beginning cluster, count the turning chain as the first stitch.

1 To work a three double crochet cluster, yarn over hook, work the first stitch, omitting the last stage to leave two loops on the hook. Work the second stitch in the same way. You now have three loops on the hook. Work the last stitch of the cluster in the same way, resulting in four loops on the hook. Wrap the yarn over the hook.

2 Draw the yarn through the four loops on the hook to complete the cluster and secure the loops.

Working puff stitches (pf)

A puff stitch is a cluster of half double stitches worked in the same place—the number of stitches in each puff can vary between three and five. When working a beginning puff stitch, count the turning chain as the first stitch.

1 Wrap the yarn over the hook, insert the hook into the stitch, yarn over hook again and draw a loop through (three loops on the hook). Repeat this step twice more, inserting the hook into the same stitch (seven loops on the hook).

2 Wrap the yarn over the hook and draw it through all seven loops on the hook. Work an extra chain stitch at the top of the puff to complete the stitch.

Working bobbles (b)

A bobble is a cluster of between three and five double crochet stitches worked into the same stitch and closed at the top. Bobbles are worked on wrong side rows and they are usually surrounded by shorter stitches to throw them into high relief. When working contrasting bobbles, use a separate length of yarn to make each bobble, carrying the main yarn across the back of the bobble.

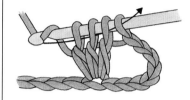

To make a three stitch bobble, wrap the yarn over the hook, work the first stitch, omitting the last stage to leave two loops on the hook. Work the second and third stitches in the same way. You now have four loops on the hook. Wrap the yarn over the hook and draw it through the four loops to secure them and complete the bobble.

Working popcorns (pc)

A popcorn stitch is a cluster of double crochet stitches (the number may vary), which is folded and closed at the top. When working a beginning popcorn, count the turning chain as the first stitch.

1 To make a popcorn with four stitches, work a group of four double crochet stitches into the same place.

2 Take the hook out of the working loop and insert it under both loops of the first double crochet in the group. Pick up the working loop with the hook and draw it through to fold the group of stitches and close it at the top.

Working around the post

This technique creates raised stitches by inserting the hook around the post (stem) of the stitch below, from the front or the back.

FRONT POST DOUBLE CROCHET (fpdc)   **BACK POST DOUBLE CROCHET (bpdc)**

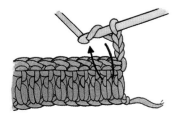   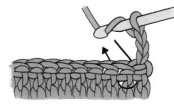

Wrap the yarn over the hook from back to front (*yo*), insert the hook from the front to the back at right of the next stitch, then bring it to the front at the left of the same stitch. Complete the stitch in the usual way.

Wrap the yarn over the hook, insert the hook from the back to the front at right of the next stitch, then take it back again at the left of the same stitch. Complete the stitch in the usual way.

Working spike stitches

Spikes are made by inserting the hook one or more rows below the previous row, either directly below the next stitch or to the right or left.

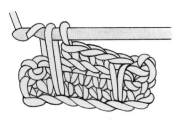

To work a single crochet spike stitch, insert the hook as directed by the pattern, wrap the yarn over the hook and draw through, lengthening the loop to the height of the working row, then complete the stitch.

Decreases

One or two stitches can be decreased by working two or three incomplete stitches together—the method is the same for single, half double, double, and treble crochet stitches.

DECREASING ONE STITCH BY WORKING TWO STITCHES TOGETHER (dc2tog)

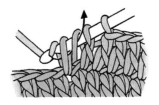   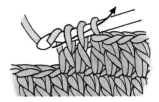

1 Leave the first stitch incomplete so there are two loops on the hook. Insert the hook into the next stitch and work another incomplete stitch so you have three loops on the hook.

2 Wrap the yarn over the hook and draw through all three loops to finish the decrease.

Two stitches can be decreased in the same way by working three stitches together. When working in double crochet, this decrease is called *dc3tog*.

Working a diagonal decrease

This type of decrease is usually worked in the center of the row of double crochet to create a diagonal line of decreases. Work to the center three stitches, skip the first stitch, work into the second stitch in the usual way, skip the third stitch, then complete the rest of the row.

Three-dimensional motifs

Initially, three-dimensional flower motifs seem a little tricky to work until you get the hang of holding the previously worked petals out of the way so you can work the foundation chains for the next layer directly behind them. This is one of those "practice makes perfect" techniques so don't give up if your first few rows of petals don't look

very neat. Try using a size smaller hook to work the chains, then change back to the normal size when making the petals. This makes it easier to insert the hook between the petals when joining the chains.

Working colorwork patterns from a chart

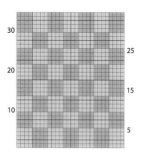

Begin by working the foundation chain in the first color, then work the pattern starting at the bottom right-hand corner of the chart, joining in new colors as they occur on the chart. See page 117 for how to join in a new yarn. On the first row, work the first stitch into the second chain from the hook, then work the rest of the row in single crochet.

Each square on the chart represents one stitch and you should always work upward from the bottom of the chart, reading odd-numbered rows (right side rows) from right to left and even-numbered rows (wrong side rows) from left to right.

When changing yarns, carry the yarn not in use loosely across the back

of the work and pick it up again when it is needed. This is called stranding and it works well when the areas of color are narrow, but when areas are wider than six stitches, use a small ball of yarn to work each color, looping the old yarn around the new one at each changeover on the row to avoid holes.

Working in rounds

Blocks worked in rounds are worked outward from a central ring of chains called a foundation ring.

Making a foundation ring

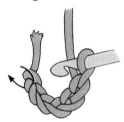

Work a short length of foundation chain (page 114) as specified in the pattern. Join the chains into a ring by working a slip stitch into the first stitch of the foundation chain.

Working into the ring

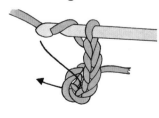

1 Work the number of turning chains specified in the pattern—three chains are shown here (counting as a double crochet stitch). Inserting the hook into the space at the center of the ring each time, work the number of stitches specified in the pattern into the ring. Count the stitches at the end of the round to check you have worked the correct number.

2 Join the first and last stitches of the round together by working a slip stitch into the top of the turning chain.

Finishing off the final round

To make a neat edge, finish off the final round by using this method of sewing the first and last stitches together in preference to the slip stitch joining method shown left.

1 Cut the yarn, leaving an end of about 4" (10cm) and draw it through the last stitch. With right side facing, thread the end in a large tapestry needle and take it under both loops of the stitch next to the turning chain.

2 Pull the needle through and insert it into the center of the last stitch of the round. On the wrong side, pull the needle through to complete the stitch, adjust the length of the stitch to close the round, then weave in the end on the wrong side in the usual way.

Blocking

Blocking involves pinning blocks out to the correct size, then, depending on the yarn fiber content, either steaming them with an iron or moistening with cold water. Always be guided by the information given on the ball band of your yarn and, when in doubt, choose the cold water blocking method below.

To block the pieces, make a blocking board by securing one or two layers of quilter's batting, covered with a sheet of cotton fabric, over a 24" x 36" (60 x 90cm) piece of flat board. Use a pencil to mark out a series of squares exactly 6" (15cm) square on the fabric, allowing about 1" (2.5cm) space between them.

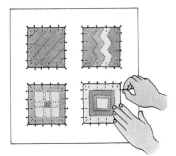

Pin out several blocks at the same time, using plenty of pins. Gently ease the block into shape before inserting each pin.

To block woolen yarns with warm steam, hold a steam iron set at the correct temperature for the yarn about ³⁄₄" (2cm) above the surface of the block and allow the steam to penetrate for several seconds. Lay the board flat and allow the block to dry completely before removing the pins.

To block acrylic and wool/acrylic blend yarns, pin out the pieces as above, then use a spray bottle to mist the crochet with cold water until it is moist, but not saturated. Gently pat the crochet to help the moisture penetrate more easily. Lay the board flat and allow the crochet to dry completely before removing the pins.

Joining blocks

Blocks can be joined either by sewing or by crocheting them together with a hook. Always block the pieces before joining and use the same yarn for joining as you used for working the blocks.

Begin by laying out the blocks in the correct order with the right or wrong side of each one facing upward, depending on the joining method you have chosen. Working first in horizontal rows, join the blocks together, beginning with the top row. Repeat until all the horizontal edges are joined. Turn the work so the remaining edges of the blocks are now horizontal and, as before, join these edges together.

Seams

Working a woven seam

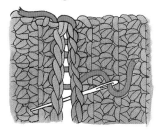

Lay the blocks out with the edges touching and wrong sides facing upward. Using matching yarn threaded in a tapestry needle, weave around the centers of the stitches as shown, without pulling the stitches too tightly. Work in the same way when joining row ends.

Working a back stitch seam

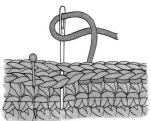

Hold the blocks to be joined with right sides together, pinning if necessary. Using matching yarn threaded in a tapestry needle, work a back stitch seam along the edge.

Working a slip stitch seam

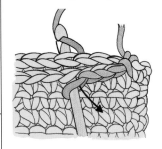

Joining blocks with wrong sides together gives a firm seam with an attractive ridge on the right side. If you prefer the ridge not to be visible, join the blocks with right sides together so the ridge is on the wrong side. Work a row of slip stitch (page 115) through both loops of each block. When working this method along side edges of blocks worked in rows, work enough evenly-spaced stitches so the seam is not too tight.

Working a single crochet seam

Work as for the slip stitch seam above, but work rows of single crochet stitches from the right or wrong side, depending on your preference.

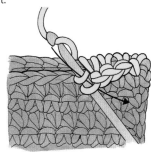

Edgings

Working directly into the afghan edge

Single crochet edging is worked directly into the crochet fabric, unlike the other edgings shown here which are worked separately and then stitched or crocheted in place. Work one or more rounds of single crochet edging right round your afghan. You can change the yarn color at the end of every round if you want to make a striped border.

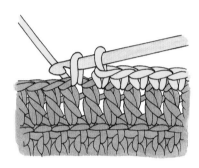

Holding the afghan with the right side facing you, make a row of ordinary single crochet stitches into the edge, spacing the stitches evenly all the way round and working three stitches into each corner stitch. When working this edging around blocks with chain spaces round the edge, work one single crochet into the chain space for every chain. Join the round with a slip stitch into the first single crochet. To work the next and subsequent rounds, work one chain, then work one single crochet into each stitch of the previous round, working three stitches into the center stitch of each three-stitch corner group.

Working a separate decorative edging

The decorative edgings shown here are worked in rows across the width of the strip so you can make them any length by simply repeating the pattern as many times as you require. Make the strip long enough to go around your afghan, allowing extra to gather or pleat around the corners so the edging will lay flat when it is attached. Pin the edging in place, making sure that the corners are neat, choose a matching yarn color and stitch or crochet it in place.

Shamrock edging

FOUNDATION CHAIN: Ch 9.

FOUNDATION ROW: (wrong side) 1 dc into 4th ch from hook, 1 dc into each of next ch 2, ch 2, skip next ch 2, [1 dc into last ch, ch 2] 3 times, 1 dc into same ch, turn.

ROW 1: Ch 1, [1 sc, 2 dc, 1 sc] into first ch 2 sp, [1 sc, 3 dc, ch 2, 3 dc, 1 sc] into next ch 2 sp, [1 sc, 2 dc, 1 sc] into next ch 2 sp, ch 2, 1 dc into each of next 3 dc, 1 dc into top of turning ch, turn.

ROW 2: Ch 3 (counts as 1 dc), 1 dc into each of next 3 dc, ch 2, [1 dc, ch 2 into next ch 2 sp] 3 times, 1 dc into same sp, turn.

Rep rows 1 and 2 for desired length, ending with a second row.

Fasten off yarn.

Deep mesh edging

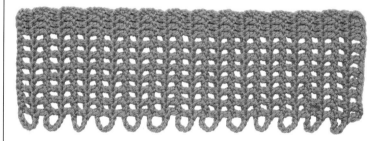

FOUNDATION CHAIN: Ch 20.

FOUNDATION ROW: (right side) 1 dc into 4th ch from hook, 1 dc into each of next ch 2, *ch 1, skip 1 ch, 1 dc into next ch; rep from * to end, turn.

ROW 1: Ch 7, 1 dc into first dc, [ch 1, 1 dc into next dc] 7 times, 1 dc into each of next 2 dc, 1 dc into top of turning ch, turn.

ROW 2: Ch 3 (counts as 1 dc), 1 dc into each of next 3 dc, *ch 1, 1 dc into next dc; rep from * to end, turn.

Rep rows 1 and 2 for desired length, ending with a first row.

Fasten off yarn.

Scallop edging

FOUNDATION CHAIN: Ch 5.

FOUNDATION ROW: *(wrong side)* [3 dc, ch 3, 3 dc] into 5th ch from hook, turn.

ROWS 1 & 2: Ch 3, [3 dc, ch 3, 3 dc] into ch 3 sp, turn.

ROW 3: Ch 5, [3 dc, ch 3, 3 dc] into ch 3 sp, turn.

ROW 4: Ch 3, [3 dc, ch 3, 3 dc] into ch 3 sp, ch 2, [1 dc into ch 5 sp, ch 2] 5 times, [1 dc, 1 sc] into next ch 3 sp, turn, ch 3, 2 dc into next ch 2 sp, *sl st into next ch 2 sp, ch 3, 2 dc into same sp; rep from * 3 times, 1 sc into next ch 2 sp, ch 3, [3 dc, ch 3, 3 dc] into next ch 3 sp, turn.

ROW 5: Ch 3, [3 dc, ch 3, 3 dc] into ch 3 sp, turn.

ROW 6: Ch 5, [3 dc, ch 3, 3 dc] into ch 3 sp, turn.

Rep rows 4 to 6 for desired length, ending with a fourth row, omitting instructions after working 1 sc into ch 2 sp.

Do not break yarn.

Turn edging so RS is facing and scallops are along the bottom edge, and beg working across top of edging.

NEXT ROW: *Ch 3, 3 sc into next ch 3 sp; rep from * to end, working last 3 sc into top of beg ch 5, turn.

NEXT ROW: Ch 1, 1 sc into each sc of previous row, working 3 sc into each ch 3 sp, turn

NEXT ROW: Ch 1, 1 sc into each sc of previous row.

Fasten off yarn.

Narrow shell edging

FOUNDATION RING: Ch 4 and join with sl st to form a ring.

ROW 1: *(right side)* Ch 3 *(counts as 1 dc)*, [3 dc, ch 2, 4 dc] into ring, turn.

ROW 2: Ch 3, [3 dc, ch 2, 3 dc] into ch 2 sp, 1 dc into top of turning chain, turn.

Rep row 2 for desired length.

Fasten off yarn.

Shell & lace edging

FOUNDATION CHAIN: Ch 12.

FOUNDATION ROW: *(right side)* 4 dc into 4th ch from hook, ch 3, skip next 3 chs, 4 dc into next ch, ch 3, skip next ch 3, 1 dc into last ch, turn.

ROW 1: Ch 6, 4 dc into first st of first 4 dc group, ch 3, 4 dc into first st of next group, turn.

ROW 2: Ch 3, 4 dc into first st of first 4 dc group, ch 3, 4 dc into first st of next group, ch 3, 1 dc into 3rd of ch 6, turn.

Rep rows 1 and 2 for desired length, ending with a second row.

Fasten off yarn.

Making a fringe

You can make a fringe directly into the afghan edge or first work one or more rows of single crochet edging round the afghan to give a firm edge.

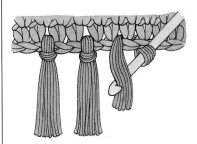

Cut the yarn twice the required length of the fringe plus about 2" (5cm) extra. Take four or more lengths and fold in half. Insert a large hook through the crochet edge from back to front and draw the folded end of the yarn through to make a loop. Hook the ends through the loop and gently tighten the knot. Repeat at regular intervals along the crochet edge, then trim the ends evenly with sharp scissors.

Abbreviations

Standard crochet abbreviations

alt	alternate
beg	beginning
ch(s)	chain(s)
cont	continue
dc	double crochet
foll	following
hdc	half double crochet
lp(s)	loop(s)
patt	pattern
rem	remaining
rep	repeat
sc	single crochet
sk	skip
sl st	slip stitch
sp(s)	space(s)
st(s)	stitch(es)
tr	treble or triple crochet
yo	yarn over

Special abbreviations

beg cl	beginning cluster made from 3 dc sts
beg pc	beginning popcorn made from ch 3 and 4 dc sts
beg pf	beginning puff st of hdc3tog
bpdc	back post double crochet
bpsc	back post single crochet
cl	cluster made from 4 dc sts
dc3tog	work 2 double crochet sts together to make cluster
fpdc	front post double crochet
MB	make bobble (work 4 open dc in same st leaving 5 loops on hook, draw yarn through all 5 loops at once)
pc	popcorn made from 5 dc sts
pf	puff st of hdc4tog
sc3tog	decrease 2 sts by working the next three sc together
sp	spike (insert hook 1 row below next st, pull up loop of yarn, insert hook into top of next st, yo, draw loop through, yo, draw through all 3 loops on hook)
tr2tog	work 2 tr together

Useful hook/yarn combinations

Sport weight (4ply) B-E (2.5-3.5mm)
Double knitting (DK) E-G (3.5-4.5mm)
Worsted weight (Aran) I-J (5-6mm)

Yarns

Choosing yarns

Each block in the book can be worked with your own choice of yarn. As well as using different colors (see pages 20 and 21 for more information on choosing color combinations), fiber composition is also a choice you have to make. Pure wool yarns are considered preferable when crocheting, but there are times when synthetic yarns are better, particularly for baby items that may require frequent washing. You might also prefer the feel of an acrylic or wool/acrylic blend when you are working. The choice is up to you.

The swatches show block 173 Big Round, (page 102), worked in three different yarn weights. By using different yarns, the appearance of the block changes considerably, from light and lacy to thick and chunky. Swatch 1 is worked in Rowan 4ply Soft using a 3mm Inox hook and, after blocking, the swatch measures 4 ½" (11.5cm) across. The next swatch is worked in Jaeger Matchmaker Double Knitting which is the same weight as the yarns used to make all the blocks in the directory. Worked with a 4mm Inox hook, the swatch measures 6" (15cm) across after blocking. The last and largest swatch is worked in Jaeger Matchmaker Aran with a 5mm Inox hook and, after blocking, it measures 7 ¾" (19.5cm) across.

Calculating yarn amounts

The most reliable way to work out how much yarn you need to buy for a specific project is to buy a ball of each yarn you are going to use for your project and make some sample swatches. The amount of yarn per ball or skein can vary considerably between colors of the same yarn because of the different dyes that have been used, so it's a good idea to make the samples using the actual colors you intend to use. Using the yarn and a suitable size of hook (see page 124 for a yarn/hook compatibility chart), work three blocks in each pattern you intend to use, making sure that you allow at least 3" (8cm) of spare yarn at every color change. This will compensate for the extra yarn you'll need when weaving in the ends.

Pull out the three blocks and carefully measure the amount of yarn used for each color in each block. Take the average yardage and multiply it by the number of blocks you intend to make. Don't forget to add extra yarn to your calculations for joining the blocks together and for working any edgings.

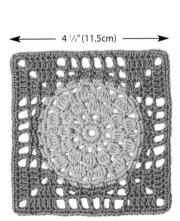

Worked in Rowan 4ply Soft
using a 3mm Inox hook

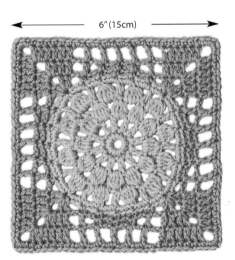

Worked in Jaeger Matchmaker Double Knitting
using a 4mm Inox hook

Worked in Jaeger Matchmaker Aran
using a 5mm Inox hook

Yarn colors

When creating the blocks in this book, colors were chosen from a wide palette of over seventy shades of double knitting (DK weight) yarn. Here's a list of the actual yarns used, arranged by color. Most of the yarns are made from pure wool, but where the exact shade was unavailable in a woolen yarn, a small number of acrylics and wool/acrylic blends in the same weight were used.

white King Cole Anti-Tickle Merino DK shade "White" (blocks 25, 26, 27, 28, 65, 66, 67, 68, 169)

cream Jaeger Matchmaker DK shade 662 or King Cole Anti-Tickle Merino DK shade "Aran" (blocks 7, 9, 12, 16, 24, 38, 39, 40, 46, 47, 69, 77, 78, 91, 93, 94, 95, 103, 108, 131, 132, 135, 139, 148, 150, 154, 165, 169, 174, 178, 182, 187, 193, 196, 208, 211)

oatmeal Jaeger Matchmaker Merino DK shade 663 "Oatmeal" (blocks 48, 70, 93, 102, 106, 110, 114, 139, 141, 145, 179, 194, 200, 204, 207)

acid lemon Jaeger Matchmaker DK shade 895 (blocks 5, 30, 31, 53, 54, 61, 63, 81, 84, 85, 88, 161, 170, 194)

pale yellow Jaeger Baby Merino DK shade 205 (blocks 45, 97, 100, 136, 140, 163, 166, 170, 194, 209)

sunshine yellow King Cole Anti-Tickle Merino DK shade "Gold" (blocks 48, 49, 50, 51, 52, 76, 87, 112, 116, 133, 137, 166, 170, 183, 186, 190, 194, 200, 204, 205, 209)

amber King Cole Anti-Tickle Merino DK shade "Amber" (blocks 45, 48, 63, 64, 70, 127, 131, 151, 155, 170, 190, 200, 204)

sand Sirdar Legend DK shade 666 (blocks 102, 106, 169)

camel Debbie Bliss Merino DK shade 255103 (blocks 38, 39, 40, 69, 95, 102, 150, 154, 165, 179, 184, 193)

mustard Jaeger Matchmaker DK shade 862 (blocks 1, 2, 3, 46, 61, 62, 63, 71, 76, 94, 155)

light orange King Cole Big Value DK shade "Inca" (blocks 13, 16)

orange Jaeger Matchmaker DK shade 898 (blocks 1, 18, 20, 48, 49, 50, 61, 62, 63, 73, 74, 76, 96, 136, 140, 166, 170, 190, 200, 205, 209)

burnt orange Jaeger Extra Fine Merino DK shade 979 (blocks 3, 12, 95, 127, 131, 151, 155, 193, 209)

salmon King Cole Anti-Tickle Merino DK shade "Salmon" (blocks 9, 11, 58, 60, 91, 117, 121, 141, 145, 192, 196, 198, 202, 207, 211)

pale coral Jaeger Matchmaker DK shade 881 (blocks 12, 57, 58, 59, 92, 117, 121, 128, 132, 192, 198, 202, 211)

coral King Cole Anti-Tickle Merino DK shade "Coral" (blocks 59, 60, 89, 90, 172)

dark coral Jaeger Matchmaker DK shade 870 (blocks 9, 12, 59, 60, 91, 110, 114, 117, 120, 121, 128, 132, 192, 196, 198, 207, 211)

scarlet Jaeger Extra Fine Merino DK shade 985 or King Cole Anti-Tickle Merino DK shade "Scarlet" (blocks 13, 15, 25, 26, 27, 28, 49, 50, 75, 126, 130)

cherry King Cole Anti-Tickle Merino DK shade "Cherry" (blocks 65, 66, 67, 68, 149, 153)

raspberry Jaeger Extra Fine Merino DK shade 943 (blocks 1, 13, 15, 73, 76, 149, 153)

light raspberry King Cole Anti-Tickle Merino DK shade "Raspberry" (blocks 77, 78, 119, 120, 123, 153, 178, 208)

dark raspberry Patons Diploma DK shade 06139 (blocks 33, 36, 77, 212)

elderberry Jaeger Extra Fine Merino DK shade 944 (blocks 73, 75, 109, 113, 125, 129, 132, 140, 149, 153, 180)

pale pink Jaeger Baby Merino DK shade 221 (blocks 33, 35, 36, 77, 80, 97, 98, 103, 108, 119, 123, 125, 129, 130, 178, 212)

variegated pale pink Jaeger Baby Merino DK shade 212 (blocks 78, 164, 174, 178, 212)

dusk pink Jaeger Matchmaker DK shade 863 (block 59)

dawn pink Jaeger Matchmaker DK shade 883 (blocks 42, 44, 111, 115, 160, 171, 195)

clover pink King Cole Anti-Tickle Merino DK shade "Dusky Pink" or Patons Diploma DK shade 06158 (blocks 14, 15, 33, 36, 86)

fuchsia Jaeger Matchmaker DK shade 896 (blocks 33, 34, 83, 88, 109, 113, 125, 126, 129, 130, 140, 143, 147, 168, 172, 185, 197)

variegated fuchsia Jaeger Baby Merino DK shade 193 (blocks 35, 86, 87, 144, 148)

cyclamen pink King Cole Big Value DK shade "Fiesta" (blocks 13, 15)

magenta Jaeger Matchmaker DK shade 887 (blocks 13, 15, 33, 35, 36, 119, 124, 144, 148, 168, 172, 181, 185)

bright aubergine Jaeger Matchmaker DK shade 894 (blocks 33, 88, 110, 114, 119, 123, 181, 185)

dark aubergine Jaeger Matchmaker 4ply shade 701 used double (blocks 181, 185)

amethyst Jaeger Matchmaker DK shade 897 (blocks 15, 16, 43, 44, 107, 111, 115, 125, 129, 138, 144, 148, 160, 164, 171, 181, 191, 197, 201, 208, 212)

antique violet Jaeger Matchmaker DK shade 626 (blocks 191, 195, 197, 201)

dark violet Debbie Bliss Merino DK shade 225605 (blocks 49, 50, 126, 151, 155, 171, 180)

lavender Jaeger Matchmaker DK shade 888 (blocks 41, 42, 43, 44, 77, 79, 84, 111, 115, 118, 120, 122, 124, 143, 147, 160, 164, 167, 171, 172, 176, 180, 195)

mauve Jaeger Matchmaker DK shade 882 (blocks 44, 97, 100, 103, 108, 167, 171, 191, 197, 201)

variegated purple Jaeger Baby Merino DK shade 194 (blocks 44, 144, 148, 171, 195)

dark purple Cygnet Superwash DK shade 2999 or Jaeger Matchmaker DK shade 856 (blocks 42, 44, 119, 126, 130, 167, 171)

blackberry Jaeger Extra Fine Merino DK shade 945 (blocks 21, 22, 49, 50, 81, 84, 105, 112, 118, 122, 143, 147, 159, 163, 171, 176, 180, 206, 210)

pale blue King Cole Anti-Tickle Merino DK shade "Sky Blue" (blocks 24, 53, 108, 112, 116)

variegated blue Jaeger Baby Merino DK shade 213 (blocks 21, 22, 81, 187, 206, 210)

sky blue Jaeger Matchmaker DK shade 864 (blocks 7, 8, 21, 83, 84, 97, 99, 134, 142, 146, 182, 210)

powder blue Debbie Bliss Merino DK shade 225213 (blocks 159, 163, 177)

marina blue Jaeger Extra Fine Merino DK shade 986 (blocks 18, 20, 84, 138, 162, 168, 172, 173, 177, 196, 199, 203)

mid blue Jaeger Matchmaker DK shade 889 or King Cole Anti-Tickle Merino DK shade "Bluebell" (blocks 21, 22, 23, 24, 29, 32, 54, 56, 81, 82, 101, 105, 112, 116, 120, 124, 134, 138, 159, 182, 187, 198, 202, 206, 210)

cornflower blue Sirdar Wash 'N' Wear DK shade 300 (blocks 5, 6, 7, 21, 101, 105, 152, 156)

larkspur King Cole Anti-Tickle Merino DK shade "Larkspur" (blocks 83, 142, 146)

royal King Cole Anti-Tickle Merino DK shade "Royal" (blocks 21, 49, 50, 51, 65, 66, 67, 68, 152, 156, 172)

Capri blue Debbie Bliss Merino DK shade 255202 (blocks 91, 104, 177, 183, 196)

denim blue Jaeger Matchmaker DK shade 629 (blocks 21, 29, 53, 55, 182, 187)

petrol blue Patons Diploma DK shade 06212 (blocks 9, 29, 104, 107, 118, 122, 157, 161, 183, 186)

pale turquoise Jaeger Matchmaker DK shade 884 (blocks 5, 7, 9, 10, 11, 18, 20, 43, 89, 97, 100, 103, 104, 111, 117, 121, 138, 146, 158, 162, 173, 177, 183, 186, 194)

mid turquoise King Cole Anti-Tickle Merino DK shade "Turquoise" (blocks 17, 61, 63, 91, 101, 104, 107, 117, 118, 120, 124, 143, 147, 183)

variegated turquoise Jaeger Baby Merino DK shade 192 (block 186)

bright jade King Cole Anti-Tickle Merino DK shade "Green Ice" (blocks 5, 7, 53, 55, 89, 90, 156, 182)

emerald King Cole Anti-Tickle Merino DK shade "Emerald" (blocks 25, 27, 28, 49, 50, 51, 172)

grass green Cygnet Superwash DK shade 2817 (blocks 152, 156)

linden green King Cole Anti-Tickle Merino DK shade "Linden" (blocks 42, 58, 85, 87, 110, 115, 128, 129, 132, 141, 145, 181)

lime green Debbie Bliss Merino DK shade 225503 (blocks 101, 114, 142, 146, 157, 161, 172, 195)

pea green Patons Diploma DK shade 06125 (blocks 113, 170, 184, 188)

asparagus Jaeger Matchmaker DK shade 886 (blocks 18, 19, 20, 29, 31, 46, 54, 55, 61, 63, 78, 88, 105, 133, 137, 147, 158, 162, 184, 189, 199, 203)

sage green Jaeger Matchmaker DK shade 857 (blocks 4, 32, 107, 116, 128, 130, 131, 137, 157, 158, 170, 189, 193, 199, 203)

bronze green King Cole Anti-Tickle Merino DK shade "Bronze Green" (blocks 18, 189, 193, 199)

pine green Debbie Bliss Merino DK shade 225506 (blocks 31, 137)

olive green King Cole Anti-Tickle Merino DK shade "Olive" (blocks 3, 18, 20, 29, 31, 142, 146, 170, 188)

variegated green Jaeger Baby Merino DK shade 191 (block 188)

pale coffee Cygnet Superwash DK shade 4315 (block 169)

dark natural Jaeger Matchmaker DK shade 784 (blocks 20, 69, 70, 72, 93, 94, 175, 179)

mink King Cole Anti-Tickle Merino DK shade "Mink" (blocks 12, 39, 60, 69, 71, 94, 102, 127, 141, 145, 154, 165, 169, 175, 179, 184, 205)

cocoa Jaeger Extra Fine Merino DK shade 972 (blocks 12, 69, 127, 131, 145, 184, 188)

pale gray Jaeger Matchmaker DK shade 885 or King Cole Anti-Tickle Merino DK shade "Silver" (blocks 37, 39, 93, 106, 118, 122, 123, 139, 169)

steel gray Jaeger Matchmaker DK shade 892 (blocks 29, 106, 109, 169)

flannel gray Jaeger Matchmaker DK shade 782 (blocks 39, 40, 93, 135, 139, 150, 154)

clerical gray Jaeger Matchmaker DK shade 639 (blocks 37, 109, 113, 169)

Index

Suppliers

American suppliers
Cygnet Yarns
Showers of Flowers
6900 West Colfax Avenue
Lakewood, CO 80215
http://showersofflowers.com

Debbie Bliss Yarns
Knitting Fever, Inc.
35 Debevoise Avenue
Roosevelt, NY 11575
www.knittingfever.com.
In Canada: Diamond Yarn (see Canadian suppliers)

Jaeger Yarns
Westminster Fibers,
4 Townsend West, Unit 8
Nashua, NH 03063
In Canada: Diamond Yarn (see Canadian suppliers)

King Cole
Cascade Yarns
PO Box 58168
Tukwila, WA 98188
    www.cascadeyarns.com

Rowan
Westminster Fibers,
4 Townsend West, Unit 8
Nashua, NH 03063
www.knitrowan.com.
In Canada: Diamond Yarn (see Canadian suppliers)

Sirdar
Knitting Fever, Inc.
35 Debevoise Avenue
Roosevelt, NY 11575
www.knittingfever.com.
In Canada: Diamond Yarn (see Canadian suppliers)

Canadian suppliers
Diamond Yarn
St. Laurent, Ste. 101
Montreal, QC H3L 2N1
www.diamondyarn.com.

Patons
Patons/Spinrific
320 Livingstone Ave. South
Listowel, ON N4W 3H3
www.patonsyarn.com